Born After

PSYCHOANALYTIC HORIZONS

Psychoanalysis is unique in being at once a theory and a therapy, a method of critical thinking and a form of clinical practice. Now in its second century, this fusion of science and humanism derived from Freud has outlived all predictions of its demise. **Psychoanalytic Horizons** evokes the idea of a convergence between realms as well as the outer limits of a vision. Books in the series test disciplinary boundaries and will appeal to scholars and therapists who are passionate not only about the theory of literature, culture, media, and philosophy but also, above all, about the real life of ideas in the world.

Series Editors
Esther Rashkin, Mari Ruti, and Peter L. Rudnytsky

Advisory Board
Salman Akhtar, Doris Brothers, Aleksandar Dimitrijevic, Lewis Kirshner, Humphrey Morris, Hilary Neroni, Dany Nobus, Lois Oppenheim, Donna Orange, Peter Redman, Laura Salisbury, Alenka Zupančič

Born After

Reckoning with the German Past

Angelika Bammer

BLOOMSBURY ACADEMIC
NEW YORK • LONDON • OXFORD • NEW DELHI • SYDNEY

BLOOMSBURY ACADEMIC
Bloomsbury Publishing Inc
1385 Broadway, New York, NY 10018, USA
50 Bedford Square, London, WC1B 3DP, UK

BLOOMSBURY, BLOOMSBURY ACADEMIC and the Diana logo are trademarks of
Bloomsbury Publishing Plc

First published in the United States of America 2019

For legal purposes the Acknowledgments on p. 238 constitute an extension of this
copyright page.

Cover design by Daniel Benneworth-Gray
Cover image: Author, age three, in war-ravaged Rüdesheim, 1949

Library of Congress Cataloging-in-Publication Data
Names: Bammer, Angelika, author.
Title: Born after : reckoning with the German past / Angelika Bammer.
Other titles: Reckoning with the German past
Description: New York, NY : Bloomsbury Academic, [2019] |
Series: Psychoanalytic horizons | Includes bibliographical references and index.
Identifiers: LCCN 2019007347 (print) | LCCN 2019011256 (ebook) | ISBN
9781501336430 (ePub) | ISBN 9781501336447 (ePDF) |
ISBN 9781501336423 (hardback : alk. paper)
Subjects: LCSH: Bammer, Angelika, 1946- | German American women–Biography. |
Diplomats–Germany–Family relationships. | Bammer, Walter–Family. | Nazis–Family
relationships. | Memory–Germany. | World War, 1939–1945–Personal narratives,
German. | Holocaust, Jewish (1939–1945)–Germany–Velen. |
Velen (Germany)–Biography.
Classification: LCC E185.63 (ebook) | LCC E185.63 .B35 2010 (print) |
DDC 940.54/8243092 [B] –dc23
LC record available at https://lccn.loc.gov/2019007347

A catalog record for this book is available from the Library of Congress.

ISBN: HB: 978-1-5013-3642-3
          ePDF: 978-1-5013-3644-7
          eBook: 978-1-5013-3643-0

Series: Psychoanalytic Horizons

Typeset by Integra Software Services Pvt. Ltd.
Printed and bound in the United States of America

To find out more about our authors and books visit www.bloomsbury.com
and sign up for our newsletters.

You, who will emerge from the flood
In which we have drowned
Be mindful
When you speak of our failings
Also of the dark time
From which you escaped.

Ihr, die ihr auftauchen werdet aus der Flut
In der wir untergegangen sind
Gedenkt
Wenn ihr von unseren Schwächen sprecht
Auch der finsteren Zeit
Der ihr entronnen seid.

—Bertolt Brecht, "To Those Born After" (1939)[*]

It is Thanksgiving evening. I am sitting with my son in his room. The house is quiet. We are the only ones awake. We have been talking, but it's late and we have fallen silent. I feel the comfort of shared trust as night folds in.

"I want to read you something," I say, getting up. I return with a folder holding hand-written, loose-leaf pages. My German story, as I have started calling it. I turn the desk light on and start to read. When I pause, my son says, "Keep reading." So I keep reading. It's the first time I hear out loud the words I have written.

"Who is this for?" he asks with a seventeen-year-old's directness. I hesitate, not sure of my answer.

"For people who look at me and wonder, 'what did your parents do in the war?'" I say. "Who hear German and right away think Nazi. People who wonder what being German feels like, given what they … what we … what Germans did."

My son looks at me. His face is shadowed and his hair is light.

"Yes, I know," he says.

We are both silent. After a while, I resume my reading. My life is a story and I revisit scenes. I read on and on into the night, curled up in a chair in my grown son's room, until I run out of material to read him.

"Is there more?" he asks.

"That's it for now." My voice is hoarse and my feet are freezing. It is a.m. I turn the desk light off. "Time to sleep."

My son cocoons into his covers and smiles good night.

But just as I am about to leave the room, I turn back to him. His question, who is this for, still resonates. And now I have another answer.

"Who am I writing this for? For you," I say. "I am writing it for you and your sister. For you who inherited German history from me. I am writing it for my parents, who tried to answer when I had questions, even when they didn't know where to find the words. I am writing it for the person I myself became over a lifetime of reckoning with the history I was born into. The child whose parents saw in her the promise of a world they could reclaim. The six-year-old who was hated for being German. The fourteen-year-old who could read Celan but not say Jew. The twenty-year-old who left Germany on a one-way ticket without understanding what that leaving meant. The mother whose children were called Nazis because of her. And I am writing it for people like me who live with the legacy of a shameful past."

I was twenty years old when I left Germany, but I still remember the girl I was then. Is it the day itself I remember or the photograph of that day? They have become inseparable. The space between the image and the *experience has collapsed in time. It was in Chicago, a bright and sunny winter day. I see her standing next to a waterless fountain by the Art Institute. The wind is blowing. It has blown a wisp of hair across her face. She smiles at the camera, her eyes wide open. She looks so young.*

I find the picture and get it out. Who was I then? I stare at the girl by the fountain, her hair still dark, not yet white like mine now. I remember her, but I can't go back to her. She is in the past.

But I can see her future. For the girl in the picture has my daughter's eyes and her uncertain smile is my son's.

Contents

Prologue
Swastika Raincoat

German weather, my American friends called it. *Hundewetter*, dog weather, as we said in German. But that November when I was twenty, a student of literature at the University of Heidelberg, even the dogs seemed to stay inside. The sky was heavy and lightless and the air gray and drizzly cold. Yet when an American friend and I went out on the town, I didn't mind the rain. It was a chance to wear my brand new outfit: a white vinyl raincoat with a matching hat. I turned my collar up and pulled the brim of my hat down. I was Ingrid Bergman in *Casablanca*.

The pub we chose was nothing fancy, just a place for a beer and bratwurst. It was crowded with the usual mix: students, people from the neighborhood, and a group of Americans I assumed were tourists. It was loud and smoky, but the warmth felt good. We left our coats on the bulging coat rack, along with other damp and dripping clothes, sat down, had a drink, and got the menu. But the smoke was bothering me, my eyes were burning, so we paid and got up to leave.

"I'll get the coats," I said. In the crush of rain gear, mine stood out: light and bright and shiny. But as I got closer, I felt confused. Was this my coat? It didn't look right. Then I realized there was something on it. Stick figures, I first thought, little people in a row joining hands. Then I saw that it wasn't stick figures: it was swastikas. All over the white coat's surface and all around the white hat's brim someone had inked row upon row of little swastikas.

Who had done this? My chest felt tight, my body hollowed out and empty. I stared at the grim parade of swastikas. I grabbed the coat, my face on fire with shame, and shoved my arm into a sleeve. The hat I left behind on the coat rack. When we stepped out, the rain had turned icy. I walked to the car in silence. I couldn't think of anything to say.

Back at the dorm, I stuffed my coat into the garbage chute. The suck of air as it hurtled down made me shiver. What had happened? None of this made sense. I had been hit by a stray bullet in someone else's fight, a shot that came out of nowhere. Someone angry or bored or resentful sought a target, and I was there.

A lifetime later, I still feel the impact.

When I told people what had happened, no one knew what to make of it. The standard reaction was, "Who would do something like that? And to you—a German in Germany!" It made no sense. Was it a drunken prank? A random act of violence—what the writer André Gide had called an *acte gratuit*? Or just some idiot in a pub with a ballpoint?

I could never explain it. Nor could I let it go. I returned to that night in the pub as if to the scene of an unsolved crime, retelling the story, looking for reactions, trying to analyze how I reacted. I reviewed the sequence of events. What had I missed? What could anyone in the pub that night have known of me? They were all strangers. No one could even have identified me as German, as the English I was speaking with my friend was accent-free. They couldn't have known anything about where I came from, much less whether anyone in my family could be called a Nazi. They couldn't know it, because I didn't yet know anything about Nazis in my family myself. I was young, I lived in the present, and when I visited the past it was usually in fantasy, like pretending to be Ingrid Bergman that night.

No matter how often I return to that night in Heidelberg, I remain puzzled. Not just by what happened, but by my response. I had been violated, my clothes defaced, but I felt no outrage. I didn't want to know who had done this, make accusations, or make a scene. I wanted to hide my face and not be seen.

Instead of getting angry, I felt ashamed and guilty, as if I was the one in the wrong, as if the person who had defaced my coat had revealed a secret, something shameful I could not disclose. Sometimes others even seemed to think likewise. Underneath their professed outrage when I told the story, I sensed doubt. No one ever said, "Well, you're German, after all … So maybe they weren't all that random, those swastikas. Maybe, in the end, they were a kind of truth." No one said it, it, but I felt the implication hover.

It sometimes seems as if the swastikas have always been there, from long before they showed up on my raincoat to long after I had moved to the United States. I caught them in a glance, a tone of voice, a sentence that wasn't finished. They were like the rush of air when a door is opened. "Where are you from? Are you German? What about your parents? Where were they during the war?" In the questions asked and the ones left unasked, I felt the chill.

I got rid of that raincoat long ago. But in my mind I never let it go. I wore it secretly, a coat of shame that no one else could see.

This is the story of that coat and the girl who felt ashamed as she grew up in the shadow of the swastikas. It is the story of a time that began before her birth and extends through her children's generation, so I tell it in the past, present, and future tense, and in a chronology that is discontinuous.

During a visit to Germany fifty-five years after the Third Reich ended, the journalist Gitta Sereny was struck by the fact that even half a century later "the past seems always present."[1] It didn't need to be provoked or summoned. "It is," as Sereny put it, "just there."

I have tried to understand what that "always present" means, what the "just there-ness" of that German past feels like. *Born After* is my attempt to find the words.

Part One

The Trouble with German

Who are we that this could have happened?
　　　　　　　—Eelco Runia, *Moved by the Past* (2014)[1]

"Those Germans," my father would sometimes say, as if he—as if we—weren't part of them. Whenever "they" did something that made him feel ashamed, he would seek distance, disavow belonging. "A terrible people" (ein schreckliches Volk), he would mutter and look disgusted.

　　"But," I would counter to provoke an argument, "what about you? What about me? Where do we fit in? … And what about our entire family?"

　　I always knew what his answer would be. Silence. It was an argument that we never had.

Angelika Bammer, second grade, St. James Catholic School, Toronto, 1952.

In the Aftermath

We longed for your arrival, my parents told me.
We waited and waited, but you didn't come.
You were waiting also.
You were waiting for the war to end.

I was born on September 26, 1946, in the aftermath of World War II. The fighting was over. Soldiers were again civilians. Murderers had fled their stations and destroyed their evidence, as best they could, while survivors faced the challenge of surviving. A thousand years of heralded German glory had collapsed into twelve years of shame.

My country was no longer a country. Still called Germany, it was actually a chessboard of occupied zones—American, British, French, and Soviet—with military commanders in place of an elected government.[1] The former leaders had been deposed. Some were dead—either executed or by suicide. Others had fled or gone into hiding. Many were in prison or awaiting trial. In the words of *Life* magazine's first postwar editorial, "a nation of 80,000,000 people in the heart of an overpopulated and machine-dependent continent" had just been eliminated.[2]

During the Nazi years, a trick question had often been inserted into apprenticeship examinations: "What comes after the Third Reich?" The answer was supposed to be "nothing," as the Third Reich had been declared eternal, a sort of heaven on earth. But if the candidate fell into the trap and assumed that the Third Reich would logically have to be followed some day by a Fourth Reich, he would be failed for having answered incorrectly.[3] The postwar irony was that the correct answer, "nothing," had unintentionally been proven right. For in May 1945, when the Third Reich ended, what was left of Germany seemed indeed to be nothing.

Some, like the American Secretary of the Treasurer, Henry Morgenthau Jr., thought this was good. Germany should be dismantled, disabled as a modern state, blasted back to the agrarian age, and kept there.[4] Across much of Germany, including the industrial regions of the Ruhr and Silesia, this reduction of a modern industrial state to a "country primarily agricultural and pastoral in nature," had de facto already happened. "There are no cities left in Germany," *Life* magazine reported, going on to describe "a destruction the likes of which has not been seen since ... Genghis Khan ... wiped out whole nations ... from China to Bulgaria."[5] The destruction was "on a scale without historical precedent," the writer W.G. Sebald later recalled.[6]

Germany was in a shambles, its economy collapsed, its industry at a standstill. There was no work, no heat, and no food.[7] People were living in makeshift shelters in bombed-out ruins, without electricity, running water, or sanitation. The stench of rotting bodies under tons of rubble poisoned the air. Other bodies had been burned to ash. Conditions were "[i]ndescribably wretched," the British publisher Victor Gollancz wrote after a visit to Düsseldorf in October 1945.[8] Cities had become wastelands. People were bloated from hunger. The monstrous had come to seem normal.

"Germany is perishing," my father wrote in his diary in September 1946. "They won't let us work. Or give us raw materials to work with … Underground, the coal lies untouched. Above ground, industry dies and people shiver."[9] What was left? "The Germans have a word for it—*Dreck*," a May 1945 *Life* magazine editorial concluded. "*Dreck* means junk, dirt, debris, rubble—and that is what the country of the Thousand-Year Hitler Reich is today."[10]

I was born into a time of shadows. Life itself seemed to flicker on and off, while the dead were counted and the missing sought. In the wake of World War II and the Holocaust, during which Europe had almost self-destructed and the future of the world had been put at risk, the enormity of the losses overwhelmed all scales of measurement. In Europe alone, the human catastrophe surpassed anything the world had ever seen. Around 6 million Jews and 21 million Russians had perished, and over 40 million people had been displaced. The perpetrator nation was also suffering. Mass suicides marked the end of a regime that had chosen *Heil* (salvation) as its official watchword, and 13 million ethnic Germans had been expelled from lands in the east. When "Germans stopped killing others [they] … began killing themselves," a reporter's terse dispatch noted.[11] It was "as if the blood of a thousand wounds had drained into this land," the photographers Otto Hagel and Hansel Mieth wrote in 1950 when they revisited the Germany they had last seen in 1930.[12]

After World War II and the Holocaust, the nature of crime had to be rethought. A whole new category—crimes against humanity—was created to describe the magnitude of the harm that had been done. By the end of the war, many Germans came to see their own government as their worst enemy. "It has come to this," my mother wrote in her April 1945 diary, "that we are more likely to see our own government … as the enemy than those we were taught to fear."[13]

It was as if the flow of time had been disrupted. The "transition from the past to the present" seemed blocked.[14] "When the sun came over Germany it was a wonder that it did not stand still," *Life* magazine commented on the day that Germany surrendered, "for it saw events there which blotted out one function of the sun: the marking of time. The age of science, the twentieth century, the present time vanished."[15] Never had time seemed more out of joint than at that moment. People talked of null time, annulment time, a "Zero Hour"[16] (*Stunde Null*) that was not just a breach of history, but a "spiritual caesura" between Evil and Good itself.[17] In this transition from one to another time, mine was the hinge generation,[18] tasked with bridging the gap between what had preceded us and the aftermath to come.

Not surprisingly, it was a time marked by silence, for the confusion and chaos of the postwar world had disrupted language. With tens of millions of displaced people trying to settle in new places or make their way across the continent to their homes, Europe had become a maelstrom of languages and dialects. The writer Primo Levi gave a vivid sense of the situation in his description of the transit camp in Belorussia, where he stayed after his release from Auschwitz on his odyssey home to Italy via Poland, the Ukraine, Belorussia, Romania, Hungary, Germany, and Austria. "In July 1945," he wrote,

> ten thousand persons were staying in Slutsk … There were Catholics, Jews, Orthodox, and Muslims; there were whites and yellows and various blacks … German, Poles, French, Greeks, Dutch, Italians, and others; and also German who claimed to be Austrians, Austrians who declared they were Swiss, Russians who called themselves Italians.[19]

In this Babel of languages and cultures, communication was difficult and record-keeping all but impossible. There was no common language in which to talk, no authorized language in which to keep records.

But even if they could find the words, people had lost their faith in language to communicate. How could you communicate experience that you couldn't make sense of yourself? How could you understand someone else's experience when you didn't know, and couldn't imagine, the conditions? Should you speak anyway? Or remain silent? And what was the cost, emotional or social, of either choice? Often the gap between people's experiences simply seemed "too big to be bridged."[20] Silence hung in the balance like a dead weight.

This is how Levi described his first encounter with Germans after his release from Auschwitz in January 1945. On October 15, 1945—after thirty-one days of travel, eight and a half months after leaving Auschwitz—he and his Italian comrades arrived in Munich. Soon they would be home in Italy. But here, in Germany among Germans, they found only silence. The former inmates of the camps couldn't speak about their experience, and Germans, "deaf, blind, and mute," were unwilling to ask or listen. The shock of that silence still resonated over sixteen years later. "It seemed to us that we had something to say," Levi recalled, enormous things to say, to every single German, and that every German should have something to say to us. We felt an urgency to sum up, ask, explain, and comment … Did "they" know about Auschwitz, about the silent, daily slaughter, a step from their doors? If so, how could they go along, return home, and look at their children … If not, they had to listen, they had a sacred duty to listen, to learn from us, from me, everything, immediately.

Like a swarm of "insolvent debtors," he concluded, they refused to pay.[21]

For Germans the problem was compounded by the fact that Nazi rhetoric had made their language a semantic minefield. I watched my mother blunder into that minefield one day when we were making fruitcake and she was adding candied lemon peel to the mix. "*Judenspeck* (Jew fat)," she said without thinking, as she popped a jellied lemon cube into her mouth. As soon as she realized what she had said, she looked horrified, the shock on her face mirroring the shock on mine. "It's what we called *Zitronat* (candied lemon peel) in the Nazi years," she stammered, blushing.

So many words no longer meant what they claimed to mean—"relocation" (*Umsiedlung*) meant deportation, "special treatment" (*Sonderbehandlung*) meant assassination, and "final solution" (*Endlösung*) meant genocide—that Germans no longer trusted their own language. This distrust carried over into the postwar world. Words were serviceable for simple, material things like shoes, coal, bread, butter, and cigarettes. But when it came to ideas they were suspect. Abstractions—concepts or principles like home (*Heimat*), loyalty (*Treue*), or heroism (*Heldentum*)—had been drowned in what the philologist Victor Klemperer called the "brown sauce" of Nazi rhetoric.[22] The poet Paul Celan used an even harsher term. His mother tongue had become a language of murderers, a *Mördersprache*.

Klemperer and Celan believed that the German language had been irredeemably infected by the Nazi virus. No one who used it could be immune. As Klemperer noted, language isn't just out there as a social medium. It is in us. We think and feel it. We ingest it, word by word, until we embody it and it has become us. "Like tiny doses of arsenic," its effect is cumulative and eventually "the toxic reaction sets in."[23]

Psychoanalysts remind us that "[w]hen the guarantees of speech have been destroyed," we no longer know "how to construct an Other to whom to speak,"[24] and we risk losing our sense of self in the process. The East German writer Christa Wolf described the dilemma of postwar Germans in these terms. After Auschwitz, she wrote, even "the tiny word 'I'" had become "unbearable."[25] The identity "German" no longer had a clear reference point. Some Germans had been renamed Aryans, some recast as non-German

Jews,[26] while ethnic Germans who had been citizens of other countries had been made German in the course of the war. With such a mutable category, it wasn't clear anymore what being German meant.

As language disintegrated, the unspoken dissolved into forgetting. Those who had done harm tried to leave what they had done behind. Those who had suffered it often tried to do likewise. Those who had stood by and let it happen, the "herds of dreamy, militant sheep,"[27] did what they had done before: nothing. Many memories were too painful to live with, even as they were too urgent to forget. So records were sealed, memories entombed, and emotions shuttered, and the archives of oblivion began to fill.

Some who needed to remember went to other lands where they could speak in a different tongue. Some who needed to forget bartered language so they could mourn and try to heal in silence. But what seemed like silence was not silence. It was not vacant space. It was the edge of the precipice of language where memory hung. It was the sigh in a wisp of smoke from a winter chimney, the intake of breath between words. It was the unquiet ground where the dead lay, the murmuring at the bottom of ash-filled lakes.

I was born into a burnt and broken world. War had raged across Europe, scattering bodies from Normandy to the Katyn Forest and leaving a "chaos ... of crushed cities" in its wake.[28] But it had passed over my natal village lightly. "A miracle!" my mother wrote in her diary. "Our little town of Velen has been spared."

My father had returned from the war in November 1945. In the postwar redrawing of borders he had lost his family home, as the Sudeten territory was returned to Czechoslovakia and ethnic Germans expelled, but he had found a new home in Westphalia with my mother's family. Now, alongside millions of other postwar veterans, he had to reenter civilian life. Most importantly, he needed a job and income. Until then, he kept busy and tried to contribute as best he could. "I worked hard in the garden," he noted in an August 1946 diary entry. "Planted strawberries, kale, Brussels sprouts, and spinach ... After that I worked on my English." Given Germany's multinational occupation, perhaps his language skills would lead to something.

The war was over, but the present was far from secure. Of immediate concern was the prediction of a long, hard winter, a prediction that would soon come true. Winter came that year with the force of avenging Furies and the death toll it exacted was high. Some put it in the hundreds of thousands, others say millions. It would be remembered as the Hunger Winter: extreme cold, lack of food and heating fuel, and a resulting rise in tuberculosis. But in September, when I was born, life in Velen was still abundant. Rabbits bred in backyard hutches, geese and chickens scratched and pecked in yards, and pigs fattened in sties next to kitchens. Rye and barley fields ripened, apple and plum trees hung heavy with fruit, and sugar beets were the size of footballs.

With my first intake of breath, I inhaled the smells of village life. The sewage smell from the ditches where I later fished for tadpoles. The bread smell from Kremer's bakery, where I got Sunday morning rolls. The blood smell from behind the butcher shop, where pigs were slaughtered. On the day I was born, I might have smelled the roses in the cemetery, where my grandparents would one day be buried. Perhaps a whiff of incense from the church where my parents had been married even blew my way. The day I was born the air would have carried a mix of diesel fumes, mud, and manure stink, the green of Westphalian pastureland, the dust of harvested grain, and the rich loam of freshly ploughed furrows. It was my first experience of what home would smell like.

I was one of seventy-five children born in Velen that year, in a village of under two thousand.[29] We were the children of the aftermath, the generation of those born after. Our parents' need to believe in the promise of new beginnings—that was our birthright. But along with that birthright came a debt they also left us: to repair the damaged world they had left behind. In the journal that my parents kept as a record of my first year, my father wrote, "You, our child, were our promise. You were the promise of a new time." This promise marked the path that my life took, even as memories of the time before dogged my steps.

The announcement of my birth that my parents sent out included a line from Psalm 91: "For he commanded his angels over you, to protect you on all your ways."[30] "It was our prayer for you, our first-born," they wrote in my journal. Years later, I learned that Psalm 91 had also been my father's prayer as a soldier, the words he turned to when overwhelmed by fear.

> You shall not be afraid of the terror by night,
> Nor of the arrow that flies by day,
> Nor of the pestilence that walks in darkness,
> Nor of the destruction that lays waste at noonday.
> A thousand may fall at your side,
> And ten thousand at your right hand;
> But it shall not come near you.

He knew the psalm by heart. He had lived its terrors: the arrows that flew by day, the pestilence that walked in darkness, and the destruction that laid cities to waste at noon. And over six long years of war, while he had lived with death, been wounded and awarded medals, he had seen thousands and tens of thousands fall. But he had survived, and now the angels who had guarded him on his ways—from Russia to Normandy, from West Prussia to the Ardennes—were to guard his daughter on her way. This was my father's prayer.

Yet he also knew that prayer was a wish, not a guarantee. He knew that fate, as much as God, had a hand in the outcome of who lived or died, and what became of them. He knew that many, like him, had prayed for protection, yet they had not been heard. They had been left to the terrors that came at night and assailed them in the light of day. Paul Celan's 1945 poem "A Song in the Wilderness" was a bitter lament for those who had been abandoned, even, as it seemed, by God. For the abandoned, prayer is pointless. When "[t]he angels are dead and the Lord has gone blind,"[31] heaven, like the world, is empty. No one hears them. No one sees them. No one cares.

I was baptized four days after my birth—*Angelika* (for the angels who watched over me) *Maria Hildegard* (for my parents' mothers)—in a gown of lace from my mother's bridal veil. My godmother was my maternal grandmother, Maria Bushoff. My godfather Manfred Förster wasn't there. Saxony, where he lived, was in the Soviet zone, and Velen, where we lived, was in the British zone. The borders between us had become impassable.

There was much I didn't know about them until years after they had both died. Only then did I learn that my grandmother had been a Nazi and my godfather had been a Jew, as if these facts had been incidental to who they were to us personally. It would be years before questions of the personal and the political would weigh on me. The day of my baptism, I was still graced with ignorance—of history and the effect of borders, of Nazis and the meaning of the word "Jew." While Vicar Mengering welcomed me into the Catholic community "in the name of the Father and of the Son and of the Holy Ghost," as he traced the sign of the cross on my forehead, I lay secure in my grandmother's arms and slept.

The next day, on October 1, 1946, in a city in the south of Germany, what one of the presiding judges called "the greatest trial in history" came to an end.[32] It had begun on November 20, 1945, ten days after my father was released from an American prisoner-of-war camp, when the four victorious Allied governments convened an International Military Tribunal in Nuremburg to put political, military, and industrial leaders of Nazi Germany on trial. Ten months later, the first Nuremberg Trial concluded with the judges' verdicts.[33] Of the twenty-three men who had been put on trial, twelve were sentenced to death, three to life imprisonment, and four to prison sentences from between ten and twenty years. Three were acquitted.[34]

While my father was planting Brussels sprouts and working on his English, and my mother was washing diapers and sewing curtains, a group of their countrymen were convicted of "war crimes, crimes against peace, crimes against humanity, and conspiracy to commit these crimes." And while eleven men in Nuremberg were hanged for war crimes,[35] I, born in the aftermath of that war, drank in life.

Discarded statue, Lapidarium, Berlin-Kreuzberg, 1992. Used between 1978 and 2009 as a museum, storage, and restoration site for statues removed from public spaces, the Lapidarium was closed to the public in 2010 (Photograph by author).

Three short lines in my father's diary from October 1, 1946 mark this moment of disconnect between events on the big stage of history and the banal matters of everyday life. "My child is six days old," he wrote. "She has plump little cheeks and is drinking eagerly. I worked in the garden." Then he adds, without further comment and set off by a simple dash: "11 death sentences in Nürnberg, 3 pardons."[36]

"So it goes," as Kurt Vonnegut put it in *Slaughterhouse-Five*, his rendering of the firebombing of Dresden that took between 35,000 and 135,000 lives. Catastrophes, massacres, genocides happen, while ordinary life plods on. Everyday necessities claim our attention, banalities consume our time. Bakers bake, farmers farm, butchers butcher, hangmen hang. Children grow, people work. The sun shines. We grow ill. We get well. We die. Suffering is not removed or distant. It is commonplace, it is everywhere, it is right here where you and I are. We don't see it because we're busy or have other things on our mind. Perhaps we are "eating or opening a window or just walking dully along." But whether we notice it or not, the suffering is there. While the ploughman ploughs and the fisherman fishes and "the dogs go on with their doggy life and the torturer's horse/Scratches its innocent behind on a tree," the "dreadful martyrdom" of other people's suffering runs alongside.[37]

Lost in the Past

There is a place I have never been to, yet I know it well. I know it from the inside, how it feels. I often go there in my dreams and each time I have the same experience.

I am in the mountains, on a path by an abyss, a rock ledge rises up behind me. I am alone. The sky is empty. Everything is still. It's as if the world had temporarily stopped breathing. Then everything is in motion on fast-forward speed. I am running, slipping, climbing, clambering up and over rocks, as a sense of dread overwhelms me. I am terrified of something I can't see. Yet I can feel it closing in all around me.

That's when I wake up and remember where this dream comes from: it's a scene from a film by Leni Riefenstahl, the pioneering filmmaker often labeled "Hitler's film director."[1] My dream scene is from *The Blue Light*, one of her early mountain films, and the one that launched her career, winning the Silver Medal at the 1932 Venice Biennale. More consequentially, it caught the attention of the man who, a year later, would be elected Reich Chancellor of Germany: Adolf Hitler. Riefenstahl's bold aesthetic and Hitler's grand vision were in sync and they worked together from Venice onward. He gave her the resources she needed to make the extravagant, expensive, and innovative films she envisioned as an artist, and she gave him films like *Olympia* and *Triumph of the Will* that elevated his vision of the world beyond propaganda to the level of art.[2]

I don't remember when or where I first saw *The Blue Light*, and I remember the plot only vaguely. The heroine (played by Riefenstahl) is a child of nature, who lives in the mountains and only occasionally comes to a village to trade her potions for necessities she cannot procure herself. The villagers tolerate her; some even find her wild vitality alluring. But they keep their distance. Her freedom threatens their complacent order, and one day they band together to cast her out. Their rage escalates and finally becomes murderous.

The scene that follows is the scene I relive in my dream. Pursued by a lynch mob, the heroine flees into the mountain wilderness, scrambling up and over rocks like a hunted animal. I feel her panic, the terror of being caught, the loneliness of being outcast. My heart is racing and I am struggling for breath. And just as I have almost escaped to safety, I slip and plunge to my death.

The sense of falling is what always wakes me. Once I'm awake and my breathing steadies, I remind myself that it's just a dream, just a scene from a film I saw once. It has nothing to do with me. But it isn't just a dream or a film scene. It's a memory of a place I know. I recognize the mountains: I've been there. It was long ago and my memory is hazy, but it has marked my unconscious with feelings that haunt me in dreams.

In 1949, the summer before I turned three, my parents took me on a trip to Bavaria. It was their first vacation since the end of the war, a break they had long wanted and saved for.

After months of looking for work, my father had finally found a job that paid enough and for which he was qualified. There were times when he had almost given up. "A man can't work for nothing," he wrote despairingly in his August 1946 diary. "If I could only find a way to support my family." He had traveled all over the British and American zones, making contacts and sitting for interviews to no avail. In the multilingual context of occupied Germany his fluency in four languages would be potentially useful, but the Allied powers governing Germany at the time couldn't use his law degree from the Charles University, and the Germans trying to rebuild from the ruins wanted practical skills. Erudition was of little interest. What mattered was not what you knew, but what you could do.

In light of that question, my father decided to learn a trade and became apprenticed to a furniture maker in Velen. "If I can't find other work," he wrote in his diary, "I can at least be a carpenter." He built a rabbit hutch, a goose pen, and passed his first apprenticeship exam by making two small tables with decorative wood inlays, before shaving off part of his left thumb with a wood plane put his carpentry career on hold.

In November 1946, a more suitable job opened up. He was offered a position in the newly opened Foreign Trade Office in Frankfurt with a monthly salary of 500 Reichsmark. My mother was jubilant. "Hurray, my little girl!" she wrote in my journal. "The job in Frankfurt is secure! We have made it to the top of a big mountain."

But the mountain hadn't quite been scaled yet. There were the practical matters of food and housing, all rationed and controlled by permits. Food ration permits required proof of employment, and employment required proof of a housing permit. It was the Catch-22 of Germany after World War II: to get food, you had to prove that you had a job; to get a job, you had to prove that you had housing; to get housing, you needed money, for which you had to have a job.

To make matters worse, housing permits were as hard to get as job offers, particularly in Frankfurt. Around 70 percent of the city had been destroyed by air raids, transforming what had once been one of the most beautiful medieval inner cities into a landscape of rubble and dust. Only fifty buildings in the old part of Frankfurt had survived intact and half of the city's inhabitants had been rendered homeless. Through perseverance, luck, and connections, my father finally found a room that served our little family of three as living quarters. For the next two years this single room was our Frankfurt home.

It was a time of making do and learning to do without. Food was scarce, particularly in the cities. The November we moved to Frankfurt, a dispatch from Germany reported that "[i]n Wuppertal there was no bread at all for 10 days."[3] Fats and animal protein—meat, fish, or eggs—were luxuries, Victor Gollancz reported, and many Germans lived "on no more than 1,000 calories, and some of them, from time to time, on considerably less." These were conditions, he noted, that could "be characterized as slow starvation."[4]

As I reread my parents' postwar diaries, I am struck by how consistently they mention hunger. They always seemed to be hungry, while I never seemed to get enough. I suspect that my life-long uneasiness about food—worrying whether I'm being greedy and hoarding or whether I'm being stingy and should share—must date back to this time. Growing up, even at home in my own family, I never felt I could just help myself to food when I was hungry. I had to ask permission. It was as if there might not be enough.

In a time of too little, the demands of a growing child must at times have overwhelmed my parents. I was too hungry, too needy, too greedy for the life that to them still felt tenuous. Food wasn't the only problem. Everything in postwar Germany was scarce. The "shortage of everything ... that babies need" was particularly "appalling," a shocked Victor Gollancz wrote.[5] When he noted that diapers "*to all intents and purposes, simply do not exist*," he underscored his dismay in italics. Sometimes my mother tried to find the humor in the situation, musing in my baby book whether "in the future when you read about this time, you will find the absence of even such basic things as diapers funny."

The final straw was that I started walking three months too early to get shoes. Shoes were a luxury item that required ration cards and you had to be at least a year old to qualify.[6] Since I was only eight months old, I had to go shoeless. Fortunately, it was spring.

And so, in fits and starts, we became a family. During the war, my parents had dreamed of starting a family and making a home. "When the war is over," their letters said. The future they had dreamed of had now come. They had survived the war. They were together. They had a strong and healthy child. We had a place to call home, even if it was just a room in an attic.

By 1949 a new sense of normality was gradually being restored in Germany. The occupation status had been lifted, and the Western Allies (the United States, Great Britain, and France) had granted a fledgling West Germany limited sovereignty within their zones.[7] Germans were again citizens in their own country, not just subjects under foreign rule. They had a new flag (the disgraced swastika had been replaced by the black–red–gold tricolor of the

Weimar Republic), a revised national anthem (even if only the third verse could officially be sung),[8] a new currency (in June 1948 the Deutschmark had replaced the Reichsmark), a new constitution that affirmed the "inviolable dignity of every human being" as its founding principle,[9] and a new capital city, Bonn. A newly elected West German parliament convened that summer, and a new chancellor, a horse-faced, beanpole of a man with the lilting accent of a born-and-bred Rhinelander, took the reins of the new government that fall.

At the time, my father couldn't have known that this man, who during the previous regime had been on the government's hit list, would soon be his boss. He couldn't have known that within two years he would be working in the West German Foreign Ministry and that Konrad Adenauer would not only be Germany's first postwar Chancellor, but its first postwar Foreign Minister as well. What my father knew in the summer of 1949 was that things were improving and that he could afford to take a vacation with his wife and child.

He chose a place far from the ruined cities, with a landscape that the war seemed not to have touched: the Bavarian mountains. They reminded him of his native Bohemia, where he had gone skiing and hiking with family and friends. The photographs my parents took that summer have a playful feel. In one set, my mother and I are playing hide and seek: I have just "found" her, she is laughing, and I am clapping my hands with delight.

Her face is aglow with summer and her gray-green eyes seem to shine with light. Her hair is pinned back, the way my father loved it, and she is wearing the dress she made during the first postwar summer, when every day was the day she hoped her Walter would come back. On that day, she dreamed, her war would be over. "It is a particularly pretty dress," she had noted in her diary. "I know that Walter will be happy to see me in it."[10]

This happiness is evident in the photographs from that summer. Our poses are easy, relaxed. In one picture, I am sitting on a log pile beside my father, my socks and boots miniature versions of his. His arm is around me as he smiles down at me. I imagine my mother, behind the camera, smiling too. I feel the lean of my body against my father's, the sheltering curve of his arm against my back. The closeness between us is palpable.

But as I look at this picture now, across the distance of many years, I also think how German he looks: canvas rucksack, leather hiking boots, and knee-high wool socks. And from that same distance I see myself in the picture as a German girl: hair braided into two short pigtails, tied with ribbons above each ear, and an embroidered dirndl with a small white apron. The dark skin and black hair I was born with ("You looked like a little negro," my aunt Lotti teased me) have made way for the light hair and fair skin commonly

Me and my mother in Bavaria, summer 1949.

associated with being German. The only break with the German stereotype is my hazel eyes. German eyes are supposed to be blue.

Half a century later, I am sitting beside my father again, his arm around me as in the picture when I was two. It is 2005 and I am visiting him in the retirement home where he has lived since my mother died a decade earlier. We are going through old photographs stored in a shoebox. One of them catches my eye and I pull it out.

It is a small black and white picture of me on a mountain path. The path is narrow and the incline steep. A rock ledge rises up behind me. To my left is an abyss with just a thin iron rail for protection. The sky is cloudless, empty.

I feel a jolt of recognition. This is the place from my dream. As I stare at the picture, the sense of dread from my dream overcomes me, as if something dangerous and threatening were close by. I can't name it, but I feel it hovering, closing in. I turn the picture over and on the back is a note in my mother's hand: "On top of the Wendelstein."

"Where *is* this place?" I ask my father, handing the photograph to him. He glances at it. "Around Berchtesgaden," he says, as he hands it back to me. Then he adds, after a pause, "Where Hitler came from."

I am in Bonn, where our family has lived since the 1960s, when my father worked for the Foreign Ministry, and where I spent most of my secondary school years. I am sitting on the couch that used to be in our family living room. My mother's tea set is on the table in front of me, and on the walls are photographs and paintings from our family home. I am in a familiar place with familiar things next to my father.

Yet I feel disoriented, lost in a past I don't understand, in a place I remember but don't recognize. I want to feel as I did when I was two years old, secure in the shelter of my father's arms, but I feel confused and alone and frightened, overwhelmed by feelings that I can't explain.

How did a place *around Berchtesgaden*, a scene from a Riefenstahl film, and a vacation from my early childhood, morph into a mix of memories and feelings that overwhelm and haunt me in a nightly dream? And what does this sense of dread come from? Berchtesgaden was "where Hitler came from," my father told me. Factually, that's not true, of course. But even if it wasn't where he came from, it was where he frequently went: the place in the Bavarian mountains of his summer retreat. It was at the Berghof, on what Hitler liked to call his "Holy Mountain," that he was told of the Allied landings on the Normandy beaches when he finally awoke, having given instructions not to be disturbed. It was here that his deputy, Reich Marshall Göring, commanded the remains of the Luftwaffe at the end of the war. And it was here on his Holy Mountain, while German armies were in an agony of slaughter and German cities were going up in flames, that Hitler slept in, watched films, and enjoyed the scenery.[11]

Me and my father in Bavaria, summer 1949.

How do you remember things you didn't experience, that happened to others or before you were born? And how do you know that you actually know things when you are unable to put them into words?

Philosophers, psychoanalysts, and theologians try to answer such questions, explaining that knowing can fall outside language and remembering can run forward and backward through time.[12] Neuroscientists provide lab-tested evidence that memory and experience aren't congruent. Yet I find the "mysterious unavailability of much of our knowledge" unsettling.[13] What am I to do with things that I know, but can't access? And how does their lack of access affect me?

My mind is a confusing tangle of things that I experienced, things I learned about, and things I imagined: a family vacation, a film, and scenes from Nazi history. I can't explain the connections rationally. When I try, they dissolve in the way that dreams and memories do. But they are real to me, as real as the ghost was to Hamlet when it urged him to take responsibility for acts "most foul" he had inherited from his parents' time.

Drawing on his experience as a psychoanalyst working with autistic and schizophrenic children, Christopher Bollas shows how we can know things without knowing what it is we know. Emotionally and cognitively, he explains, children absorb parts of their parents' lives without understanding what they are absorbing. They don't do so consciously or intentionally. They don't even know that a transfer of experience is happening. The child simply experiences parts of her parents' lives as part of her own life. But it is a part of her life that she can't access. She can't explain or understand it. She can just feel it. It is a knowing that "is not to be thought."[14] It cannot be thought. It can just be lived.

I put the photograph of me on top of the Wendelstein back in the shoebox. My father pats my hand.

"Your tea's cold." He smiles at me. "Let me make some fresh."

Following the Clues

I didn't plan to do it, and I didn't do it consciously at first. But before I even knew what I was doing, I looked for clues. I proceeded carefully: no direct questions, just pay attention. Watch … listen … listen well. Attend to their tone of voice, their shift of eyes, their body language. And listen for what they left unsaid.

I knew that something big had happened. I could tell that it was on their minds. But they wouldn't talk about it in my presence. It hung between us like a screen I couldn't see through. What were they hiding? Why was it secret? To stay connected, I needed to know.[1]

By the time I was five, I had figured out that it had something to do with our family. Wherever we went, it went too. When we moved to Canada in the early 1950s, it followed us there. That's when I found my first clue: whatever had happened had to do not just with our family; it had something to do with hate. A child on the playground had said, "I hate you," when I told him where my family was from. I hadn't heard this word before, but I immediately knew it was a clue to the secret. "Hate" tore a hole in the screen I could see through. It was the first English word I remember learning.

It was the early 1950s and Germany's recovery as a nation had begun.[2] Its people were being reeducated, its cities rebuilt, and its economy was being restarted. In West Germany, the $1.5 billion of the Marshall Plan was reviving industrial production. Coal mines in the Ruhr were again operative.[3] The vaunted Economic Miracle had begun. Meanwhile, countries that had broken off diplomatic relations with Nazi Germany were starting to resume them with its postwar government. The country that just a few years earlier had stood "at the bottom of the list of civilized nations," as *Life* magazine's postwar "victory" issue had noted,[4] was being readmitted to the community of nations.

The speed and extent of Germany's reinvention of itself was bracing. Some found it promising, others disturbing. My father's position was clear. The emerging new Germany was the one he believed in and the one he wanted to help build. In March 1951, when a newly founded West German government opened its first Foreign Ministry,[5] he applied for a position. This time, his language skills and law degree were an asset and he was accepted. A few months later his postwar career as a West German diplomat began.

His first overseas posting to Canada came quickly. Diplomatic relations between Germany and Canada had resumed earlier that year, first on a consular, then ambassadorial, level, and on November 8, 1951, the day before what officially came to be called Germany's Destiny Day (*Schicksalstag*), the new West German embassy in Ottawa opened. The historical significance of this German Destiny Day was unmistakable. It recalled the pride of November 9, 1919, when the first German Republic was announced in Weimar and a fledgling democracy ushered in, and it recalled the shame of November 9, 1938, when the fiery pogrom known as *Kristallnacht* set the stage for the genocide we know as the Holocaust. When the German embassy in Ottawa opened almost exactly thirteen years after *Kristallnacht*, the traumatic memory of the Holocaust was still raw, and the deliberate modesty of the embassy's appearance—a simple house in a simple residential neighborhood—was a small, but resonant, gesture of contrition.

On September 14, 1951 my father boarded the SS *Giuseppe Garibaldi* in Genoa and landed in Halifax twelve days later, arriving in a country that would be our home for the next decade. Snapshots from onboard ship show my father to cut a dashing figure—hair slicked back, Clark Gable mustache, and silver-tipped cigarette holder in his hand. Three days after he arrived in Canada, I celebrated my fifth birthday in Velen with cocoa and cake.

When my mother, one-year-old sister, and I followed the next spring on the SS *Ryndam*, we weren't as dashing. Storms over the Atlantic slowed our journey for over a week. Desperately seasick, my mother lay on her bed, a damp cloth covering her eyes and forehead, while I wandered about the ship unattended. My favorite place was the lower deck, where the dogs were kenneled. Behind bars in their wire cages, they seemed as lonely as I felt, but when they pressed against the bars and licked my fingers, and when their fur rubbed against my skin, we comforted each other. They were my secret refuge on the ship. When we finally landed, my anxious father was shocked to see the "pitiful little boat ... [that] was dwarfed by all the other ships around it."[6]

We had crossed the Atlantic Ocean and arrived in Canada. What would this New World be like for us?

Only years later did I realize that we had crossed much more than an ocean. We had crossed into another world. In 1951, almost exactly a year before me, another five-year-old girl had, like me, left from Le Havre and arrived in Halifax with her family of Polish Jews who had come to Canada by way of France. She would later describe the world they had left behind as "'the cemetery' that was ... a good part of Europe."[7] But for the Borensztejn family (anglicized in Canada to the less Slavic, but ironically more Germanic, Borenstein), Europe was not just a "cemetery" they were glad to leave. For the Borensztejns, as for countless other émigrés including my family, what we were leaving behind was also our home. Canada was a foreign country to us, and we were foreigners, whether we came as refugees, immigrants, or guests.

However, as Germans, we had special status. We weren't just foreigners. We were suspect foreigners, accused by the history we trailed in our wake. The war was over, but people weren't at peace yet. Memories were bitter and emotions raw as the world took the measure of the devastation Germans had wrought under Hitler. Even politically, things remained unsettled. The war had not concluded with a peace treaty, just an armistice. Legally speaking, Germany and the Allies were still at war.

In May 1952, a month after our arrival in Canada, a major step in the direction of peace was taken with the German Treaty. Signed by West Germany and the Western Allies, it was designed to bridge the period between Germany's military capitulation and an eventual peace treaty that would bring World War II to a formal and conclusive end.[8]

This is not what happened. World War II didn't end the way we expect wars to end: with a peace treaty. It ended in a way that could not have been foreseen at the time of the German Treaty. Less than a decade after World War II, the geopolitical situation had radically changed: the Germany of World War II no longer existed and the former Allies were no longer allies. The heat of World War II hadn't yet cooled when the Cold War began, and in this new conflict a divided Germany became the frontline between the newly configured East and West blocs. In these changed circumstances, it wasn't clear who should make peace with whom and with which sides the two Germanies were allied. The resulting conundrum made a peace treaty impossible, so it was quietly—and indefinitely—postponed.

A few decades later, the situation changed again in ways that no one during the Cold War could have predicted: the two Germanies reunited. This unification (or as some preferred to call it, reunification) of West and East Germany, of a capitalist democracy and a socialist state under cadre control, did not just end the Cold War but also the hot war that the armistice of 1945 had merely suspended. When the four former Allies—the erstwhile Soviet Union, United Kingdom, United States, and France—came together in 1990 to recognize the united Germany as a "democratic and peaceful state" and "an equal and sovereign partner in a united Europe," the matter of war and peace in relation to Germany was effectively settled.[9] It had taken almost half a century, but peace, or at least the "foundation for the establishment" of peace, as the Treaty on the Final Settlement more cautiously put it, had finally, de facto, been achieved.[10]

Myths were rife for the making in the postwar world, as people and entire regimes eagerly remade themselves to accommodate new expectations. The first thing to be remade was usually the past. In Germany, all things Nazi seemed to disappear as soon as the Hitler government was discredited. Victor Klemperer described the zeal of this transformation: "War criminals are being executed, 'little Pgs' ... are being removed from office, nationalist books are being withdrawn from circulation, Hitler Squares and Göring Streets are being renamed. Hitler oaks are being felled."[11] Under the previous regime, Germans had been pressured to become Nazis, whatever "being a Nazi" meant at the time. Now they were expected to be something different. Exactly what they were supposed to become was hard to define. The easiest solution was to be "no-longer-Nazi," or, even better, to never have been one. From diplomats to housewives, hardly anyone seemed to be a Nazi anymore. Even more surprisingly, hardly anyone ever seemed to have been one.

On the national level, the most emphatic evidence of a break with the past was proffered in September 1952 in the form of the Reparations Agreement between the Federal Republic of Germany and the State of Israel. Known in

German as the *Wiedergutmachungsabkommen* (literally, the "Agreement to Make-Good-Again"), it promised to indemnify Jews for the loss of property under Nazi rule and cover the cost of integrating Jewish refugees into Israel.[12] This Agreement was supposed to signal to the world that the new Germany of the Bonn Republic had decidedly left its Nazi past behind.

The problem with this rehabilitation story is that it wasn't true. Not only were so many former Nazis back, but so many never seemed to have left in the first place. While Hitler oaks were felled and Hitler Squares renamed, shopkeepers kept the shops they had "inherited" from Jewish owners who had "disappeared." Meanwhile institutions, from government to industry, restocked their offices with experienced hands from the previous era. The Federal Chancellery itself set the tone by appointing a man who had served Hitler as a top aide and legal advisor to the same position in Chancellor Konrad Adenauer's postwar cabinet. The well-known fact that Adenauer's "dear Herr Globke" had been one of the legal architects of the infamous Nuremberg Laws, notably the Reich Citizenship Law that stripped German Jews of their German citizenship, was treated as little more than a minor embarrassment.

When my father, recalling his early years in the Foreign Ministry, boasted that he was "the first German diplomat who was not a Nazi," I heard echoes of the postwar myth that the past was past. True, he was not a Nazi and never had been. He had been a soldier in the German army, but never a member of the Nazi party or any Nazi-affiliated group. But he couldn't have been "the first German diplomat who was not a Nazi." In order to weed out former (or current) Nazis, all civil servants in the new West German government, particularly those just starting a public service career, were reviewed politically. And even if the system was imperfect, he couldn't have been the only one who passed.

I understand my father's insistence on his non-Nazi credentials. We all want to be among the good guys; he did too and he had the record to prove it. Yet his insistence served another purpose. By claiming that he was "the first" person in the Ministry who was not a Nazi, he punctured the myth that the postwar German government was Nazi-free. On the contrary, he implied, it was full of them. An early review of the Foreign Ministry in its first year corroborated my father's contention. Almost half of those recruited for higher-ranked positions were former members of the Nazi party. In the legal department alone, eleven of the seventeen senior hires were former Nazis, and as the Ministry sought experienced professionals for its top positions, this percentage eventually even increased.[13]

Nevertheless, the public image of the Foreign Ministry as "the shining white knight among German institutions in the Federal Republic,"[14] uncontaminated by the Nazi past, prevailed for almost sixty years. It was not debunked until 2005, when Foreign Minister Joschka Fischer tasked an international team of historians to investigate the Ministry's Nazi history. The commission's report, *Das Amt und die Vergangenheit: Deutsche Diplomaten im Dritten Reich und in der Bundesrepublik* (The Foreign Office and the Past: German Diplomats in the Third Reich and the Federal Republic), five years late and 880 pages long, was a sensation. It became a bestseller overnight.[15]

The findings were scandalous. Even to those who had called for the study, the Ministry's fall from grace was a shock. The Foreign Ministry had not been the beacon of integrity it had claimed to be, "untainted by the crimes of the Third Reich" or free of former Nazis rebooting their careers.[16] Like most other institutions in the new Germany, it had been compromised from the start. In fact, the report suggested, it had been worse than most. Large numbers of diplomats who had served under Hitler had been rehired,[17] while "high-ranking positions in particular were again staffed with members of the 'old guard.'"[18] The sobering conclusion was that "[n]o federal ministry [had] maintained as direct a continuity with its Nazi past as the Foreign Ministry and no other ministry [had] repressed that continuity as thoroughly."[19] My father's boast about his exceptional non-Nazi status turned out to be truer than I had granted. He was not the first, much less the only, postwar German diplomat without a Nazi stain. But among the many with a tainted past, he stood out.

Caught between a past it had officially rejected and a future it wasn't yet free to choose, as a non-sovereign state, Germany in the early 1950s was a "precarious nation."[20] What it stood for had to be reconfigured. The question was how, and by whom? The Foreign Ministry had an answer: culture. Cultural relations would be the cornerstone of foreign policy.[21] Instead of missiles, Germany would send musicians. Bach and Beethoven instead of bombs. Werner Herzog instead of Wernher von Braun.[22] Not only would such a policy make Germany more attractive to other nations, it would help "build trust in our country around the world."[23] Most importantly, a focus on culture would restore Germany's image as the fabled "land of poets and thinkers"—a civilized nation.

This was a mission my father fully endorsed. Cultural exchange, he thought, was what politics should be about. Even chamber music was, for him, political, in its ability to connect people across their separating differences. He often came home from work excited about a new book by a German author, or a new German film or play, wondering how they might convey a measure of what Germany was about to the outside world. As we discussed these things in the evening, over supper or a glass of wine, my intellectual education took shape. I learned about Joseph Beuys and Werner Herzog from my father before they became household names, and I heard of works by new German writers before they had even been published. When I was thirteen, my father read me passages from a new novel that had just come out and, decades later when I was a professor of literature and taught Böll's *Billiards at Half-Past Nine*, the memory of my father reading it to me deepened its meaning. In this way, my father's postwar perspective shaped my professional life as well. Culture, for him, was more than mere enrichment, more than an add-on to the necessities of daily life. For him, the arts and literature weren't optional, much less a luxury. They were foundational to human life. At his most optimistic, he even hoped they might bend the arc of history away from violence. I inherited that hope from him.

The year that Germany and the Western Allies signed the German Treaty, establishing the foundation for a more lasting state of peace, I turned six and started first grade in Ottawa. The school (or perhaps just my teacher) used a negative incentive system: good students sat in the front and bad students in the back. If you were good or did well, this helped you get better; if you were bad or did poorly, this arrangement made things worse. And because, not speaking English, I couldn't do well, I was seated at the very back. Fortunately, in my case, the negative incentive backfired. Shame worked. My goals in first grade were simple: I had to get out of the back row. I had to move as close to the front as possible.

While Germany was trying to rehabilitate itself on the international stage and be readmitted to the community of nations, I was doing something similar on a small and personal scale. I too wanted to be accepted. I wanted others to like me and I wanted to fit in. I didn't know about Nazi history or postwar politics, reparations or collective guilt, but I knew that being German was a problem. Even as Germans were trying to put the past behind them, the weight of that past was still sinking in for the rest of the world.

I couldn't change who I was or where I came from. What I could change was my presentation. The first step was not to speak German, at least in public. I had to learn English fast.

I began by collecting words: big words, little words, silly words, words in English that reminded me of German words, and words that I just happened across. It didn't matter if I knew their meaning. All that mattered was that I liked the sound. Some people collected stamps or butterflies; I became a word collector. Words were my talismans, my magic spells, my weapons. They were tools with which to shape the world. They were my dominion; the place where I aspired to rule.

Words weren't abstract to me. They were physical. I felt them on my tongue, rolled them around inside my mouth, and watched them change who I was when I spoke them. Looking out of the car window on a drive somewhere, I saw the world streaming by in the form of images and the images would morph into words. I broke the words into syllables and arranged the syllables into metric patterns. I composed them. I conducted them. I played them as if they were instruments. First a walking pace, andante: *te-le-PHONE-pole, blink-ing-STREET-light, big-truck-PASS-ing, when-are-WE-there.* Then accelerate, allegro molto: *Mer-CE-des, Ford-PICK-up, Volks-WAG-en, Chev-RO-let.* End with a coda when it was time to stop: *FREIGHT-TRAIN-RED-LIGHT-DRIVE-WAY-FRONT-DOOR-HOME.*

Hate was a coda word. It ended things. It was hard like a rock or a fence post, closed like a fisted hand. When a child in the playground said to me, "I hate you," I didn't know what it meant or what to do with it, but I felt *hate* like a door slammed shut. When I asked my mother what *hate* meant, she didn't answer me. But her silence was the clue I was looking for: *hate* had something to do with our being German.

That's when I realized that words weren't the answer to my questions. What had happened? What had Germans done? They wouldn't tell me what we had done that sent words like *hate* our way, or why no one was willing to tell me. If adults weren't giving me answers, I had to figure it out myself. I had to look for answers outside words. Silence, my mother had shown me, was an answer too. It was the space between words left unspoken.

I started to listen for what people weren't saying and look for what they tried to hide. Games offered the perfect opportunity. One game in particular served my sleuthing goal: "I see something that you don't see." It was a game we often played on car trips. We were barely in the car when I began.

"I see something that you don't see," I shouted from the back seat. "And it's red," I added, offering my first clue.

I picked random objects, like the tongue of the car's speedometer (clue: red), or the pearl in my mother's earring (clue: round). The trick was to find something that everyone could see, yet seemed unimportant and could go unnoticed. I didn't care about winning the game. I just wanted to understand how and what we see. How we don't see what is right in front of us. We look right past it. Even when it touches us, we might not see it. The car game was a lesson in seeing. I was teaching myself how to look.

More than anything, I wanted to see what my parents saw. I literally tried to put myself in their place. When it was my mother's turn, I pressed against her, put my eye next to her eye, and rubbed my cheek against her cheek. "Stop that," she twisted away from me. Her tone was brusque, her irritation evident. But I persisted. I had to know what it was she saw. Perhaps if I could see the world through her eyes, I could see how *hate*, silence, and being German were all connected.

Decades later, when my son was the same age I had been when I was hit by *hate* in the playground, I watched him go through a similar process of

Me and my mother on a visit to Montreal, August 1952.

looking for clues. A book I was teaching had caught his attention, probably because it didn't look like the books I normally taught. It was a book with cartoon drawings of animals: mice and cats and pigs. They weren't in color, like the picture books he usually read, and they included quite a bit of text. But at first glance, it could have been seen as a book for children. Even though some of the animals looked menacing, particularly the cats with their teeth and claws, they didn't look scarier than Maurice Sendak's wild things.

Nicolas was hooked. He couldn't read words yet, but he could read the pictures. There were cats in German uniforms carrying weapons, shouting orders, and beating mice. There were pigs forcing mice off the sidewalk or taunting them as they walked by. There were mice alone, mice in groups, mice in families, mice talking, eating, hiding, running, cowering. There were mice on city streets wearing Jewish stars on their clothes, mice in concentration camps in striped pajamas, and naked mice in line for group showers. There were mice corpses stacked in piles.

The book that Nicolas had found on my desk was *Maus*, Art Spiegelman's story of his parents' experience as Jews in Nazi-occupied Poland and his own experience as their American-born, postwar son. He had told the story in the form of a comic book with Jews as mice, Germans as cats, and Poles as pigs.

Nicolas couldn't put the book down. He read *Maus I*, which I had in paperback, and *Maus II*, which had just come out in hardback. When he had finished them, he started over. He studied the images, slowly and closely, frame by frame. It was as if he was committing them to memory. He never asked me to read them to him. He read them in silence, on his own.

I kept telling him, "They have to stay in my study. I need these books for my class." But invariably I found them in his room, on his bed or on the floor with his Legos. He didn't ask me any questions about these books, and I didn't offer any answers. I don't think we ever talked about them. We just passed them, back and forth, without words.

Friends who learned that my five-year old son was reading *Maus* were appalled and worried. "He's way too young to be exposed to such things," they objected. But their objections came too late. Whatever damage could be done had been done by then. He had found the books and started reading them before I stopped him, even before I stopped to think that perhaps I should.

I have often pondered our silence about the *Maus* books. We always talked about books that we shared. Why not this book? My son had a five-year-old's insatiable curiosity and asked about everything. Why not this story? And why did I, who set few limits on what I talked about with my children, stay silent on the story of *Maus*?

There are reasonable explanations for my silence. Nicolas was too young to learn about the Holocaust or Nazi Germany, even if cast as a story of cats and mice. It was too complex a history to burden a young child with, and simplifying it didn't seem truthful. But the deeper truth was that I didn't know how to talk about this history. For *Maus* wasn't about just any history. It was about a history that had to do with me. Not just me, but my parents and even my children. If children of victims, as Spiegelman documented, inherit the trauma of their parents' experience, didn't children of perpetrators inherit their parents' shame? I probably reasoned at the time that we would talk about all this some other time, just not yet. The right time would come along later.

Yet when later came and he seemed old enough to learn about the history he had inherited through me, I was shocked to discover how much he already knew. No one had talked to him about it directly. No one had told him in so many words. He had figured it out by studying the pictures. Like me at his age, he had not asked questions. He had found answers by following the clues.

Family Ties

My father used to tell me, "Angelika, family is all there is." It was meant to reassure me, but it sounded threatening. What I heard was, "Only family will be there for you. If something happens, good or bad, no one else will care."

But counting on family was problematic. To begin with, our family was small. In Canada, there were only four of us: my father, mother, sister, and me. All the others who made up family in the larger sense—grandparents, aunts and uncles, a few cousins and some relatives I hardly knew—were an ocean away. The idea of home didn't feel more secure, either. Velen, where my grandparents Bushoff lived, was on another continent and my father's home in Bohemia, on the other side of a so-called Iron Curtain, was more foreign to me than the moon. I couldn't rely on family. We were in Canada and I had to fit in there.

Being German made fitting in difficult. To our Canadian neighbors, to my playmates and classmates, even to strangers we met in shops, we were objects of suspicion, if not hostility, members of a people they didn't trust or like. They kept their distance and often turned away. Even if my father was right and family was the only reliable safe space, it was not enough for me. I needed friends. I needed to be part of a bigger community—our neighborhood, my school, the parish. I wanted to be with people who accepted me and included me in their activities. The solution, I thought, was to become more like them, to blend in and not appear different.

I shifted identities according to context. In school, I was a diligent student, a devoted Catholic in church, and at home I was a dutiful daughter, drying dishes, ironing linen and cleaning my room. I learned to be different people in private and public. I was a German girl at home with my family. In public, I became Canadian. At times I felt like a traitor, disclaiming my family behind their backs, but I was trying to balance different loyalties. I tried to shed the outward trappings of Germanness without renouncing the German daughter within. The transformation wasn't automatic. It required attention and there were many steps. The first step, which I quickly mastered, was learning English. Not just the words, but how to say them right. I thickened the l's, rounded the r's, and flattened the vowel sounds until I passed as a native speaker. When I switched to German, I just readjusted my mouth and throat.

But if changing languages was relatively easy, changing my body was not. The first challenge was becoming conscious of it as German. Not how it looked, but how it felt and what it did. How I walked or moved my arms or held my shoulders. How close I stood or sat to other people. How I smiled or how I looked when I didn't smile. These were things I did unconsciously. They felt natural, normal. But what felt natural and normal to me appeared foreign in the eyes of others. To learn the language of cultural passing with my body, I had to learn to be foreign in myself. Then practice until that foreignness felt natural.

Years later, when I came to the United States as a foreign student, I had to learn the lesson of cultural passing again. People always asked me, "What's the matter?" and I would answer, "Nothing," until I realized that they meant, "Why aren't you smiling?" To pass as an American I had to get an American smile.

I trained like an athlete for a competition. I studied technique and had a practice regimen. Locked in the bathroom, I faced the mirror and began.

"Hi, how are you?" I would say, smiling. Check the smile. Make corrections. Lift the corners of my mouth. Extend the smile and hold as long as possible. Should I show my teeth or cover them? They weren't white or straight enough to pass as American, but I had to let that go. Get the smile right and the rest will follow.

Now try talking, but don't stop smiling. "Fine, thank you," I addressed my mirror face. "How are you?" Check the smile again. Hold; and adjust as needed.

When the corners of my mouth got shaky, I let the muscles of my face relax and take a break before going for another round. I learned to contort my face into grimaces to release the tension. Sometimes I let my jaw hang slack until I drooled. When I could smile through a whole conversation, I had reached my goal. I could pass as an American and not look foreign.

As a German child in 1950s Canada, blending in was my foremost aim. In 1953 we moved to Toronto, where my father had been transferred to the General Consulate. We had a house in a sprawling suburb with treeless lawns. My father drove to work in a tan Ford Customline. My mother stayed home and kept house. I walked to school with the neighborhood children. By all appearances, we were a normal, middle-class family. Our German difference could almost be ignored.

For Germans in general, the sense of a new postwar normality was settling in. By the mid-'50s, Germany had rejoined the community of Western nations as an equal partner. The *Protocol on the Termination of the Occupation Regime in the Federal Republic of Germany*, which marked the end of West Germany's occupied status and its emergence as a sovereign state, had finally been ratified.[1] It had been admitted to the North Atlantic Treaty Organization (NATO) and was a member of the newly founded Western European Union (WEU).[2]

My attempts to be accepted as an equal by my peers and classmates had been equally successful. In St. Pius Parish, I was part of a group preparing for our First Communion. In school I was getting good grades and winning spelling bees. On the track team I was earning points as a sprinter. But my status as a peer always felt tenuous. All it took was a careless misstep, a lapse of attention, or something unexpected, to expose my foreignness. Then everyone would see that I didn't really belong; I was just pretending.

There was the time I invited some children over to play croquet. It seemed a good way to make friends in our new neighborhood. They came, perhaps as curious about this game they had never heard of as they were about the new girl on the block. We were getting the croquet set out of the garage, when a girl asked, "Does your father gamble?" I didn't know what to say. I didn't know what *gamble* meant. It was a word I had never heard before. Then I saw where her question came from: a stack of boxes labeled "Proctor & Gamble" in the garage. I had my answer. The boxes told me. "Yes, he does," I said matter-of-factly, as I grabbed the wickets. "Let's play croquet."

Language had so many pitfalls, you couldn't help but occasionally fall in. My name was often the first stumbling block. On my first day of school in Toronto the teacher paused at my name.

"Are you Anglican?" she asked, smiling at me.

Another new word. I didn't know what *Anglican* meant, any more than I had known about gambling, but I knew from the sound what the word looked like. It looked like my name. So, I quickly reasoned, I must be Anglican.

"Yes," I answered brightly, "yes, I'm Anglican." I gave her a big Canadian smile. That I was Catholic was entirely irrelevant.

I tried to solve the problem of my name by changing it. I offered, "You can call me Angie." But when I brought someone home it didn't work. For there was my mother, saying my name the German way: hard "g" and the "l" a flick of the tongue. As soon as she said it, my attempt to pass was over. I was not Angie, but a girl with a strange, foreign name.

"*Ann-gay-lee-kah* ..." They drew the syllables out slowly. "What kind of a name is that?"

"It's a German name," I explained quickly, vowing never to bring someone home again. My name embarrassed me. So did my mother with her German accent. "Don't call me Angelika," I would hiss at her, angrily, after my English-speaking friends had left. "When I'm with friends, I want to be called Angie." I actually didn't want her to call me anything. All I wanted her to do was smile.

As if to compensate, I started carrying a photograph of her around. Classmates had family pictures they would show me: a new baby, a sister in a prom dress, a brother with a football, the family dog. I wanted to have a family picture to show too. So I put a picture of my mother in my wallet.

But like my smile, it had to be adjusted and I adjusted it. Over the photograph that I had taken from our family album, I drew the mother that

I thought an Angie would have. I broadened her smile and added bright red lipstick, arched her eyebrows, and enhanced her eyes. I gave her bangs and a stylish hairdo. But the effect wasn't what I'd intended. By trying to make her look un-German, I had made her into a freak.

Even at the time, I must have known how grotesque it looked, for I don't recall ever showing the picture to anyone, even though I carried it around with me for years. Not only did I carry it around, I kept it.

It has been years since I last saw it, but I find it in a box of old keepsakes and get it out. My first reaction is embarrassment. It looks ridiculous. The crude ferocity of the disfigurement is unsettling. What kind of a child would attack her mother this way? There is something monstrous and yet pathetic about the gesture.

Memories of long-ago feelings return. There is the anger of a child at her German parents—with their German names, their German accents, their German ways—for burdening her with a German history. There is her wish to disavow her connection to them, to deny them as her German family. And

The 1944 photograph of my mother that I "retouched" in 1955.

there is her shame at the betrayal that lies in this wish to disavow the very people she most loves.

Perhaps this is why I kept the picture. Among all the forgettable family pictures of people smiling, trying to look the way we thought we should be, this one, in its very grotesqueness, was honest. The disfigurement it expressed felt real. Many of our smiles, on and off camera, were a presentation. As I look at the defaced photograph, it dawned on me that this picture didn't show my mother. It showed how I was feeling.

As I put it back in the box, I caught a glimpse of something written on the back. I took it out again to look more closely. It was a date, in my mother's hand: "December 1944." Exactly a decade before I tried to remake her. I stared at the face beneath my childhood scribblings. Who was this young woman before she was my mother. What story did this picture tell?

In December 1944, my mother, Ursula, was twenty-two. She had been living in Rumburg with my father's parents for almost two years by then, since her January 1943 wedding, but she still felt like a stranger in this eastern European world. She confided to her diary that she was homesick and often lonely. And she was increasingly worried about the war. The Red Army was steadily advancing westwards and German civilians were starting to flee. The growing uncertainty about what was to come made tempers fray, and the domestic tensions in the Bammer household—her father-in-law's harshness and his wife's unhappiness—had become worse. She missed her Velen home. Her parents seemed a world away. She missed the comfort of friends. Above all, she missed her husband, Walter. She longed to feel his arms around her, but he was off at war.

Ursula worried about Walter constantly. Over the past year, as the war unraveled, he had been shuttled from front to front in a mad effort to forestall the defeat that appeared inevitable. In June he was sent to Normandy for the American invasion. When his artillery regiment was destroyed, it was reconstituted with fresh bodies and sent to Russia to reinforce the Wehrmacht's last defense against the Soviet onslaught. Their effort was doomed from the outset. The Eastern Front had reached a mind-boggling length of 2,400 kilometers, and Germany was out of resources. Soldiers, weapons, fuel, and ammunition were at emergency levels. Along the Vistula alone, 980,000 German soldiers and 2,000 tanks faced 2.25 million Soviet soldiers and 6,500 tanks. And while the Soviets commanded 4,500 aircraft, the German Luftwaffe was virtually out of fuel. The human cost of the struggle was staggering. That summer and fall, Germany alone lost over 5,000 men on the Eastern Front each day. When Soviet troops entered East Prussia on October 18, 1944, Germany's war in the east was effectively over.

All remaining hopes were directed toward a last offensive on the Western Front. Codenamed Watch on the Rhine, it was set for mid-December in the forested region of the Ardennes, strategically located between the British and American front lines. My father had just arrived in the east when his unit was redeployed westward.

As soon as she heard of his redeployment, my mother took the first train she could get to see him. It was a full day's travel from Rumburg to the isolated military base of Gruppe in West Prussia where he was stationed, and she barely arrived in time. Walter was already packed; his unit was departing in the morning. They had just a few hours together.

One evening in Bonn, my mother shared some details of her visit to Gruppe with me. It was late October, one of those central European days of perpetual twilight, made even more desolate by the foggy cold. By the time she got there, it was dark. Even in her winter coat, she couldn't stop shivering. With nowhere else to go—there was nothing at the military base in Gruppe—Ursula got permission to meet Walter in the canteen. They sat and talked under harsh, bright, overhead lights, warming their hands around cups of hot tea.

There was an urgency to this visit that distinguished it from previous times, as if they knew there wasn't much time left. They were not measuring their time together in years anymore, but in days and even in hours. "There was no time to waste," my mother recalled. "Before he left, I wanted to know everything ... everything he hadn't yet shared."

Impelled by this sense of urgency, she dropped her usual reticence and pressed him to tell her all about his past, including girlfriends he hadn't talked about before. She wanted to know what was important to him, including what and whom he had loved. "I wanted nothing hidden between us," she told me. "I needed us to know each other fully. It almost felt like I was taking his last confession."

When they parted, she slipped a note into his pocket. "Read this later, when I am gone," she had penciled on it. It is one of the only notes from Ursula that survived the war.

Gruppe, West Prussia
31 October 1944

My dearest Walter,

I love you with all my soul. I want you to feel that I am with you at every moment. And if a time comes when things are particularly difficult, may you draw strength from the certainty of our love and the bond that holds us close forever. May you then feel me there, right by

The original 1944 photograph of my mother.

your side, sheltering your head against my breast, holding you safe with my arms around you.

Walter, my husband … sleep calmly and deeply. God be with you and he will be with us.

Your wife

When they parted, Walter promised Ursula that he would come back to her, no matter what. "Wait for me, Ursula. I will find you." These were the last words she would hear from him for over a year.

The Ardennes Offensive (or the Battle of the Bulge, as it would be known in English) was decided soon. It began on December 16 and was effectively over by New Year's Day, even as fighting dragged on through a miserable January. The German military was vanquished and Germany's infrastructure had collapsed. Telephone lines had been cut or destroyed in air raids; mail delivery was all but suspended for security reasons. News circulated in the form of rumors and word of mouth.

In the absence of any reliable information, Ursula had no idea where Walter was. He could be in France, or Belgium, or even Germany. He could be wounded, taken prisoner, or even dead. She confided her growing fear and dread to her diary: the nightmares that woke her, the sense of futility in trying to stay busy during the day. The total war that Hitler had called for had finally engulfed them. Chaos and uncertainty were all around.

What she did then seems strange, or at least surprising. She went to a photographer and had her picture taken. Could she have meant it as a Christmas present in case Walter somehow made it home? Could it have been part of a plan to return to Westphalia if the Russians came and she needed a photograph for a travel permit? Or, as she saw the world around her disintegrate, did she need to prove that she was still intact; a young woman of twenty-two with her life ahead of her?

The young woman in the photograph doesn't give me answers. She doesn't even meet my gaze. Her eyes look off to the distance, perhaps to someone only she can see in her mind. She is younger than my daughter is now. She is wearing the embroidered sweater that Walter had given her the previous Christmas, their first Christmas as husband and wife. "For when we go to the mountains on our first vacation," he had told her. She has arranged her hair the way she wore it on their wedding day: parted in the middle and gathered at the back. Her pale young face and the stillness of her body move me.

A young woman sits for her portrait in a world going up in flames. Yet, for the count of a photograph's exposure, she holds herself steady. She looks off into the distance and smiles.

Between the Word-Gaps

We returned to Germany in November 1959. After seven years as a diplomat in Canada, my father had been assigned to a position in the Cultural Bureau of the Foreign Ministry. And since Bonn, the provisional capital of the new West Germany, was the seat of the federal government, my parents told me my new home would be there.

"We'll be home for Christmas," my parents said, their voices happy. I said I was happy too, but I had mixed feelings. Canada had never felt like home to me (I always knew that we were only visiting). But Germany didn't feel like home either. I had left it at the age of five and grown up elsewhere. The country I was returning to as a twelve-year-old wasn't home to me anymore. It was the place I named when people asked me where I was from. Yet the joy of return in my parents' eyes made me feel envious. They had a sense of belonging I didn't have. They had a *Heimat*.

Heimat was a place, but it wasn't just a place. It was a sensibility, a way of feeling, a deep connection. It was usually where you came from and where your family had roots in a community they had long been part of. It was sometimes where you had moved to, formed attachments, and put down roots. But no matter how deep or shallow the roots, *Heimat* was the place where you were known and recognized for who you were, where springtime smelled familiar, and the sun on your face in summertime warmed your soul. It was where people said your name in your mother tongue and the sound of the language evoked memories.

Yet in the postwar Germany we were returning to, *Heimat* was a suspect term. With its sense of nostalgia for a lost homeland, it carried a whiff of Blood and Soil thinking.[1] As I came of age, I learned to dismiss it as sentimental and condemn it as dangerous. Progressive intellectuals strove to be world citizens, "transcendentally homeless," as the Frankfurt School theorists whom my cohort admired put it.[2] Being attached, much less bound, to a place that you called home was considered provincial, petit-bourgeois, embarrassing. To be transcendentally homeless was to be emancipated from such bonds. However, I secretly longed for such a sense of *Heimat* and tried to imagine how it might feel. In such a place I wouldn't feel foreign or provisional or suspect. I would belong there, be part of a community. I wouldn't worry about being welcome. I would be at home.

Being transcendentally homeless sounded better in principle than it felt in practice. I once read somewhere that even T.W. Adorno, the stern thinker who deemed nostalgia retrograde, secretly loved listening to folk music from his native Germany. Yet he kept this pleasure to himself, perhaps because it revealed emotional attachments to a people and place he was deeply ambivalent about for political reasons. I sometimes thought that this ambivalence even affected his choice of Adorno, his mother's Italian name, over Wiesengrund, his father's German name. Perhaps Wiesengrund, which in German means meadow grounds, was too tied, in the most literal way, to the physical materiality of German land.

Publicly, my father agreed with Adorno: nostalgia was suspect. It harbored nationalism at its core, and nationalism, as history had shown, was dangerous. But that wasn't the whole story for either man. After my father's death I discovered that, like Adorno, he had kept other, private, feelings hidden. The summer after their return to Germany in 1959, my parents went on a three-week trip through Germany, visiting people and places they had missed during the years away. In the trove of personal papers I inherited after his death, I found a small album that my father had made as a memento of that trip, with photographs and reflections on what being back in Germany meant to him. I was unprepared for the depth of nostalgia that his words revealed. The love of *Heimat* they described made his fierce rejection of nationalist attachments all the more poignant. "After the long stay abroad," he wrote,

> a great longing had grown within us for places of German culture, for the familiar landscapes we hadn't seen for so long, and for the people who by nature were close to us. In short, we satisfied what is conventionally understood as a "feeling for *Heimat.*" It is an important feeling in a person's life.

I was moved by the longing in my father's words and the ambivalence revealed by the quotation marks around "feeling for *Heimat.*" He didn't romanticize homelessness in the way Adorno did, but he accepted it as part of the war's outcome. Germany started the war and lost it, he always said, "and we lost our right to a homeland in the process." Yet his political position was in conflict with his personal feelings. He resolved the conflict by never publicly mourning the loss of his home in Bohemia after Germany lost the war or the loss of his belief in a country he had fought for. These were losses he could only mourn privately.

In the spring of 1960, after several months in Velen with my mother's parents while we waited for new government housing to be built, my family moved to Bonn. That Easter, I started seventh grade at the Liebfrauen School, a private Catholic secondary girls' school.[3]

In the fall, our regular German teacher went on maternity leave and a replacement teacher took her classes. I don't remember her name; even at the time it hardly seemed to register. She was just the *Referendarin*, the assistant teacher. No longer young but not yet old, of average height and normal build, she had short, dark hair, pale skin, and wore prescription glasses. Her appearance was unremarkable, but something about her made us uncomfortable. Unlike other teachers who showed interest in us, she kept her distance. She rarely, if ever, smiled and seemed to avoid having to look at us directly. When she had to, her hands would flutter to her face, as if to shield herself. It was as if facing us took deliberate effort.

Yet her vulnerability didn't make us compassionate. It made us mean and we attacked her. We were rude, then hostile, and finally cruel. We pretended not to hear her when she called on us and feigned ignorance when she asked a question. We mimicked her. We mocked her. We laughed at her. We stared at her hairy legs and grinned. However, one day we went too far. We were mocking her again, our snorts of laughter smooth and hard as pebbles, when she suddenly rushed to her desk, grabbed her books, and fled. She left the door to the hallway open and we heard her crying—big, raspy, gulping, throaty sobs. No one followed her. No one said anything. We just sat there, unyielding, silent.

I think back to what we did to her with a kind of horror infused with shame, the callous cruelty of the young when they band together. But now I wonder whether there was more to it than that, something sinister that we couldn't name.

At the time I only registered her discomfort with us, but I think we were equally uncomfortable. Her appearance may have played a role, a pale and haunted look at odds with the brave new world of our postwar Germany, but I think our cruelty to her was grounded in a deeper and unconscious fear. By introducing us to things we had avoided knowing and raising questions we had learned not to ask, she threatened our sense of security, and we responded by fighting back.

The censored knowledge that we found so threatening was not about sex, as one might think with adolescents. In the shadow of the Nazi years, it wasn't sex that was silenced in Germany. It was death. "Death, not sex," Ruth Kluger recalls in her memoir of an Austrian childhood under Nazism, was the secret that grown-ups tried to keep from children.[4] When our pale, new teacher cracked the door to this secret we didn't know what to do with what we saw.

One day she brought a strange little text to class unlike anything we had ever read. It was prose that sounded like poetry, a story that had no plot, a dialogue that read like a monologue. I couldn't tell whom it addressed or who was speaking, but I knew that it spoke to me. When it asked, "do you hear me" (*hörst du mich*),[5] I answered, "Yes, I hear you. I am listening."

It was called "Gespräch im Gebirg" (Conversation in the Mountains) and the author was Paul Celan, a writer I had never heard of.[6] I didn't know that he had been honored that year with one of the most prestigious German literary prizes, the Georg Büchner Prize,[7] and I couldn't yet know that his "Todesfuge" ("Death Fugue") would be hailed as the "poem of the century" (*Jahrhundertgedicht*), "the Guernica of European postwar literature."[8]

Celan burned into my awareness like a meteor from outer space. I had no context in which to read someone like him: a Jewish survivor of Nazi labor camps in which both of his parents died, a German writer who kept his mother tongue even after leaving the German-speaking world to reside in Paris.[9] "Gespräch im Gebirg" was like a coded message about a world I didn't understand.

Not until later, when I learned the history of Nazi Germany and studied European literature of the postwar world, did the meanings encoded in it yield their secrets. Only then would I learn that "Gespräch im Gebirg" had an autobiographical context: a meeting in the Swiss Engadin between Celan and Adorno, who, like him, was a German Jew, and who, like him, had left

Germany for foreign exile.[10] Even later, I learned that this meeting between the poet, who grappled with the legacy of Auschwitz by writing poetry, and the philosopher who famously claimed that "to write poetry after Auschwitz is barbaric,"[11] was a meeting that had never taken place.[12]

Even if I had known these facts at the time I first read "Gespräch im Gebirg," I wouldn't have known what to do with such information. I was too untutored to engage with Adorno just yet and ponder the problem of meaning "after Auschwitz." I didn't yet know enough to see that Celan faced the same problem of writing as Adorno did or understand why both the philosopher and the poet distrusted language, even as their distrust was the crucible that shaped their art.

Both Celan and Adorno knew language as a generative force that shaped identities, fashioned worlds, and contained values. But Nazism had shown them that language can also destroy, undoing identities, worlds, and values that we take as given. It can undo our very integrity as persons, if we aren't vigilant, by doing our thinking and even our feeling for us. Adorno and Celan responded differently to this threat. Adorno fashioned language into a dense semantic wall that could protect the work of critical thinking. Celan broke language down like rock in a quarry, trying to find pieces with which to rebuild a demolished world. Before a word had been found for what eventually would be called the Holocaust,[13] he shattered language to make the impact of the catastrophe sensible.

At the age of fourteen I didn't understand much, if anything, about Celan. But something about his approach to language resonated. It reminded me of my childhood when I used to play with words, breaking them down into sounds and syllables. Celan also played with language, even if his form of playing was work. Like a mason hewing stone, he broke German into chunks and shards, making poems with the usable pieces. Word by word, syllable by syllable, weighing silence against sound, he pieced together fragments from a world that had broken.

"Gespräch im Gebirg" didn't look like the texts our teachers usually assigned. It looked unfinished, raw; a few mimeographed pages of typescript with uneven letters and hand-corrected typos. The language was German, but it sounded foreign. I read it as if I were reading Latin: parsing words, diagramming sentences, checking meanings.

The plot was simple. Two men, Jew Klein and Jew Gross (Little and Big, in their English variants) meet by chance one day, while each is out walking on his own. They are walking *through the mountains*, perhaps the same mountains where Celan was to meet Adorno.[14] But they pause their solitary walking to talk a while, and this pause changes the world around them. It dispels the silence. For it had been *quiet, quiet up there in* the mountains. But *it wasn't quiet for long*, the text continues. *Because when one Jew comes along and meets another, then it's goodbye silence, even in the mountains.*

What do they talk about, these two Jews, Klein and Gross? They talk about where they have come from (*A good ways you've come ... all the way here*), and they talk about where they are now (a *road in the mountains*). They talk about what they lost (*the others, who were like me, the others who were different from me and just the same*), and they talk about what they loved (*I loved the candle that was burning there ... the candle that he, the father of our mothers, had kindled ... I loved its burning down*). And they talk about what there is left to say for two Jews in the 1950s, alone in the mountains, where the only links to the world they left behind are their German language and their memories of *what burned down*.

Celan was telling me things without saying them and I was spellbound. But I didn't know how to respond. The words were familiar, the language strange, and the world it depicted felt dangerous. The first sentence already unsettled me: *One evening when the sun, and not only that, had gone down, then there went walking, stepping out of his cottage went the Jew, the Jew and son of a Jew, and with him went his name, unspeakable.*

For me and my classmates, good German girls from good German families, raised to be good citizens of a post-Nazi Germany, the name that was unspeakable was *Jew*. Yet here it was, spoken directly in the very first sentence. Not just once, but insistently, a ritual three times: *Jew, the Jew, and son of a Jew.*

"Jew" was not a word a nice German girl was supposed to use. It wasn't exactly forbidden, but we knew it should be avoided. If need be, we could say "Jewish."[15] Replacing the noun "Jew" with the adjective "Jewish" turned Jewishness from an identity to an attribute, like being old or tall or good-natured. Grammatically speaking, a Jewish neighbor was just a neighbor, a Jewish writer just a writer, and a Jewish citizen just a citizen among other citizens. The adjective, Jewish, carried no historical weight.

However, the word "Jew" by itself was unspeakable. It was too forceful, too direct. It felt like a kind of summons. When I heard "Jew," I heard it echo back, "Hey, you."

The truth was, I didn't know any Jews. I hadn't known any when we lived in Canada and I didn't know any in Germany when we returned. If any of the people I knew were Jews, I wasn't aware of it. Not until years and even decades later did I realize that some of the people I had known then—family friends, acquaintances of my parents, my own godfather—had been Jewish or of Jewish origin. I wondered, in retrospect, if our seventh grade German teacher, Frau Adelman, had perhaps been Jewish. Or the substitute teacher who took her place and taught us Celan? Or Sylvia Rosenbaum, one of my classmates? Were Adelman and Rosenbaum Jewish names? These were questions I never even thought to ask at the time. I had learned to so carefully avoid asking anything that might have touched on German Jewish history that I stopped even wondering about it.

My resulting ignorance is hard to fathom and embarrassing to admit. I had been reciting poems by Heinrich Heine and reading stories by Franz Kafka long before I knew that either of them was Jewish. I didn't know that some of the thinkers who most influenced me intellectually—Karl Marx, Sigmund Freud, and Ernst Bloch, to name just three—were Jews until after I had started studying them. I invoked T.W. Adorno without knowing that the mysterious "W" in his name obscured the Jewish lineage of his father, Oscar Wiesengrund,[16] and I was inspired by Erich Auerbach's work to study literature without knowing he was a Jewish émigré from Nazi Germany. Years passed before I realized how deeply Auerbach's Jewishness had marked his work. I was rereading his landmark text *Mimesis* when the afterword brought me to sudden tears. When Auerbach implored "those of my friends ... who have survived" (*meine überlebenden Freunde von einst*) to join him in remembering the culture of a Europe they had loved and lost, the entire tragedy of the Holocaust seemed compressed into a single, haunting memory of a love that could not be forgotten and a mourning that would never end.[17]

My first memory of the word "Jew" dates back to my childhood in Toronto in the 1950s, when my parents sometimes had what they called a "German evening" with German colleagues and friends. These gatherings had a warm familiarity, the intimacy of being German among Germans in a private setting. They drank wine, listened to music, and played cards, but, above all, it was a chance to speak German together. I was never invited to join them (I was a child and was supposed to be in bed), but the warmth and laughter from the living room drew me like a moth to lamplight. I wanted to be included in their fellowship.

I got as far as the bottom of the staircase outside the living room. I crept down from my upstairs bedroom and sat on the stairs in the dark. With my feet tucked under my nightgown and my arms around my knees for warmth, I eavesdropped on their conversation. I couldn't always tell what they were saying, but I heard the ease of familiarity in their voices and the nostalgia of shared memories when they talked. Even I could feel the nostalgia in the music. When Dietrich Fischer-Dieskau sang "Die Forelle," Schubert's elegy to the hapless trout, his lyric baritone, the words of the poem that I knew by heart, and the piano accompaniment that I had heard my grandfather play, took me to a place so deep with longing that my throat constricted.

However, my favorite music was *The Threepenny Opera*.[18] From my perch on the stairs outside the living room, I learned all the bawdy songs by heart.

"Pirate Jenny," though, was the one I loved. Jenny was a prostitute and kitchen maid, but in my eyes she was a hero. She was bold and strong and fearless and believed in justice, and I wanted to be like her. When I dried the dishes and made my bed, I was Pirate Jenny. I sang, "Messieurs, you see me wash the dishes./And you see me as I make the beds." Then I lowered my voice just as Lotte Lenya did when she sang Jenny on my parents' record: "But what you don't see is who I am ... I am Pirate Jenny!"[19] When my parents had company and I had to hide in the dark, I sang "Pirate Jenny" under my breath. And when Jenny condemns to death those who mistreated her, I squirmed with pleasure. "Hang them," I whispered, "cut their heads off." And when their heads fell, I said, "Whoops," and laughed.[20]

On one of those German evenings, I was listening to the buzz of conversation from the living room, when a word pierced my attention like a shot. *Jude*, I heard someone say, *Jew*. I don't remember anything else that person said or what anyone said after that, but the stillness that followed *Jew* stayed with me. The voice of the speaker dropped and the room, for an instant, fell silent, while I sat in the dark, thighs pressed against my chest, and listened.

All I heard was the sound of my own breathing.

Six years later, when I read Celan in seventh grade, I encountered silence again. But in his story of Jew Klein and Jew Gross the silence was generative. It didn't break with language. It was a pause within it.

In "Gespräch im Gebirg" the world seems to have fallen silent. [*T*]*he stick is silent*, we read, *the stone is silent*. Except for two Jews who happen to meet on their way through a foreign landscape, no one speaks. But, Celan reminds us, *the silence is no silence, it's merely a pause, a word-gap ... a vacant space.* Language is not absent from the world. *You can see the syllables all standing around*, the text continues. In the midst of silence, language is waiting, ready to be reclaimed.

Years after I first read Celan, I was visiting an old friend from my Liebfrauen School days in Bonn. Marianne had been my upper level English teacher and we had stayed in touch. My Celan story clearly surprised her.

"Was it unusual," I asked, "to have fourteen-year-olds read Celan?"

"Very," she was emphatic. "To read Celan with students that young was unusual in and of itself. But at that time, in the early '60s ... to bring Jewish history, German-Jewish questions, into the classroom ..." her voice trailed off, "that was almost unheard of." I recalled the teacher who had given us a chance to face this history and confront these questions—her pale and frightened look, her hands that seemed to want to shield her face.

"No one," Marianne continued, "was doing that then. Not in literature classes, not in history classes ... nowhere."

"No one ... nowhere" was a bit too strong. A creative teacher could include materials that weren't part of the official curriculum, and curricula weren't uniform but varied from Land to Land.[21] Students in Hamburg weren't taught the same things as students in Bonn or Munich. Overall, however, Marianne was right. In the 1960s Nazi history and the Holocaust weren't on the agenda in German schools. This wouldn't change until the 1970s, and even then many teachers successfully avoided it by "running out of time" at the end of term. In many a classroom at the time, German history ended with Bismarck and the founding of the first German Reich.

My high school history ended with World War I. By the time we reached the Versailles Treaty, our time was up. Whatever came after 1919—the Weimar Republic, Nazi Germany, World War II, and the postwar period—was left for us to learn on our own. Or ignore.

Toward the end of my visit in Bonn, when my former teacher and I shared memories of school in the 1960s, we returned to Celan, and Marianne slipped into her old role as teacher. "What did you make of Celan back then?" she asked me. "What did you learn from him?"

I didn't know how to answer her question. I recalled my adolescent confusion, my struggle to make sense of what I'd read.

"Nothing," I finally answered, "I learned nothing."

Yet that was untrue. I had learned many things, even if at the time they weren't yet conscious. I learned that not everyone was silent about the Nazi years (the "recent past," as people vaguely put it). People talked about it when they came together, and sometimes they came together for just that purpose. When Jew Klein and Jew Gross ask why they have come all this way to meet on this road in the mountains (*What did I come for? Why and what for did you come?*), the answer, for both, is simple: *I had to talk.* Celan's Jews talked about what they had suffered, but presumably others talked about what they had done. Wasn't talking about the past—what they had done and suffered—part of what my parents' German evenings were about? Celan taught me that, while they may have been surrounded by silence, people were talking among themselves.

That begged the question, of course, about who was listening. Who was listening and talking to whom? For not only was Germany divided, Germans were divided too. Between the many who wanted to talk about what they had suffered and the few who were willing to talk about what they had done ran a torrent of unresolved feelings and a deep confusion about how to bridge the gap.

But these were thoughts I came to much later. What Celan gave me at the time was very specific, a clue to the mystery that had dogged my childhood:

What had happened before my birth that no one was willing to tell me? I knew that it had to do with being German, and the word "hate" had been my previous clue. I now realized that it had to do with a word that was even more forbidding. That word, my final clue, was "Jew."

Ambushed by History*

In 1962 my father became the first German ambassador to Gabon, a newly independent former French colony in equatorial West Africa. My parents had decided that ("for the good of your education") I should stay in Germany. Their solution was boarding school and their choice a Catholic girls' school in southern Germany. I begged them not to make me go, but they were adamant. If it turned out to be as bad as I feared, they proposed, I would only have to stay two years. It *was* as bad. They kept their promise and I left when my two years were up. But at first I had to do my time. So in the spring of my sixteenth year I went off to boarding school.

The school typified German architecture of the postwar period. A long, five-story rectangle with all the charm of a cardboard box, the school dated to the 1950s, when all of Germany seemed under construction. Roads, train lines, telephone systems, schools, hospitals, factories, housing—a whole country was being rebuilt. Resources were limited and everything was needed fast, so things didn't have to be beautiful, just functional. It was a criterion that my boarding school amply met. White walls, linoleum floors, and prefab furniture. The only adornment I recall was the chapel flowers.

We wore thin polyester uniforms that didn't fit well and gained weight from eating too much starchy food. Every day started with mass before breakfast and ended with a mumbled evening prayer. There was nothing to lift our spirits except the anticipation of a forthcoming break. As plants long for light we longed for things of beauty, and turned to fantasies for our escape.

Classmates from titled families offered ready material for those fantasies. With their Hermès scarves, Gucci loafers, and signet rings, their names that referred to places (one of my classmates had the last name Prussia), and their homes marked on the map as castles, they were objects of fascination to us commoners. The aristocracy was abolished as a legal class in 1919 when Germany adopted its first democratic constitution, but it remained alive as a social class, and the spectacle it provided was thrilling.

---

* Nguyen, *Nothing Ever Dies: Vietnam and the Memory of War*, p. 157.

The biggest thrill at the beginning and end of each term was the arrival (or departure) of Nora Liechtenstein. We jockeyed for the best position from which to watch. The white stretch limousine with the license plate *FL 1* pulled up, the chauffeur emerged, walked around the car, held the rear door open, and our schoolmate, Nora, climbed out. When I first saw her, she was a pale-faced, slightly pudgy twelve-year-old, blonde hair cut in a plain pageboy. Nothing about her signaled "princess." But when she exited the limousine with the liveried chauffeur, she was Princess Norberta of and from the Principality of Liechtenstein, and we were awestruck by the sight of royalty. At that moment, we all turned into commoners. And as commoners are wont to do, we gawked.

Sixteen was not a good age to be in boarding school. I pulsed with longings I didn't have words for; I dreamed of romance and flushed with thoughts of sex. In the hothouse culture of adolescent girls in boarding school my body became a source of torment. Dime store romances were passed around like contraband and I read the forbidden books at night with a flashlight. When scenes of doctors seducing nurses and men on horseback fondling farm girls' breasts inflamed my senses, I tried to distract my body by feeding it. But food wasn't what I wanted. The few photographs of me in that period show a girl with a sallow face and a body that is awkward and graceless.

We were housed four to a room: four narrow beds, four wooden shelves, four stools, and a four-cubbied closet. Two sinks by the door were our bathroom and communal toilets were down the hall. With no showers and advance permission required to use a bathtub (baths limited to once a week), daily hygiene was a constant challenge. A sink, a bar of soap, and a washcloth were the tools of my daily regimen.

I washed my face first, then soaped each armpit and ran the washcloth around my breasts and between my thighs. I had to avoid seeing my naked body, as that was sinful, and I couldn't let water drip on the floor, and the flimsy curtain around the sink kept gaping open. By the time I got to my feet, the water had finally warmed and I could finally indulge a sensuous pleasure: I balanced on one leg, put my foot in the sink and felt warm water caress it.

The last hour of our scheduled day, as we readied for bed before the ten o'clock lights out, was called *Silentium*, Latin for silence. It meant no speaking, no laughing, no music of any kind, nothing that disturbed the stillness. To enforce the rule, a nun patrolled the hall, a shadowy figure fingering her rosary. When we passed her on our way to the toilets no words were exchanged. Just a nod of her wimpled head on her part and quick little curtsies on ours. But if she heard talking or laughing or even whispering in a room, she responded swiftly: a loud rap on the door, followed by a sharp command in Latin, "*Silentium!*" She waited by the door to make sure that silence had been restored before she resumed her pacing. A second offense got no warning; it was punished instantly. Without bothering to knock, she opened the door and left it ajar until lights-out.

One evening, while I was washing myself, the nun on patrol heard my roommates talking and pulled our door open. In the rush of cold air from the hallway, the thin curtain around me fanned open as I stood there naked, on one leg, one foot in the sink. Long after the door was closed that night, the shame of my exposed nakedness lingered.

During my second year of boarding school, we studied modern Germany: from the Napoleonic wars and Bismarck's founding of the German Reich in 1871 to World War I and the Weimar Republic. In fact, we never got to Weimar; the school year ended with Germany's World War I defeat. But we had an additional assignment: independent research on a topic we could choose. I chose the Holocaust, although I didn't call it that ("Holocaust" wouldn't be the standard term for at least another fifteen years). The term I used still carried the baggage of Nazi rhetoric: Final Solution, *Endlösung*. "The Final Solution of the Jewish Question" was my project title.

I don't remember how I picked this topic or got permission to work on a subject we weren't covering in class. I don't remember how I did the research. What I remember is what it did to me.

Looking back, I wonder where I even found materials. There was no Internet. We had no computers. There was printed material, but my resources were limited to a provincial boarding school in a provincial town in southern Germany, and not much would have been available. Research on the history of Nazi Germany and the Holocaust was just beginning and little had as yet been published. Hannah Arendt's *Eichmann in Jerusalem* would not appear in German until the following year, and while her *Origins of Totalitarianism* had been available in German translation for some time by then, it didn't offer the kind of material I needed.[1] Alain Resnais' documentary film about Nazi concentration camps, *Night and Fog*, had been shown in theaters, but I hadn't seen it, and I didn't know that the state of Baden-Württemberg, where my boarding school was, had played a particularly ignoble role in its troubled German reception. In 1956, when France chose *Night and Fog* as its submission to the Cannes Film Festival, the German government registered opposition and wanted it withdrawn. Massive protests and the threat of international censure eventually caused the German government to back down and, in an astonishing about-face, not only endorse the film, but buy the rights to distribute it, free of charge, to the German public.[2] Yet when the Federal Ministry of Culture went as far as recommending the film for use in German secondary schools, the state of Baden-Württemberg refused. As a result, my boarding school had no access to it.

I didn't know that Hanns Eisler, who had worked with both Bertolt Brecht and T.W. Adorno and whose "Solidarity Song" I loved to belt out on car trips ("Proletarians of all nations" I would shout through the open window, "Unite and you shall be free!") had composed the music for *Night and Fog*,[3] or that Paul Celan had translated the French film script into German. And despite Celan's impact on me when I first read him in seventh grade (and although six volumes of his poetry had appeared in the meantime), I hadn't read anything else by him beyond "Gespräch im Gebirg."

What I would have known about and had information on were two landmark trials taking place around that very time in Israel and West Germany. The Eichmann trial in Jerusalem had just come to an end and the first Auschwitz trial in Frankfurt was beginning. They marked a turning point in public reckoning with the Nazi past, not just for the issues they raised, but for the intentionally public ways in which they raised them.

The trial of the man who would be remembered as the "architect of the Final Solution" ended three weeks after I started boarding school. On May 29, 1962, "Adolf, son of Karl Adolf, Eichmann," as he was officially identified by the Jerusalem District Court that tried his case, was sentenced to death for crimes against the Jewish people, crimes against humanity, and war crimes. Two days later, at midnight between May 31 and June 1, 1962 Adolf Eichmann was hanged in Ramla, Israel, and his ashes were scattered at sea.

The following December, my last year of boarding school, another event of similar historical import began in Frankfurt. The first of what were to become a total of six Auschwitz trials, it would be the biggest criminal trial in postwar Germany.[4] Although only twenty-two of the 6,000 to 8,000 people involved in the administration and operation of the Auschwitz camp, from SS members to kapos, were tried, the data assembled over the course of the trial was staggering: over 1,400 testimonies were collected and the binders of evidence stretched some 20 feet across. When the trial ended on August 19, 1965, the indictment covered 700 pages. The final verdict was six life sentences, ten sentences of between three and fourteen years, and three acquittals.[5]

Both the Eichmann and Auschwitz trials were based on the premise that history and memory are interdependent. For history to have an effect it must be remembered, and for memories to have public resonance they must enter history. As Adolf Hitler famously reminded his military commanders, who worried about the repercussions of the genocide they were about to unleash with the invasion of Poland, "Who still talks today about the Armenian genocide?"[6] A history that isn't actively remembered is a history lost.

But just as events depend on memory to be preserved as history, experiences depend on history to be preserved in memory.[7] The need to affirm the truth of their experience—what they suffered, what they did, and what they knew—impelled thousands of witnesses to testify in the Eichmann and Auschwitz trials. By contributing their individual piece to the collective story that the trials produced, the experience of each witness, in the form they remembered it, became part of history.

The final judgment of the Eichmann trial underscored its epochal significance. This trial, it proclaimed, had presented a history "of the Hitler regime in Germany and in Europe, and … the catastrophe which befell the Jewish People during that period."[8] But it offered more than a factual history. It told "a story of bloodshed and suffering which will be remembered to the end of time." Toward this end, the facts the trial disclosed had to be made public. The Israeli government's decision to have the trial covered on live television and shown around the world was predicated on this understanding.[9] Accordingly, the Eichmann trial became the first trial to be broadcast live on television, inaugurating the use of this new medium to inscribe a historical trauma into the collective memory of a spellbound world.

The Frankfurt Auschwitz trial was similarly conducted in full public view. Evidence of atrocities was presented simultaneously to the court of law and the court of public opinion on the assumption that once vetted and registered publicly, the facts could no longer be denied. Unlike the Eichmann trial, the Frankfurt Auschwitz trial couldn't be broadcast in its entirety (it was too long).[10] But it was covered regularly and extensively in live broadcasts on West Germany's main public television network.[11]

Given their extensive coverage, I could hardly have missed knowing about these trials. But I don't recall any details. Did I hear about them on the radio? Read about them in the paper? Both seem probable, even likely, but I don't recall. Years later, when I read Peter Weiss' drama, *The Investigation*, based on transcripts of the Auschwitz trial, none of what I read there seemed familiar. I don't recall seeing any part of the trials on television. Television was still new to Germany and few people, including my family, had sets at home.[12] And while it is possible that the boarding school had a television set somewhere, I don't recall ever seeing one.

With no archives to draw on, a modest library, and limited access to the information emerging live from the trials, where did I find material for my research project? People would have been the most likely source: people who had lived through the time I was studying. There was no shortage of what German calls "witnesses to history."[13] At school, there were the nuns and teachers; at home, there were neighbors and friends; there were the members of my own family—grandparents, aunts and uncles, parents. I could have talked to them and asked them about what they knew. In retrospect such a step seems obvious. But at the time it didn't seem an option. Silence had become a habit that was hard to break.

My access to information was limited, my exposure to news partial, and I can't reconstruct the exact means by which I found material, yet information about the trials was circulating and bits and pieces were filtering through to me. Even if Germans weren't sure what to call it yet, a public conversation about the Holocaust had started, and I was listening. The clues I gathered were adding up. Toward the end of the school year, I put them together and wrote my paper. Just before Easter, I turned it in.

It wasn't the kind of paper I had been taught to write in school with a thesis, an argument, and a conclusion that resolved the issue. I had no thesis. I had no argument. There was no conclusion. What I had were facts. Pages and pages of facts that I had collected and put together. I had dates and the names of places, most of which I had never before even heard of. Dachau, Stutthof, Bergen-Belsen, Auschwitz, Theresienstadt, Majdanek, Treblinka. To these dates and names of places I had added numbers.

Dachau, 1933: 200,000 imprisoned; 41,500 murdered.

Stutthof, 1939: 85,000 dead.

Bergen-Belsen, 1940 (POW camp) – 1943 (concentration camp): 52,000 murdered, 70,000 dead.

Auschwitz, 1940 (Auschwitz I) – 1942 (Auschwitz II [Auschwitz-Birkenau] and Auschwitz III [Auschwitz-Monowitz]): 1.1 million dead.

Theresienstadt, 1941: 35,440 dead, 88,000 deported to be murdered.

Majdanek, 1941: 78,000–360,000 dead.[14]

Treblinka, 1941 (Treblinka I: forced labor camp) – 1942 (Treblinka II: killing center): 1.1–1.4 million killed.

I had tried to embed the facts in explanation, using the tools of analysis I had learned, but my attempts to make sense of it all had foundered. I didn't have any explanation. Just a numbing, staggering, horrifying list of facts.

My problem was how to write this paper, what form to use. What kind of voice or style was appropriate? Beyond the facts, what was there to say? In the end, I chose a flat, impersonal style, eschewing feeling and suspending judgment. I wrote as if it weren't me writing. I was just a scribe, a keeper of accounts, an amanuensis.

Yet since the assignment included an oral presentation, I couldn't pretend I was just a scribe. I had to face my classmates and speak to them. I had to tell them what I had learned. I had to tell this "story of bloodshed and suffering" directly, publicly, in my own voice.

Abandoned graves in the Jewish cemetery on Schönhauser Allee, Prenzlauer Berg, Berlin. Dating back to 1627, this was the only Jewish cemetery in Berlin until 1880, when a second, and much larger, one was established in Berlin-Weissensee. The use of granite and marble headstones and the inscription of text in Latin, as well as Hebrew, letters reflect the increasingly assimilated culture of urban Jewry in nineteenth-century Germany. The Schönhauser Allee cemetery is no longer in use as a cemetery; it is now a memorial site. (Photograph by author, 2012).

When my name was called, I made my way to the front of the classroom, down the aisle, past the rows of desks. The teacher sat at her desk and watched me. I remember thinking, in passing, how old she looked, with her lumpy body, shapeless sweater, and grey hair, but it didn't occur to me to connect her age to my research topic, to the fact that twenty years earlier, when the "Final Solution of the Jewish Question" was decided in a secret meeting outside Berlin in the town of Wannsee, she was a German citizen in Nazi Germany. In January 1942, at the time of the Wannsee Conference, my teacher was an adult. She would have had access to information. I didn't think this consciously; it was an unease I felt.

I reached the front of the room, faced my classmates, and started reading. "The Final Solution of The Jewish Question," I began. I read the first paragraph, stiffly and mechanically, as you do when you know the words but don't quite get what the words are saying. But I read on, word following word, like knots in a rope across an abyss. I held on tight. I didn't look down. I didn't falter. I just kept going.

I still see in my mind's eye what the sheets I was reading from looked like: blue ink on white paper, a small, crabbed script covering the entire page. I had spared no line. I had left no margins. There was no space anywhere on the page to rest or breathe. I held the sheets in both hands and kept reading. Words followed words. I read the dates and the names of places. I read the numbers. I read without looking up, my eyes on the page before me. My mouth went dry and my voice got raspy, but I didn't stop to take a break or clear my throat. I just kept reading. My classmates and teacher were silent. I read on into this silence as long as I could, until it finally got so thick it choked me.

A lifetime later, I return to that room in my memory. I am that girl again reading about "The Final Solution" to her silent classmates. Her hands have started shaking, and her blouse is spotting dark with sweat. Her face is burning. She finally stops reading and looks at her classmates. They sit there, looking back at her. We are immersed in an immensity of silence. She feels her body shaking. It is a shaking that, in some ways, never stopped.

If someone had asked me at the time what these facts I had gathered meant—what these numbers and dates and place names had to do with me—I don't know what I would have answered.

What *did* they have to do with me?

Strictly speaking, nothing. I was born "after Auschwitz," to use Adorno's phrase, after "the terrible times," as postwar Germans often liked to put it.

Yet I later realized—and even at the time must have dimly known—that the numbers and dates and names of places I had uncovered had everything to do with me. From the time of my first breath, they were in the air. They were the ground I walked on.

At the end of that year, I got the top grade in my class for history. Excellent, my report said, *sehr gut*. I got the same grade on my paper: *sehr gut*. That's all my teacher wrote. A grade. Two words. No further comments.

I finally had the answer to the question that had dogged me growing up: What had happened? What had happened before I was born that made people say "I hate you" and made me afraid of simple words like "Jew"?

Now I knew. What was I to do with this knowledge? Where was I supposed to go from here? I wanted to go as far away as possible, and decided that I would leave as soon as I could.

Passing Through Bitburg

> *So kiss me and smile for me,*
> *Tell me that you'll wait for me,*
> *Hold me like you'll never let me go,*
> *Cause I'm leavin' on a jet plane,*
> *I don't know when I'll be back again,*
> *Oh, babe, I hate to go.*
> —Peter, Paul, and Mary (1969)[1]

I left Germany with a one-way ticket. But that didn't stop me from continuing to look back. It was 1969, I was twenty-two years old, studying modern languages and literature at the University of Heidelberg, and had applied to graduate schools at American universities. When asked what my plans were, I said, "I am going to America."

My answer was accurate, but it wasn't truthful. For the truth was, I wasn't *going* anywhere. I was *leaving* somewhere. I was planning to leave Germany behind.

I had booked a flight on Icelandic Airlines, which offered budget fares between Luxembourg and New York, and was heading to the Luxembourg airport with my father. It was a two-hour drive from Bonn. He drove. I looked out the window. We didn't talk much. Apart from vague memories of family excursions and a bike trip with friends some summers before, the landscape we were driving through held no meaning for me. Whatever meanings it held for my father—including memories of a war that had ended close to here for him in the mud and despair of the Ardennes offensive—he didn't share. We didn't talk about the pasts this landscape conjured, but stayed in the safe zone of present-day small talk. For long stretches we didn't talk at all.

It was a picture-perfect, blue-sky day, the kind of day we call a good day to travel. We expect our plane to take us where we are going without crashing or falling from the sky. We kiss goodbye, wish a safe flight, a last smile on parting. My father traced the sign of the cross on my forehead. I felt his arms around me one last time. I walked away, and when I turned around he was still standing where I had left him. I waved. He waved back. When I turned around again he was gone. I clutched my bag and breathed into the empty space. I had packed my bags, bought a ticket, and said goodbye. Now I was leaving. I didn't dwell on what I felt.

But feelings aren't so easily banished. They sneak up on you unawares. A melody fills your heart with longing for the person that its sound evokes. A scent carries the memory of a place where you were happy. For years the sadness I dismissed that day in Luxembourg returned to me at night in the form of dreams. The pattern was always the same.

I have a plane to catch and it's late. My anxiety rises. I am running out of time. I have to get to the airport and am still at home packing. What should I take? The suitcase is on the bed, open. My anxiety spikes. I can't do this.

The scene shifts. I am outside, on the street by a large, gray building. I have no idea where I am. Nothing looks familiar. The names on the doorbells by the building's entrance are all foreign to me. So is the street and even the building. How can I get to the airport if I don't even know where I am?

I rush back upstairs and grab the half-packed suitcase, but I can't find my ticket or my passport. I race back down to the street, too panicked to even check the time. Maybe someone out there who knows the way can take me. But the street is deserted. There is no one there.

Then I know that it's all in vain. It is too late. I will miss my plane. In fact, I have already missed it.

The scene shifts again and I am back in the room where I started. My half-packed suitcase is still on the bed. The room is a mess. But I am no longer packing for a trip. I am leaving. I strip the linens from the bed, fold them neatly, and lay them on a chair. I leave the suitcase as it is. I won't be taking it. Before I leave, I write a note and place it on the bedside table. It says, thank you for having let me stay.

By the time I left Germany aged twenty-two, I should have been a master in the art of leaving. But it didn't get easier the more I did it. It got more difficult.

I certainly didn't lack for practice. Traveling back and forth between my European and American worlds became the rhythm of my adult life. I went to Europe at least once a year to see my family and friends there; then left again to resume my new life in America. I would leave one home for the other home only to leave and return again. It was a continuous cycle of coming and going. Yet no matter how cosmopolitan a traveler I tried to be, I was stuck in an emotional time warp. It was as if all future leavings took me back to when I was five and first left what had been our home in Germany. It was a deep memory that a later parting could abruptly trigger.

Over the course of my father's work, my family moved to several different countries. First Canada, then Gabon, and finally Spain. With returns to Germany in the years between, our life was marked by a pattern of leaving places that were home for as long as we lived there. Home was where we were for the time being. Attachments were accordingly provisional. "Don't get attached to things," my parents cautioned me whenever I begged them for a dog. "When we move, you'll have to leave it behind ... and you'll be sad then."

Learning how to leave, how not to get too attached, was a lesson that my parents had learned from history. When my mother married my father during World War II she left her home in Westphalia to live with his parents in Bohemia. After the war, when my father and his family were expelled from Czechoslovakia as ethnic Germans, they learned to make a new home for themselves in West Germany. Knowing how to leave places and people without leaving one's self behind was a skill that their lives had taught them. It was a skill they tried to pass on to me.

Yet despite their best efforts and a lifetime of practicing on my part, I remain an amateur in the art of leaving, shamed by the extravagance of grief when I have to leave a person or a place I have become attached to. At such moments I am still the five-year-old girl on the boat traveling across the Atlantic, leaving the safety of a home I am familiar with for the perils of a place that is foreign. I kneel by the porthole in our cabin and look out at the world in which our ship is being tossed about. I see sky and I see water and that is all I see. I am overwhelmed by the vast emptiness that surrounds me.

Years later, when I became a parent myself, I was shocked to discover that I unwittingly passed the lesson that my parents taught me on to my children. One day, when he was five and angry, my son announced he was running away from home. "I am going to another country," he yelled. Leaving home, for him as for me, was an emigration.

In the summer of 2007—my twins had just graduated from college—we went to Europe on a family trip. My children were the same age as I had been when I went to America for graduate study and I thought it would be fun to mark this moment of transition in their life by revisiting a similar moment in my life. I proposed a drive from Bonn to Luxembourg, the same route my father and I had taken. Although Luxembourg didn't rank with London or Berlin on the list of places to visit, my children accepted my proposal, and I reviewed the route in preparation.

I got out my old road map of Western Europe and spread it across my office floor. Kneeling down—my left knee in France around Nancy and my right knee in Germany around Mainz—I marked the two cities, Bonn and Luxembourg, with stick pins. It was a large-scale map, the script was tiny, and I had trouble reading the smaller names. But as I was tracing the route, my finger stopped on a name I hadn't expected to find in this context: Bitburg. It was just a dot on my map, a small town in the Eifel region, about an hour and a half's drive from Bonn on the route that my father and I would have taken on our way to Luxembourg. In June 1969 I wouldn't have paid any attention to it. It would have been just another town we were passing through. But sixteen years later, Bitburg was no longer just another German town: it had become a symbol of Germany's unresolved Nazi past.

It had come to the world's attention in 1985 on the fortieth anniversary of the end of World War II in Europe. A variety of commemorative events had been planned, prominent among them a joint visit by the American president, Ronald Reagan, and the West German Chancellor, Helmut Kohl, to a small German military cemetery in Bitburg. This event had attracted attention for its symbolic value: former enemies standing side by side, remembering dead soldiers not as members of opposing armies, but as men who had died for their country in a brutal war. To highlight this purpose, the event had intentionally been removed from the standard circuit of nationalist pageantry, where government leaders enact gestures for media play. They had chosen a small military cemetery off the beaten track. Who until then had ever heard of Bitburg? Suddenly everyone had.

Breaking news revealed that the "simple soldiers" buried in the Bitburg cemetery weren't just regular Wehrmacht, but included forty-nine members of the Waffen-SS, the armed wing of the Nazi Party.[2] Old wounds the event had hoped to heal were torn open. Instead of closure, fresh conflict ensued. The past was not laid to rest, as the planners had planned. In a place that commemorated members of the Waffen-SS, a gesture of reconciliation between former enemies appeared unseemly, if not scandalous. At the very least, it was premature. The dead were undeniably dead, but the past wasn't. The ritual planned for Bitburg was hastily repackaged.

Before they went to Bitburg, President Reagan and Chancellor Kohl visited a former Nazi concentration camp, Bergen-Belsen, and the visit to the Bitburg cemetery was cut short. It lasted just eight minutes and was silent. No speeches, just the ceremonial laying down of a wreath. Despite these adjustments, public censure was scathing. *Time* magazine called it a "fiasco," the *New York Times* a "blunder." Bitburg would be remembered as a political scandal and public relations disaster.

However it was remembered, Bitburg was a jarring reminder of how Nazi history had redrawn the map, not just by dividing Germany, but across Europe.

The land my father and I passed through on our way to Luxembourg in June 1969, would not—perhaps ever—just be landscape. In the wake of the violence of the twentieth century, this land bled history like an unhealed wound.

Squatting over a map on the floor of my office, I was caught in a time warp with Bitburg as a critical juncture. In 1969, it was the past I had hoped to leave behind with a one-way ticket out of Germany. In 1985, it was the return of that past into the life I had made for myself in America. And in 2007, it was a reminder of the fact that my German past would be part of my children's future. In that sense, Bitburg represented my own dilemma in response to history: what should I remember, what could I forget, and how would I know when remembering or forgetting was called for? Two impulses were in competition: the wish to disclaim responsibility for Nazi history (*it wasn't me*) and the need to accept responsibility for its effects (*but I am German*). I lived the contradiction of wanting to not-be-German, even as I worked to come to terms with what being-German meant.

As I stared at the dot on my map marked "Bitburg," I realized what should have been obvious to me all along: the idea that I could leave the past behind when I left Germany was wishful thinking. Past and present could not be pried apart. What I called the past wasn't just history. It was the place that I called home. It was the family that had known and raised me. It was the person that I had become.

I knew from the map (although not from memory) that after passing through Bitburg we crossed the Sauer River and were out of Germany. The airport was under an hour away.

What did my father and I do while we waited for my boarding call? Trying to recall that time years later, my mind is blank. Perhaps we had a snack or a cup of tea at the restaurant. Perhaps we looked at postcards of Iceland, where the plane would stop to refuel. Perhaps we simply sat and waited. We must have talked, but I don't remember what we talked about, nor do I remember what I thought or felt. All I remember is wishing that my father would say, "Don't go," to me.

He didn't say that. He hugged me and said "*Gute Reise*," travel well. He didn't cry. I didn't either. I flew into what felt like nowhere, leaving the world that was familiar to me behind. The plane droned westwards, while I stared out into the night.

Decades later, long after America had become my home, I learned that my leaving had affected my parents much more than I was able or willing to see in my twenties. It was 1995, the year after my mother's death, and I had come to Bonn to see my father. We were going through old photographs that my mother had kept in a box of her favorite bath soap. I had always loved the dramatic packaging of this Maja soap: the black box with the crimson lining and the Art Deco writing in gold, the seductive flamenco dancer on the cover (Maja means "alluring," my mother had told me). It was her special soap with its own dish by the side of the bathtub. No one else in the family used it. Yet I found it irresistibly attractive: its heady scent of carnations and jasmine evoked sensual pleasures that would make me flush, secrets of the body I longed to know. If my mother knew them, she didn't share them with me. But after she bathed, their perfumed traces lingered.

As I went through the photographs in the Maja box, a faint scent of carnations recalled my mother, but the pictures themselves didn't interest me. They were mementos of my parents' travels across Europe and random snapshots of various relatives and family friends. I was bored and started to put the box away when a picture from my own past caught my eye.

It shows a girl standing by a fountain outside the Art Institute of Chicago. It is early winter or late fall. The trees are barren and her heavy coat is buttoned. She wears her hair short like the Catholic schoolgirl she once was: parted on the left, a barrette on the right side. She looks straight into the camera, smiling, her eyes wide open.

I stared at the girl in the picture. I had forgotten how young I was then. I handed the picture to my father. "Do you remember when I sent you this? It was my first Christmas in America ... the year I left."

"Yes, I remember ... " He handed it back to me. "That was the Christmas that your mother cried."

Resident Alien

I arrived in New York on June 30, 1969. It was sweltering and the humidity made it hard to breathe. The hotel where I spent the night was freezing. When I tried to open the window, it was bolted shut, so I sat on the bed and turned on the television. A preacher called me home to Jesus. I wrapped the bedspread around me and watched him. He looked back at me. In Germany it was already the next day. I heard a toilet flush. It was less than twenty-four hours since I had left Europe.

What was I doing here? I must have had reasons, but I seemed to have lost them along the way. I burrowed deeper into the bedspread. I felt numb and empty.

Years later I learned that my experience was part of the postwar story of a generation that left Germany around this time. I was astonished when I saw the numbers. Between 1965 and 1970, around a million Germans emigrated to the United States alone. Who were we? What connected us?

At the time, I didn't think about it. I didn't even know I was part of a larger cohort, a virtual movement of Germans leaving Germany. I had no interest in community with my compatriots. That's why I—and presumably others like me—had left. We didn't want to affirm our German identity. We didn't talk of home. We didn't call ourselves expatriates and certainly not exiles. We didn't seek one another out. We went the other way. We lost our accents, assimilated our names, and absorbed our new, adopted cultures. We cast our Germanness off like outworn clothes.

The writer Günter Grass offered a partial explanation for our behavior. In a series of essays written in the 1970s, he took the pulse of postwar Germany—the negative birth rate, the emigration hemorrhage—and concluded that "the Germans are dying out."[1] Rather than lament this slow extinction, he applauded it. With the blood of two wars and a genocide on their hands, he contended, Germans *should* die out. They had lost their right to be a people. I couldn't tell if he was being polemical or serious. His argument was too extreme to be taken literally. Yet it made sense to me as a matter of principle. It helped explain why so many of us were leaving Germany. And it put my decision to leave in a historical framework I couldn't see at the time.

Of course, dying out was not the only option. There was another, more constructive, response. We could recognize our debt to history and become different Germans. Just a year earlier, in 1968, when I was still a student at the University of Heidelberg, that was exactly what I thought the German student movement was about. We, who were born in the wake of the Hitler years, would make a new Germany as we came of age. With its authoritarian structures, its bourgeois morality, and its education toward obedience, the Germany we inherited from our parents was a Germany we didn't want. Enabled by a populace that had followed Hitler like "herds of dreamy, militant sheep,"[2] our parents' Germany had led the way to genocide. We would be different. Rebellious, not passive. Rude, not orderly. Resistant, not obedient. We couldn't change the past, but we would change the future. We would erase the Nazi shame through a revolution. The headiness of this vision was like a drug.

Yet the tactics on the ground were sobering. We marched five abreast down the streets of Heidelberg shouting slogans about workers' rights, even as the workers walked away when we approached them. We condemned authoritarian mindsets and power hierarchies, even as we glorified our own charismatic leaders and sized our worldview to fit their frame. Our actions didn't match our principles and the mismatch jarred me. And on a less principled and more visceral level, what we were doing scared me.

The sight of police in battle formation—their shields and face-guards, their clubs and tear gas, their armored vehicles and water hoses that could blast me against a wall—made me want to run and hide. I wanted to be in the library among the books, where it was quiet and warm and peaceful. I would inhale the dusty air and feel safe. At demonstrations I shook my fists and yelled obscenities with my movement comrades, but my rage didn't feel authentic. I felt like an actor in a play that should have been staged in a different time. The force of our protest seemed vicarious and belated, as if we were doing what we wished our parents had done.

I wanted to believe in the possibility of a brave new Germany and participate in bringing it about. But what if the enemy we were targeting was the wrong one? On my way to the university, I passed the post office and saw the Wanted posters for domestic terrorists. Three men and a woman had thrown firebombs in Frankfurt department stores to protest the "war of imperialist aggression" in Vietnam and the interests of global capital that fueled it. Andreas Baader was about my age and Gudrun Ensslin was, like me, a university student. I stared at their mugshots and wondered: What made them different from me? How we were alike?

Our tactics differed: I went on marches and they threw bombs. But we had the same goal: to disrupt the machinery of a war that we thought was criminal. By the late 1960s, this shared goal had spawned a global movement, and across West Germany groups of urban guerrillas had risen up. The proximate cause was the war in Southeast Asia, but capitalism, imperialism, and militarism were the deeper cause, the foundation we aimed to dismantle. In the shorthand of movement rhetoric we called this foundation "the system," and to many of us this system was fascism revived: just suits and ties instead of *Sieg Heil* and jackboots. In Germany, the cry of fascism rang alarm bells.

No one took this alarm more seriously than the Red Army Faction (RAF, for short). Commonly known as the Baader-Meinhof Group (or "Gang," in the more pejorative version) after two of its founders and most influential leaders—the high-school dropout turned small-time criminal, turned political radical Andreas Baader, and the left-wing journalist and activist intellectual Ulrike Meinhof—the RAF soon captured the popular imagination. Reckless, romantic, dangerous radicals with a sexy edge, they combined the revolutionary romance of Che Guevara with the outlaw erotics of Bonnie and Clyde, and I was smitten.

Over the twenty-eight years of its existence, the RAF became a virtual underground army, conducting assassinations, kidnappings, bank robberies, and fire-bombings across Germany in the name of anti-militarist, anti-capitalist, anti-imperialist, and anti-fascist struggle. They were held responsible for thirty-four deaths. By the fall of 1977, the West Germany government considered them such a threat that it declared a state of national emergency.

In 1968, when I was in Heidelberg, this degree of violence wasn't yet evident, but even as it escalated, I continued to sympathize with these so-called terrorists. In many ways, I identified with them. They, like me, were of the postwar generation, raised in Christian families with the traditional values of German bourgeois culture. They, like me, had inherited a past they were ashamed of and, like me, envisioned a future that would end that shame. We read the same texts, debated the same theories, and were inspired by the same models: Karl Marx and Mao, Che Guevara and Ho Chi Minh, the Black Panthers, Angela Davis, the Tupamaros. At a critical juncture, our paths diverged. I turned to books and envisioned change through learning. They took up arms and fought for change through violence. But even as I disagreed with the path their actions took, I admired their willingness to put their principles into practice and risk their lives to put them to the test.

The one I admired most was Ulrike Meinhof. An intellectual who didn't compromise her principles and a writer whose work inspired change, she modeled my own aspirations. I first read her work in one of the informal study groups in the alternative university we had created. Open to all and free of charge, it had no lectures, grades, or professors. No syllabi, papers, or exams. We decided what and how to learn. We selected the texts we wanted to read, mimeographed copies, and distributed them among ourselves. We met in cafes or in communal rooms over wine or tea or coffee, smoking dark Gitanes, to debate politics and discuss theory. We were the vanguard in the revolution we dreamed of. Along the way toward this revolution, Meinhof was one of my guides. Her essay on Jürgen Bartsch, which I read soon after it appeared in the leftist journal *konkret*, changed the way I thought about justice.[3]

Identified as the villain in one of postwar Germany's most sensational crimes, Jürgen Bartsch was universally reviled as a sadistic serial killer. Born in 1946 as Karl-Heinz Sadrozinski to an unwed mother who died soon after his birth, he was adopted by a childless couple who ran a butcher's shop. Jürgen, as the Bartsches renamed him, was put to work in the shop. A photograph shows the little boy by the meat counter in a long bib apron, standing at attention, his face expressionless, his gaze unsmiling. As he grew older, Jürgen started rebelling against his father's authoritarian rule and his mother's quasi-incestuous coddling. By the age of ten, he was remanded to correctional institutions: first a home for boys, and then a Catholic boarding school, where he was taught that homosexuality was "disgusting," while one of the supervising priests abused him sexually. When the adolescent Jürgen was returned to his adoptive home, he was apprenticed to his father in the butcher trade, working long hours with minimal pay. The slaughtering, as he told the court at his trial, "never gave him pleasure."

He committed his first murder aged fifteen, when he lured eight-year-old Klaus Jung into an abandoned mine that had served as an air raid shelter during World War II. He tortured and sexually abused him, then killed him and left his mutilated corpse to rot. Over the next four years, Jürgen Bartsch committed three more murders. All of his victims were boys: a thirteen-year-old, a twelve-year-old, and an eleven-year-old. His last intended victim, another eleven-year-old, managed to escape and lead the police to the crime scene. Jürgen Bartsch was arrested and tried for murder and the abduction and sexual abuse of children. He didn't deny any of the charges, but he couldn't provide a motive for his acts. He hadn't meant to harm his victims, he insisted. What he felt for them, he maintained, was love.

Although legally still a juvenile (he was nineteen when he was arrested), Bartsch was tried as an adult and, on December 15, 1967, a regional court in North-Rhine Westphalia sentenced him to life imprisonment. A few years into his sentence, it was reduced to ten years' juvenile detention and he was moved to a clinic for psychiatric treatment. When therapy failed, Bartsch agreed to undergo surgical castration, believing that this was the only way to regain his freedom. But he was given the wrong anesthesia and died during surgery. He was twenty-nine years old.

When Meinhof's essay, "Jürgen Bartsch and Society," appeared in 1968, she couldn't yet know how his case would end. But she offered a radically different perspective on the crime. Whatever the outcome, she posited, within the existing social conditions justice could not be served and Jürgen Bartsch was not the only criminal.

What shocked me when I read her essay weren't the lurid details; what shocked me were the questions she asked. How did Jürgen Bartsch become a murderer, and what did his life and death and crime have to do with me? Meinhof's answer to these questions was bracing. Bartsch's life, death, and horrific crimes, she proposed, implicated all of us. From the stigma of illegitimacy as the child of an unwed mother, through childhood as a ward of the state, to a marginal existence as a menial laborer, he was treated as a burden that was expendable. He wasn't valued or respected. He wasn't supported or protected. When the verdict of life imprisonment was announced, people in the courtroom shouted "bravo" and applauded. If Jürgen Bartsch became a criminal, Meinhof's essay asked, weren't the rest of us part of the crime?

Meinhof's suggestion of moral complicity in the crimes of others had particular resonance in the German context. My generation had inherited the legacy of crimes that our parents had allowed to happen, even if technically—or legally—they weren't guilty. They weren't murderers, but they shared responsibility for murders committed in their name no less than the people around Jürgen Bartsch shared responsibility for his death and that of the boys he murdered. Meinhof reminded me that doing nothing, standing by, and allowing things to happen were also actions. Most importantly, she proposed, the moral responsibility that our parents had neglected had become our obligation to assume. Her quiet outrage felt more true to me than the protest slogans I shouted. "Class" was not a category of analysis to her. It was the texture of a person's life. Instead of referring to "the system" in abstract terms, she talked about right and wrong in human terms, on the level of the individual.

My first lesson in human rights came from Meinhof. It began with Article 1 of the Basic Law, the founding document of West Germany's postwar constitution. The first line spelled out the principle on which the new democratic Germany was founded: "The dignity of each human being is inviolate." Everything followed from this first principle, including "the power of the state [which] is dedicated to honor and protect" that human dignity. But, Meinhof argued, the promise of the Basic Law is not kept. The dignity of each human being is not respected. As the cases of people like Jürgen Bartsch showed, it is often violated by the very state pledged to protect it.[4] However, we can't just blame the state (or "the system"), Meinhof maintained. When human rights are violated, we are all guilty.

In June 1972, Meinhof was arrested and charged with attempted murder in the prison break of Andreas Baader that she helped orchestrate. Sentenced to eight years in prison, she was eventually transferred to the maximum security federal prison of Stammheim outside Stuttgart, where she and other members of the RAF were held in a special prison block built especially for them. The following spring, when the Stammheim Trial began, the world watched Germany grapple with questions foundational to its very existence: state authority, security, violence, and the people's right to resistance. Was Germany a police state that should be resisted, as the RAF and its followers claimed? Or was the RAF a terrorist organization that threatened the stability of a democratic state?

In the end, state power won. The RAF was prosecuted as perpetrating domestic terrorism. The four defendants in the Stammheim trial—Ulrike Meinhof, Andreas Baader, Gudrun Ensslin, and Jan-Carl Raspe—were charged with five counts of murder,[5] fifty-four counts of attempted murder, armed robbery, and the formation of a criminal association. Meinhof did not live to receive the verdict. On May 9, 1976, a year before the trial concluded with life sentences for the other defendants, she was found dead in her cell.[6] Officially her death by hanging from a knotted towel was declared a suicide, but many believe to this day that she was murdered by the state for exposing its failure to protect the vulnerable in favor of the powerful.

By the time Meinhof died, I had been living in the United States for seven years. I had moved from Indiana to Texas to Tennessee to Wisconsin, earned a Master's degree in French, and was working toward a PhD in comparative literature. In my American world, neither RAF nor Red Army Faction held meaning. RAF was the Royal Air Force of our British allies and Red Army Faction sounded vaguely Russian. When the German terrorist group was mentioned, they were called a gang: the Baader-Meinhof Gang. I always wanted to object, *they weren't a gang*, and talk about the Ulrike Meinhof I admired, but I couldn't retrieve what she had taught me from the contradictions her life became, so I said nothing.

I often wish that I had at least said something. I might have proposed that some of those called terrorists were good people with good intentions. They wanted to be the good Germans our generation was supposed to be. The problem was that we didn't have good models.

Our parents had been good Germans by the rules and expectations of their time. They had kept the law, obeyed orders, respected authority, and been dutiful citizens. They had been good Germans all the way to genocide. The response of my generation was to go the other way. We vowed to disrespect authority, disobey orders—even break the law—and question duty as a civic virtue. In the Nazi order good Germans watched neighbors, colleagues, friends, and relatives deported, exiled, and even put to death, while they looked away and busied themselves elsewhere. In the postwar order good Germans rebuilt their cities and returned to work, trying to forget what the previous order had led to. We, the children of these good Germans, distrusted order as a social principle.

In the confluence of movements that brought students, workers, and antiwar activists together in the movements of 1968, the authority of all established orders was put in question. Our parents had been wrong, so we must be right, we told ourselves, and our sense of rightness kept our doubts at bay. But those doubts gave an edge to our voices, often turning them from loud to shrill as we staved off fears that we wanted to keep unspoken.

These fears bound us to the very history we longed to shed. What if somewhere, in our collective psyche, a hidden Nazi lurked? If we weren't vigilant, could we become the very people we condemned? We didn't talk about these fears or even admit to them, but we anxiously watched for any signs that they might be valid. Had the stranger in the Heidelberg pub who had inked swastikas on my coat revealed a truth I couldn't bear to face? Could a Nazi gene be carried in the German bloodstream?

Like talismans against these fears we adopted personae that would prove our innocence. We identified with peasants fighting colonial armies with machetes and bamboo stakes,[7] and Native Americans suffering in silence as their land was taken. We pinned sepia-toned portraits by Edward Curtis on our walls next to images of napalm-burned children in Vietnamese villages.

The pictures signaled that in the conflicts of history we sided with the victims, not the perpetrators.

But among the victims of history we identified with and whose presence we symbolically invoked, one group was notably absent. There were no images of Jews, past or present, on our walls. No iconic reminders or gestures of solidarity. No rituals of identification that I recall. Jews were the hole in our collective memory, the silence that our slogans didn't fill.

Our relationship to Palestinians was particularly striking in this regard. We didn't just identify *with* them; we identified *as* them. In the historical drama in which we cast ourselves as the avengers of historical wrongs, the good guys to our parents' bad guys, Palestinians were our favorite role. The *keffiyehs* worn by men in the intifada soon became the standard German student movement garb. Wrapped around our necks, covering nose and mouth when the police used tear gas, these black and white (or sometimes red and white) headscarves symbolized our connection to a people whose lot we took as our cause.

At the time, I understood our identification with Palestinians to be based on our critique of the state. Palestinians, a people without a state, were oppressed in the name of a state, and we objected. I agreed with this critique, yet the identification with stateless victims of history felt false and made me uncomfortable. I carried my *keffiyeh* to demonstrations, but I couldn't bring myself to put it on.

Something else about the *keffiyeh* bothered me that I couldn't put my finger on at the time. It was the sleight of hand with which we substituted one group of historical victims (Palestinians) for another group of historical victims (Jews), conveniently replacing the one that reminded us of our German guilt with another that allowed us to feel righteous. As a compensatory intervention for German sins of the past, our stance was compelling. We couldn't repair the past, but we could stand up for victims of injustice. Yet identifying with—much less as—victims of history also served us well: it allowed us to avoid our historical blind spot. Adopting the victim side was one way we tried to deal with a past that haunted us. Another was to vent our anger at the generation responsible. Anyone of a certain age was a ready target.

One day it was an English professor whose course I was auditing. He was a popular lecturer, an authority on Renaissance literature, and the lecture hall that day was packed. From the back where I was sitting, he looked small, almost like a child, as he walked across the stage to the lectern. Several hundred students in rising tiers watched him enter, our notebooks out. With his shuffling gait and the cautious movements of an old man, he reminded me of my grandfather. He took his notes out, put his glasses on, and adjusted the microphone. But before he could speak, several young men, who identified themselves as student activists, came up and stood next to him on the podium. Crowding around the lectern, they seemed to be arguing with him about something. Then one of the students grabbed the microphone and addressed the room.

"We want an open discussion of issues relevant to us today, not some lecture about a bygone culture."

But the professor didn't relinquish the microphone. Whether he was stubborn or afraid or just needed to hold on to something, he clung to it even as the students who had been crowding him started shouting and pushed him aside. He was still clutching it when the lectern fell over.

Then he fell himself. I saw it like a scene in slow motion—his glasses sliding off his face, his free arm flailing, his lecture notes scattering, his hand finally letting go of the mike. I felt the shock of his body crumbling as he hit the floor. For a moment, there was absolute silence as an old man with thinning hair lay on the ground. I remember his hand groping for his glasses. Then he got up and left the room, walking stiffly, leaving his notes strewn across the floor. Several hundred students sat in silence and watched him. I was one of them.

I had thought of leaving Germany off and on for the past few years but hadn't progressed beyond a vague intention. But that day at the university, when I watched an old man pushed and fall, while a roomful of people did nothing, something broke for me. Perhaps it was the illusion that the postwar generation was inherently different from the one before, that we would redeem ourselves from the sin of Nazism and be better people. Perhaps it was the belief that we were creating a new Germany in which the dignity of each human being was inviolate. That wasn't the kind of Germany I saw that day.

It was around then that my plans to leave became definite.

A few weeks before I left, I had an argument with a fellow student, a member of a Maoist Red Cell. It was about Joan Baez and why I liked her music. I had her records and knew most of her songs by heart, but my radical friend was scornful. "She sings and lets others do the fighting," she exclaimed. "How do the songs of a pacifist change anything?"

I had no good answer. All I could say was that I liked her voice. But the truth was that she made me happy. When she sang I wanted to sing too. She reminded me that there is more to life than struggle and violence and suffering. There is joy and tenderness and grace. There are days when your heart is dancing, and the calf bound for slaughter isn't all there is. There are the sky and the wind and the swallows. They are winging through the sky, "proud and free." I longed for that release of lightness and sang along with Joan in my room,

How the winds are laughing,
they laugh with all their might.
Laugh and laugh the whole day through
and half the summer's night.[8]

With a generous fellowship in Comparative Literature from Purdue University, I moved to West Lafayette, Indiana that fall. I didn't know much about the university and had to look up West Lafayette on the map, but I was ready for this new adventure. I was assigned to teach English composition and half the football team showed up for my class. I had never seen a group of men this size before, but everything here seemed over-sized, from the giant milkshakes and double-decker sandwiches to the showers and air-conditioned cars. Yet if my students initially seemed strange to me, I was clearly equally strange to them. While they slouched in their black and gold sweatshirts, trying gamely not to fall asleep, I played them Bach for inspiration in free writing. I aspired to a radical pedagogy like that of Paolo Freire,[9] but that wasn't how it came across. As one of my students wrote in response to my Bach idea, "I can't believe we have to listen to this crap."

By the time winter came and we walked to class through heated underground tunnels while icy winds whipped down from the north, everything around me felt foreign. My familiar world seemed very far away and I felt lost. My solution was to find friends who were foreign too. There was Andres from Buenos Aires, with whom I listened to classical music, and Nadette from Toulouse, with whom I spoke French. Our foreignness was the bond that connected us: we read foreign books in foreign languages, watched foreign films, and ate food that in West Lafayette was called foreign.

I was spending the winter break in northern Wisconsin with my American boyfriend, and we invited Nadette to celebrate Christmas with us. He picked us up in his red '65 Plymouth and it was "Jingle Bells" all the way to Wausau. Nadette was going to make a traditional French Christmas cake—a *bûche de Noël*—and she had brought a list of what she needed. The local supermarket had everything except the key ingredient: butter. We needed sweet—or, as Nadette stonily insisted, *normal*—butter. But what was normal in Toulouse wasn't normal in Wausau. In Wausau normal butter was salted. We drove all over, checked every dairy aisle in every store. Store managers even checked their inventory. But there was no sweet butter in all of Wausau. On our way home, Nadette sat in the back seat of the car, close to tears.

She made her *bûche de Noël* anyway and it was the centerpiece of our Christmas table: a beautiful cake in the shape of a log with fork-drawn ridges in the chocolate icing to resemble bark. Plastic toadstools and two smiling plastic gnomes sat on top. The *bûche* looked perfect and you couldn't even taste the salt.

Nadette's attachment to her French traditions seemed provincial to me back then, but secretly I was envious. Her embrace of tradition, her proud belonging to a culture she loved, were positions I had foreclosed. I couldn't admit, even to myself, that I missed Germany, so I recast my lack of nostalgia as cosmopolitan and tried to feel superior.

As the electric lights on our American Christmas tree blinked colors, while the radio played American Christmas songs, I thought of the German Christmas Eves that had marked my childhood: the room aglow in the light of candles, the smell of resin from the tree, the scent of my mother's traditional vanilla and almond cookies. While the candles on the tree burned and flickered and the gold star at the top of the tree shone, my father read the Nativity story from St. Luke's gospel. A census had decreed that everyone go to their hometown to be counted.

That night in Wisconsin, my first Christmas in this new world, I wondered where would I go now to be counted.

Proof of Ancestry

I had moved to America, but Germany followed me like a reputation I couldn't shake. No matter how well I learned to pass as an American or how carefully I hid my roots, people always found me out eventually. I held my fork in the wrong hand; I crossed my sevens; I closed the door behind me when I entered or left a room. My name was usually enough. When I said *Un-gay-lee-ka* instead of the expected *Ann-jelly-ka*, people asked me, "Where are you from?" and I usually answered, "Germany." There would be a pause, sometimes an "oh," but often that's when they brought up my parents.

"Where are *they* from?"

My answers varied. Sometimes I said, "My father is from Czechoslovakia" (without explaining that he wasn't Czech). Sometimes I elaborated, "He is from a German region in what used to be Czechoslovakia." Sometimes I just said, "My father is from Bohemia" and let them wonder what a bohemian father was like. The one thing I never said was, "He is from the Sudetenland," although that would not have been wrong. But Sudetenland was a name my father hated. "It's a Nazi term," he protested. "It doesn't name the place I am from."[1]

My mother's case was more straightforward. "She's from Westphalia" ("in West Germany," I sometimes added). If I wanted to elaborate, I might say that her village was so close to Holland you could get there in half a day by bike.

Yet whatever my answers, embellished or plain, I always felt that I wasn't answering the real question. Perhaps it was my self-consciousness about being German and what that meant in the world at large, but I always imagined people wondering whether my parents had been Nazis (weren't all Germans ... or at least all Germans their age?). What were they guilty of? Nobody asked such questions directly, but I answered them anyway. Not in words, but physically—with a tightened throat, a flush of sweat, a knotted stomach. I changed the subject as soon as I could.

Of course, I could have answered questions about origin genealogically instead of geographically, offering branches from my family tree. But I didn't know what my family tree looked like until both of my parents had died.

After my father's death, in a drawer of albums and ledgers, I found a record of my family's history. It had an unassuming form: three small booklets bound in imitation vellum, each no more than forty pages long. Embossed on each cover, in thick Gothic letters, was the word *Ahnenpaß* (Ancestry Passport). I immediately recognized one of them as mine by the initials in the top right corner: an ornately intertwined *AB*. A second was my mother's. She had entered her information on the cover page: "Ursula Bushoff, married name Bammer," resident of Velen, Westphalia. My father's was the third. "Dr. iur. Walter Bammer," he had written, resident of Rumburg.

The familiar sight of my parents' hand—my father's casually elegant penmanship, the breathless quality of my mother's writing—flooded me with memories. For years, their letters to me in America (in the first year, sometimes once a week), had sustained a sense of home for me connecting me to the family I had left. Sometimes a letter from them was all it took to make a birthday special or release the homesick tears I'd been ashamed to shed. But the rush of nostalgia evoked by their writing on the Ancestry passports was quickly tempered by a sense of dread. These weren't just family records. They were records from a Nazi past.

The Gothic script was the first indication. The issuing institutions were the final clue. My mother's *Ahnenpaß* was issued by the Reich Association of Civil Registrars of Germany (Reichsbund der Standesbeamten Deutschlands); my father's and mine by the C.A. Starke press, publisher of Genealogical Research and Heraldry (Verlag für Sippenforschung und Wappenkunde) in Görlitz. *Reichsbund* and *Sippenforschung* confirmed the Nazi context, when Germany defined itself as the Third Reich and based membership on racially marked bloodlines. To be a proper member of the German Reich under Nazi rule, Germans had to establish an "Aryan" lineage going back at least five generations and provide genealogical evidence of the history of their tribe (*Sippe*). Administered through a Byzantine network of administrative offices, from church and civil registries at the local level to the Reich Interior Ministry at the top, the results of this research were issued in the form of these Ancestry passports.

My first reaction when I found these documents was excitement. They offered a key to a secret room of family history, promising to tell me things about my past that I hadn't known. But the word *Sippenforschung* evoked the Nazi practice of kin liability (*Sippenhaft*) used to put political pressure on resistant subjects.[2] Placing my family history into this context filled me with anxiety.

But, having found the key, I had to open the door, so I did.

And there it was, on the first page: the Nazi link between blood and race and claims to German supremacy. In decorative script, my passport featured a preamble by Adolf Hitler himself. It was an excerpt from his address to the German Reichstag on January 30, 1937, the fourth anniversary of his confirmation as German Chancellor, prophesying the glorious future of the German people under his leadership. Nazism, he proclaimed, was a revolution unlike anything the world had ever seen. Copernicus had changed people's view of the world by showing that the earth revolved around the sun. National Socialist doctrines would be even more transformative. In their wake everything—knowledge, history, time itself—would be redefined.

For a moment I just stared at the beautiful calligraphic lettering; the black, white, and red color scheme of Nazi symbolism;[3] the name *Adolf Hitler*. My personal family tree framed by Nazi blood and race rhetoric, my ancestry record introduced by Adolf Hitler. It felt surreal.

The passport itself looked straightforward enough. Thirty-one entries documented my lineage to 1800, going back the five generations required by Nazi blood laws. They covered the standard genealogical landmarks from birth through marriage and offspring to death. In my parents' passports every entry had been checked by a local official and verified with a swastika-adorned seal. In my mother's book, many of the entries had been signed by Franz Hardeweg, the head of Velen's Nazi Party.

In my book, the signatures and seals were missing. By the time I was born, Aryan registration had been discontinued and Ancestry passports were a relic of the past. I had no idea how my parents even got a blank one or why they decided to use it for their child. They probably thought nothing of it; it was just a convenient way to keep a record. The only sign that they might have been uneasy about my passport's provenance was that they kept it from me and buried it in their own files.

But now that I had it, I was eager to learn about the people I had come from, where they had lived, what they had done. The names already told part of the story. The multiple spellings of my paternal grandmother's family name—Miřovský, Meržovsky, Mirziowsky, and Miržiofski—reflected the hybrid culture of Central Europe during the time of the Austro-Hungarian empire, when people inhabited more than one language and culture at once:

German, Polish, Czech, Hungarian, Austrian. In contrast, my mother's family reflected the homogeneity of a sedentary people in rural Westphalia. As far back as 1728 (the earliest entry in my mother's Ancestry passport), the members of her family had lived and died in a radius of under 50 miles from where she was born.

The passport didn't ask what people did for work. "Occupation" was not a required category. But my parents had included this information, anyway. I learned that some of my ancestors had been small property owners (my paternal grandfather was identified as a "citizen and house-owner"). Some had been tradesmen (a brandy distiller, a cloth dyer, a shoemaker, and a miller). There had been teachers, inn-keepers, merchants, a forest ranger, and some who were just identified as "neighbors." The women weren't identified as anything other than daughters, mothers, or wives.

But while "occupation" was not a category in this document, "religion" emphatically was. It was asked, over and over, in each entry. What religion were you born into? What religion did your parents have? When and where were you and your parents baptized? When were you married, what was your religion, and what was the religion of your spouse and your spouse's parents? When someone in your family died, what was their religion? And which records could verify this information? Through each generation and centuries back, each person's religious affiliation was identified, checked, cross-referenced, and rechecked.

At first, this obsession with religion was puzzling. Then I realized what the purpose was. The questions about religion were a way to ferret out Jewish ancestry. You might claim to be a Catholic now, but were you born as one? What about your parents and their parents before them? Or the person you married, what were they? In Nazi Germany, *what is your religion* meant *what is your race*, and the only safe answer was "Christian."[4]

This connection between religion and social valuation reminded me of an incident from my Catholic childhood. Around the time of my First Communion, when I thought that Catholicism was the only true religion (as my catechism encouraged me to think), a friend of my sister's was mean to her and I defended my sister. "Leave her alone," I yelled. Then I attacked the offender. "What religion are you, anyway?" I asked.

"Protestant," she answered, puzzled.

"I should have known," I sniffed.

This recollection of my youthful zealotry shamed me. Having set out to uncover Nazi prejudice, I discovered my own. I needed a break from questions about history and identity and put my Ancestry passport away.

Later that day I recalled a conversation with my father after my mother died. He was living alone, and we had established a ritual of talking on the phone every Sunday. It was our special time together once a week. Talking about family one Sunday, I asked how far back his family line went. Not far, he said: three generations.

"And then?" I asked.

"Then come the gypsies."

I was startled. Perhaps he was joking, trying to avoid saying that he didn't know. So I followed up.

"What do you mean, gypsies?"

"Three generations ... then come the gypsies and the family line ends." His response was calm, deliberate, factual. Then he added, almost as an afterthought, "Gypsies weren't legally registered, you know, so family records don't go past that point."

I didn't know what to say, so I laughed instead. "That could explain our wanderlust," I quipped. But I was flustered. What did his comments mean? Did he really have gypsy ancestors, or was this a metaphor for something else he wanted to tell me?

He had always expressed a sense of kinship with those for whom home wasn't fixed or stable. "What's wrong with being unsettled?" he once exclaimed. "Look at our family. We're unsettled too." Rootless people were as legitimate as settled ones, he insisted. Tying identity to territory was dangerous. "That's what the Nazis did. It always leads to violence."

When I was a child, my father once shocked me by declaring that in history there were just two sides: perpetrators and victims. "In the end," he said, "you have to choose your side." This impossible choice had filled me with foreboding. Perhaps, I now thought, claiming gypsy ancestry was my father's attempt to escape the perpetrator/victim dilemma. Or perhaps he was choosing the side of the victims, trying to repair history by siding with those whom social norms had condemned. Historically, gypsies had definitely been condemned, not just by Nazis who targeted them for extermination, but by the prejudice of settled people for migrants.[5]

Whatever the reasons for his gypsy claim, I now had our Ancestry passports and could check the record. I found that my father was right on one score: his line went back three generations. It stopped (or, counting forward, began) with a woman named Anna Bammer. There was little information on her: no birth date, no death date, no marriage date, no parents, no residence of record. All the record showed was her name, her religion (Catholic), and the fact that she had a son, whom she named Johann. He was born on May 13, 1824, in a town called Alservorstadt, and, contrary to the usual custom of waiting several days, was baptized that same day. From this mother and her fatherless son, the Bammer line evolved. Yet from just these few dots on a plotline—the year and place of a birth, a hasty baptism, and an unnamed father—a story of gypsy origins could be drawn.

In 1824, before it was incorporated into Vienna, Alservorstadt was an industrial town with a munitions factory (one of the largest in Austro-Hungary, it boasted) that employed workers from the extended region, including migrants from Eastern Europe who came for work. It was also home to the famous Vienna Foundling Home for unwed mothers and their young children. When Johann Bammer was born, it was the second-largest institution of its kind in Europe, caring for as many as 4,000–5,000 children at a time.[6]

The story of Anna Bammer and her son could have started in the shadow of the munitions plant and the Foundling Home. Maybe Anna fell in love with (or was seduced by) a man who worked in the factory. Maybe he was one of the Croats, Slovenes, or Slovaks who came to Alservorstadt for work. Maybe she got pregnant but couldn't marry him, because her German family found a "Slav" unacceptable—as bad as a gypsy—so she had her child out of wedlock in the Foundling Home.[7]

Later that summer, this story of gypsies took a strange and unexpected turn. I was in Germany visiting my brother, who lived in a village outside Hannover at the time. When I arrived, he had a surprise for me: "You're going to be staying in our gypsy wagon!"

For two weeks, I lived in a wooden trailer parked under a tree in his yard. It had three little windows, a creaky door with a giant key, no electricity or running water. Next to the bed was the enamel bowl in which our mother had mixed bread dough. "If you need to pee in the night," Thomas instructed me, "use the bowl." I didn't know what to make of this strange coincidence. My father makes a comment about gypsy forebears and the next thing I know I'm in a gypsy wagon.

I asked my brother if he knew about the Bammers and the gypsies. He didn't know what I was talking about.

"What do you mean?"

When I told him what our father had said on the telephone, my brother was as puzzled as I had been. After a long pause, he asked, "Do you think he was serious?" I said I did, but not what he was serious about.

Thomas looked skeptical. Then, like me, he laughed. "Well," he shrugged, "it's either a good story ... or an unhappy romance."

At the end of the summer, before returning to the United States for the fall semester, I spent a few days with my father in Bonn. In the evening, before supper, we often walked by the Rhine, along a path right next to his building. He leaned heavily on his cane, sometimes stopping to catch his breath and gaze at the slow-moving river. I told him about my brother's gypsy wagon, but it was the family story I wanted to return to.

My parents, the summer before their engagement and my father's deployment to Russia in Operation Barbarossa, 1941.

"Tell me more about the Bammers and the gypsies," I said. He took my arm and I felt his weight as he leaned against me. We shuffled on, arm in arm, as he gripped his cane. His feet hurt from a childhood injury.

"What do you know?" I persisted. "Where did these gypsies that you mentioned come from? How do they fit into the Bammer family?"

He didn't answer me. He stopped and looked out across the water at a group of ducks. An angry mallard was pursuing a rival, and there was much quacking and flapping of wings. Moments later, the victorious drake swam off with his hen.

"So, how does the story of the Bammers and the gypsies start?" I repeated a third time. "Did someone fall in love with someone?"

The mallards were peaceful now and the sun had set. My father finally turned to me, smiling. "Isn't that how it all begins, always?"

I felt the warmth of his arm in mine and smiled back.

Part Two

Walking to Buchenwald

You who live safe ...
Ponder that this happened.

— Primo Levi, "Shemà" (1946)[1]

Self-portrait at the entrance to the Italian Pavilion, State Museum of Auschwitz-Birkenau, Oświęcim, Poland. (Photograph by author, 1999).

Into the Past

They say that hindsight is 20/20, but it doesn't work that way in regard to history. Feelings blur our vision. The present gets in the way. Fantasy looks like fact from our perspective. It's hard to focus when angle and distance aren't fixed.

A trip with my father brought this home to me in ways I had not expected. Instead of bringing the past in closer, as through a telescope, so we could see it from the shared location of our present moment, our trip kaleidoscoped into shifting patterns of memories, histories, and stories.

It was 1990. Both World War II and the Cold War were fading to memory and the Berlin Wall had just come down. Borders across Eastern Europe were not just opening, they were being erased. Europe felt alive with movement. As travel restrictions that had been in place for decades were lifted, the world my father came from suddenly seemed accessible and I wanted to see it. I wanted to visit the parts of Czechoslovakia where he had lived, attended school, vacationed, studied law, got his first job, and had his first romance. I asked my father, who had recently retired, to go with me and he agreed. We planned a ten-day trip in August.

My job was to decide the route. I was hampered by my out-of-date roadmap marked by borders that had recently been removed, but the general network of roads and highways was still operative. From Bonn, I mapped a route south to Frankfurt and Bayreuth, then east to cross the border at Marktredwitz. The part of Czechoslovakia we would be traveling in had been partly, if not entirely, German until the end of World War II and my German roadmap from the 1980s still listed place names in both languages: Czech first, then German in parentheses. Our route went through Cheb (Eger) and Kynšperk (Königsberg) for a first stop in Karlovy Vary (Karlsbad), the famous spa that the Holy Roman Emperor and King of Bohemia, Charles IV, had made a royal city in 1370, and where the likes of Czar Peter the Great, Goethe, Beethoven, and even Karl Marx and Sigmund Freud had sought therapeutic treatment.

After Karlsbad, we entered the landscape of my father's youth. First came Chomutov, the German Komotau of his childhood memory, where he spent summers with his maternal grandparents, helping in the vegetable garden or perched on a kitchen stool watching his grandmother cook. From Komotau, our route went east to Leitmeritz (today's Litoměřice), where he had been a boy, then north to Rumburg (today's Rumburk), where he lived through the end of high school. The last leg of the trip went south to Prague, where my father studied law at the Charles University and, in 1937, got his first job in the private practice of attorney Karl Schönbaum.

With the route planned, I wanted to trace the chronology of my father's life and looked for the place on the map where he had spent his earliest childhood years: Leitmeritz.

That's when I discovered Theresienstadt.

I was tracing the coordinates for Leitmeritz when they converged on two names. To the north Litoměřice/Leitmeritz. To the south Terezín. Two small dots side by side, just millimeters apart on my roadmap, separated by the thin blue line of the river Elbe (Czech, Labe). I noticed that Terezín was the only place on my map in this area without a German name. It had only its Czech name: Terezín.

I thought it couldn't possibly be the Terezín I knew by its German name, Theresienstadt. That Theresienstadt, a military garrison from the eighteenth century named by the Austrian emperor, Joseph II, in honor of his mother, Maria Theresa, was converted into a ghetto/concentration camp by the SS in 1941. So overcrowded that "you couldn't stretch without touching someone,"[1] it was a breeding ground for epidemics (encephalitis, jaundice, gastroenteritis, diarrhea) that regularly swept through the camp, taking countless lives.[2] However, most of those deported to Theresienstadt didn't stay long enough to fall ill; they were sent on to other Nazi camps to be killed. Described as "the stable that supplied the slaughterhouse,"[3] Theresienstadt served as holding pen and transit station for an estimated 140,000–155,000 Jews.

That Theresienstadt I knew from Holocaust history. This couldn't be that place. My father would have told me beforehand. Then I realized that, of course, it *was* that place. I just hadn't expected to find it on the map of my personal history.

As I stared at the two adjacent dots on the map, Leitmeritz and Terezín, my initial confusion turned to incredulity. How could my father not have told me that he once lived across from Theresienstadt? How could he have kept something this important from me, leaving me to discover it on my own, and without warning? His silence felt like a betrayal, as if he had abandoned me on the way to the past without guideposts.

What I did next made no sense, but I wasn't thinking. I rushed to tell my father of my discovery. He was in his study, listening to Bruckner. I knocked. He turned the sound down, and I went in.

"Did you know that Theresienstadt is across the river from Leitmeritz?" I blurted out, as if I half-believed that he might say to me, *But that's impossible! If I had known, I would surely have told you.* But he hadn't told me. And of course he knew, just as he knew that he hadn't told me.

If he had, would it have mattered? Would anything have changed? When an American friend asked me why the proximity of these places troubled me ("So what," she said, "if Leitmeritz is across from Theresienstadt? Neither, really, has anything to do with you"), I couldn't answer her. I could have reasoned, as perhaps my father had, that it was just a geographical coincidence, not relevant to our family history, and that I was fabricating a connection where none existed. Yet it did matter to me. The proximity between my father's childhood home and this Nazi concentration camp made the connection between the two personal.

On both sides of a narrow river, separated by a bridge I could walk across, Theresienstadt and Leitmeritz marked two axes that had framed my life: my family history and the legacy of Nazi Germany. They were distinct, but they didn't feel separate. For my father, they marked a time of innocence, the place where he had been a child. For me, they marked a site of violence, a way station on the road to genocide.

In 1913, when my father was born, Leitmeritz was part of the Austro-Hungarian empire. A mid-sized city of around 14,000, halfway between Prague and Dresden, it had been culturally German since the Thirty Years War, when Catholic forces under German leadership defeated local Protestants and the native Czech population was displaced. My father lived there with his parents until 1920, when his father took a job in the new state of Czechoslovakia representing the interests of German industry. The family moved to Rumburg, a majority-German city of around 10,000 in the industrial north, heart of the textile, steel, and glass manufacturing industries. Rumburg was Walter's home from first grade through graduation from high school.

A photograph of my father's class from 1930, two years before their Abitur, shows twenty-two young men in parallel rows of wooden desks, two students side by side per desk. The lone female student has a desk to herself in the first row. My father is in the bench behind her.

I look at his cohort: backs straight, neatly dressed in white shirts and wool sports coats, they pose for the camera, hands folded on their desks. Who had they been, these young men of my father's generation, who came of age in the 1930s under Nazi rule and went to war under the sign of the swastika? When it was over, many had died, some had been deported, and most of them had lost their homeland. The picture didn't give any answers.

When I asked my father what he remembered of the young men in his class, he scanned the picture. He had forgotten most of the names, even many of the faces. Yet a few vivid memories returned.

"That's our teacher, Professor Langhans," he pointed to the back row. "In the seat closest to him is my friend, Heinz Patzner … And these," his gaze lingered on three of faces, "these were my best friends: Heinz, Helmut, and Erich."

Heinz Vatter is in the first row next to my father. With his even features, his thick, brown hair combed straight back, and his white shirt with the open collar, he has the clean good looks of a young James Dean and the confident air of a boy from a well-off family. He stares at the camera, arms folded across his chest. "I spent many a school-year weekend with Heinz Vatter," my father recalled, "listening to music, playing tennis, partying. And since the Vatters didn't live in Rumburg, but in Schönlinde,[4] the neighboring town, I often just stayed the whole weekend."

An only child, Heinz was slated to run the family hosiery factory and studied engineering after his Abitur toward that end. But history intervened. After the war, when ethnic Germans were expelled from Czechoslovakia and the Vatter factory was appropriated by the new Czech government, Heinz moved to the West, where he started a new life for himself and his family.[5]

Helmut Stein and Erich Orlik are in the second row. Neither of them look at the camera. Helmut—thick, wavy hair and an open face—affects a casual air. Of all the students, he is the only one smiling. Erich—dark hair and wire-rimmed glasses—looks formal in shirt and tie.

Both Helmut and Erich were Jewish, my father notes. Erich followed in his father's footsteps and studied medicine, choosing a profession over his avocation, theater. "He loved the theater," my father remembered. "It was a love that he and I shared." When the Nazis came to power, Erich moved to Palestine, but when Palestine became Israel, he didn't stay.

"Why? What happened?" I asked.

"When we reconnected after the war," my father explained, "Erich told me that Israel felt too much like the Germany he had just fled. *It promoted the same blood and soil ideology as Nazi Germany*, Erich wrote in his letter, *just this time in the name of Jews*." So Erich left Israel and emigrated to Canada, changing homelands a second time.

Helmut Stein was the only friend of my father's who stayed in Rumburg, where he survived both Nazi rule and the war. When I wondered how he, as a Jew, was able to avoid deportation, my father wasn't sure. Perhaps, he speculated, because Nazi laws didn't treat him as a "full Jew" (*Volljude*) but rather as "mixed-race" (*Mischling*)? Perhaps he was protected because his wife was Catholic and Czech? "Perhaps we can ask him when we see him," I suggested. When we got to Rumburg, we were going to spend two days with the Steins.

"And who's that next to you?" I asked my father, pointing to his seat-mate in the class picture, a slight young man with cropped, blond hair and eyes so pale they looked almost sightless. He sat erect, one arm stretched behind my father's back. My father was leaning slightly forward, as if to avoid contact with that arm.

"That's Krehahn." My father's answer came quickly. "He became a fanatical Nazi," he added.

I stared at the pale young man next to my father, as if the photograph could tell me more. My father was silent.

"And his first name …?"

"I don't remember."

When we got to Rumburg, we went straight to the Steins'. I was looking forward to meeting my father's old friend, hoping to learn more about the Nazi years from his perspective. Perhaps he would tell me what "that time" had been like for him.

They lived in a grey, Soviet-era building that looked as if it hadn't been maintained in years. Helmut opened the door, the two men embraced, and we were welcomed into the living room where Frau Stein had set the table for afternoon tea. A giant painting of Mary and Jesus hung over the sofa. A crucifix hung on a side wall.

The sight was startling. For the past weeks, my father had been referring to Helmut Stein as "my Jewish friend." This insistence on his old friend's Jewishness had made me uncomfortable (what was he trying to tell me?), yet I had come to think of Helmut Stein in those terms too. Mary and Jesus and the crucified Christ didn't fit the picture. This household, I realized, was not Jewish.

Nor, as I discovered, was Helmut Stein. It was the Nazis who made him Jewish, he explained, over coffee and pastries. It was a typical German-Jewish story of assimilation and segregation, of identities defined between force and choice. Helmut's father, the son of Jewish parents, had fallen in love with a Catholic girl and converted to her faith when they married. When their son was born, they baptized and raised him Catholic. Yet by the time Helmut came of age, Nazi racial laws annulled his Catholic identity and turned him into a Jew (albeit just a "half-Jew" because of his Catholic-born mother). Meanwhile, the same racial laws turned Helmut's father—a German Catholic—into a non-German Jew.

While Helmut reviewed his family history, Frau Stein showed us pictures of their son and his family. Their son, like his parents, was Catholic, Frau Stein explained, as were his wife and children, even as Helmut volunteered that their son looked "quite Jewish" on some of the pictures. I gazed at the handsome man in the photographs—dark hair, dark eyes, and arched nose— and wondered what to make of Helmut's comment. What did "looking Jewish" mean? There was no corresponding "Catholic" look. Yet, worn familiar through centuries of use, the stereotypes signified, whether we rejected or accepted them or feigned indifference. Philip Roth's protagonist in *American Pastoral* looked at his mother one day and was shocked to find that she "looked Jewish," just as I was astonished to learn that my Polish friends, as blonde and blue-eyed as the Madonna in the Stein's painting, were also Jewish. They didn't look it!

What did it mean to "look" like anyone in particular, I wondered. To look Jewish, say. Or German. Or Black, in contemporary America. Could "looking like" someone marked in racial terms ever be neutral and not carry a sting? When I was sixteen, I met an American girl who asked me where I was from. When I told her, Germany, she frowned as if I was mistaken. "But I thought all Germans were tall, blonde, and beautiful," she said. "What happened to you?"

I had brought questions about history on this trip with me, but on our visit with Helmut Stein I held them back. Instead of asking, I listened. I sat on the sofa in the Steins' living room and watched my father and his friend recall times that came alive again in shared memory. Neither the distance of years nor the difference of experience seemed to have erased the familiarity between them, the closeness of having been young together. As they exchanged memories of *that street where …* or *the girl who …* or *the time when …*, I recalled my father's curt response to some of my questions. "I don't like to dwell on the past," he had insisted. "What matters is where we are now."

He didn't want to leave the past behind entirely. There were parts he wanted to retrieve. He wanted to retrieve who he had been before the Nazi years and affirm who he became in the years afterwards. It was the in-between time—the "terrible time," as his generation dubbed it—where he didn't want to dwell.

Yet that was the very time I wanted to take him to. Perhaps, I thought, if people like my father and Helmut Stein could tell me what that time had been like for them—how they experienced it, how they lived through it, what it had done to them—part of the break between our generations could be bridged. Things that seemed unfathomable from our postwar perspective might make sense if we could see them from theirs. I wondered what my father and Helmut Stein remembered of the Nazi years and how those memories affected their friendship.

For example, did they remember October 1937, when the popular department store in Dresden, Rika, posted notices on all its entrances that it was now an "Aryan store" and establishments in Rumburg quickly followed suit? Walter would certainly remember his shock in September 1938, when Jews were officially barred from practicing law and, two months later, had their bar association membership annulled. As a newly minted attorney in the private practice of a Jewish lawyer, these measures affected him directly. I was sure that both Walter and Helmut remembered the increasing restrictions on

Jews' participation in cultural life; Helmut directly, by being barred or made unwelcome, Walter indirectly through his father's engagement in the arts community.[6] And obviously both Walter and Helmut remembered the fate of Sudeten Jews under Nazi rule, most of whom either fled or emigrated, while those who stayed faced arrest or deportation. Within a short period, almost all of the 20,000 Jews in the area were gone.

My father and Helmut Stein didn't talk about these things. They avoided any mention of the Nazi years. But they didn't talk about the anti-German backlash either. Everything I learned about that part of German history, I learned from books.

It began even before the official end of the war. On May 5, 1945 long-standing resentment of Czechs against German rule erupted into violence that spread across the Sudeten region and continued into June. With the call "Death to the German occupiers!" (*Smrt nemeckym occupantum!*), self-declared revolutionary guards raged against a history of German domination. In the ensuing "May days" Germans were rounded up and detained in movie theaters, schools, and barracks. They were imprisoned in concentration camps recently vacated by Nazis and consigned to forced labor in the countryside and construction sites in the ruined cities. Some were tortured and killed.

Komotau (today's Chomutov), where Walter spent childhood summers with his maternal grandparents, was the site of a particularly gruesome massacre. On June 9, 1945, local Czechs rounded up several thousand German residents and, for the public's amusement, tortured a number of them to death on the local soccer field.[7] A few weeks later, on July 31, in Aussig (today's Ústí nad Labem), Germans, who were now easily identified by the white armbands with the letter "N" for *Němec* (Czech for "German") that Czech authorities required they wear, were beaten to death, shot, or drowned in the River Elbe.[8]

Politically, the aim was to return the areas appropriated by Nazi Germany to Czechoslovakia and remove all ethnic Germans from Czech lands. Plans for a postwar order based on ethno-nationalist principles had been laid early in the war. Already in 1941, Edvard Beneš, President of the Czechoslovak Government in Exile, had proposed a "New Order in Europe" that would include the expulsion of ethnic Germans from Czechoslovakia, and the Allies had in principle agreed. The postwar Potsdam Conference fashioned policy out of this principle. When the American president, the British prime minister, and the Soviet premier met for two weeks in July 1945 in the town of Potsdam, they decided that the postwar European order would be based on nation states stabilized by an ethnic foundation. To implement this plan, the Potsdam Agreement issued on August 2, 1945 proposed what a historian has called "a demographic experiment on a scale unprecedented in human history."⁹ Somewhere between 12 million and 14 million people would be permanently displaced. In particular, the Agreement announced, "[t]he transfer to Germany of German populations ... will have to be undertaken." The question was, how to implement this plan in the "orderly and humane manner" the signatories had pledged to follow.¹⁰

In an eerie echo of the 1935 Reich Citizenship Laws that had stripped German Jews of their German citizenship, President Beneš marked the official beginning of this "transfer to Germany of German populations" by retroactively annulling the Czechoslovak citizenship of all those who had identified as ethnic Germans since 1929, the date of the last census. The Allied Control Council estimated that some 2.5 million ethnic Germans would have to be evacuated from Czechoslovakia. By the end of the year, around a million people had already been expelled.

Unofficially, this process had begun much earlier. In early May, word went out in Rumburg that all ethnic Germans had to leave the city. Walter's parents and Ursula hastily packed belongings in a wooden handcart and headed into the woods outside the city. They spent the night there, huddled in blankets, only to learn the next morning that the expulsion order had been false. It was the first in a series of similar rumors. However, the threat of expulsion was real. Throughout that spring, summer, and into the fall, rogue police, military, and paramilitary groups instigated a wave of so-called "wild" expulsions. Although officially unauthorized, they were no less final. In the night of May 30, the entire German population of Brünn (today's Brno)—around 30,000 men, women, and children—were driven from their homes and forced to leave town. As many as 1,700 lost their lives in the process.¹¹ In early June, around Tetschen (today's Děčín), less than 20 miles from Rumburg, the Czechoslovak Army rounded up some 1,300 Germans and dumped them in the Soviet zone. At the height of these "wild" expulsions in the summer of 1945, some 5,350 ethnic Germans were expelled from Czechoslovakia each day and shipped by the trainload to cities across Germany and Austria.

In retrospect, it was patently absurd to expect that my father and Helmut Stein would talk about the war and Nazi years or even the immediate postwar period. We were sitting in the Steins' living room over coffee and pastries. It was a social visit, not confession or therapy. Neither the tortured history of German–Jewish relations nor the ethno-nationalist politics of the postwar period had undermined their friendship. Among the shifting categories that had marked their mutual history—Czech, German, Aryan, Jew—"friend" had been the only constant.

Rather than dredge up painful pasts that could cause tension they returned to a time before the war, when they were young and their world still seemed innocent. They retrieved a past that connected the boys they had been to the men they hoped to have turned into. I watched, as through an inverted telescope, as two old men became young again in memory.

They adopted the personae of the dashing young men they had once fancied themselves to be, with salacious references to "ripe young girls" and "pretty women." In a local restaurant that evening, I watched them trade in the gallantries of a bygone time, complimenting the hostess, winking at the waitress, being charming. Even as this glimpse of their youthful selves moved me, I was embarrassed by my father's behavior and annoyed by his air of self-righteous confidence. When a group of German tourists who had come for dinner moved a table so they could sit together, our Czech waitress confided to Frau Stein, in Czech, "how awful those Germans are," and when Frau Stein told us what the waitress said, my father agreed with her. "I would never dream of doing such a thing," he said, indignantly. At that, my annoyance turned to anger. "What's so awful about pushing two tables together?" I exclaimed. "They aren't causing any trouble or doing harm."

I felt trapped between two equally bad choices. I could join him by distancing myself from "those awful Germans," or I could distance myself from him by siding with them. Either choice felt false. We were all "those Germans"—me and my father, Helmut Stein and the table-pushers. We were "them."

The last evening of our trip, over a bottle of Bohemian Riesling, my father filled in a chapter of the story we had set aside: his relationship with Manfred Förster.

Of all the people that my father was close to, Manfred was one of the few he truly loved. He trusted him as a friend and confidant and relied on him as a mentor and older brother, even as Manfred's role in the Bammer family complicated their relationship. For Manfred wasn't just my father's friend. Ten years older than Walter and already a successful businessman at a time when my father was still in high school, Manfred was also a friend to Walter's father, advising him on business matters and working with him to forge ties between the business and the arts communities. Finally—the most entangled knot of all—he was the man Walter's mother fell in love with as her marriage cooled.

In the album that my parents made as a record of my early years there is a photograph of Manfred Förster. The caption reads: *Manfred Förster. Born November 21, 1902. Died July 1952.* The same picture stood, framed, on my father's desk. He is a handsome man: dark eyes under thick, low eyebrows, a strong, straight nose, dark hair above a prominent forehead. His lips are sensuous and his gaze intense.

When he died, I was six years old. We were in Canada, where my father had been posted to the West German embassy. Manfred was in the other Germany, on the eastern side of the Cold War divide. Underneath the photograph in my album, my father wrote in memory of his friend,

> *You haven't seen much of your godfather, as the political division of Germany since 1945 kept us apart physically. In him, our family lost a noble and selfless friend. Happiness was meted out to him sparingly, but bitterness and suffering in abundance. Remember him. Always honor his name. We, your parents, do likewise.*

I never knew my godfather in person. I just had this photograph and my father's stories. Accounts of the trip to America that Manfred paid for when my father got his Abitur: across the Atlantic by boat, then by train across the continent to California. Descriptions of the elegant Förster lifestyle: their four-story villa, the private lake complete with swans, the terraced gardens, soirées, and chamber concerts in the music room where my grandfather introduced new compositions, and sometimes performed on the piano himself.

But there was a dark side to the Förster story that I hadn't known about until that last evening of our trip when my father talked. I learned only then that the "bitterness and suffering" mentioned in my album entry had a Nazi backdrop: Manfred had been classified a "Quarter Jew" (*Vierteljude*).[12] His grandfather, Friedrich August Förster, had married a Jewish woman, and from that time forward the family was marked, its Aryan purity tainted.

This taint notwithstanding, the Förster business was an entrepreneurial success. Pianos made by the August Förster Piano Manufacturing Company became the instrument of choice for concert pianists from Giacomo Puccini to Elton John and world-famous opera companies like La Scala and the Moscow State Opera. It began with a carpenter who fell in love with a musical instrument.

Friedrich August Förster was a carpenter in Löbau, a small industrial town between Görlitz and Dresden, who first learned about pianos by repairing them. Yet as he worked on them, he became fascinated by them as instruments and finally decided to build one for himself. He apprenticed to two Löbau piano builders to learn the basics of piano building and took piano lessons to learn how to play the instrument. His four journeyman years were spent honing his craft. In 1859, after his journeyman travels were over, he returned to his hometown, where he built his first piano himself from scratch. The erstwhile carpenter had become a master piano builder. Within three years, he was running his own piano manufacturing business. When

Friedrich August Förster died in 1897, his son, Cäsar, took over the company. Cäsar was Manfred Förster's father.

In 1915, when Cäsar Förster died, Manfred was a boy of twelve and his brother, Gerhard, a few years younger. But like their father before them, the brothers grew into the family business and stepped into their father's and grandfather's shoes. Manfred studied economics and managed the business. Gerhard learned piano building and oversaw manufacturing. The company not only flourished, but new designs brought them international acclaim. At the 1928 Leipzig Fair they presented a Quartertone Grand that they had created in collaboration with the Czech composer Alois Hába, and five years later they introduced the first electronic piano, the Electrochord.

My father paused and poured another glass of Riesling. "Did you know that I was supposed to join the company?" His question startled me.

"How was that?" I was puzzled. "Your degree was in law."

"It was. But there was a problem."

The problem lay in Nazi race laws. In the wake of the 1935 Nuremberg Laws, Manfred's Jewish grandmother put the company at risk. Over the course of the 1930s, this risk increased exponentially as pressure mounted on all sides. Under the watchword "Aryanization," banks imposed credit restrictions on Jewish businesses, consumers boycotted Jewish-owned stores, and local papers publicized the names and addresses of non-Jewish patrons frequenting Jewish establishments. Many businesses were expropriated outright,[13] while nervous Jewish owners often sold their businesses at a fraction of their value as threats of expulsion from the Reich pressured them to emigrate. By 1938, an official Property Transfer Office had been created to handle the systematic expropriation of Jewish assets. The goal was to "de-Judaize" the Reich economy—and ultimately the entire Reich—by not only liquidating Jewish assets, but also destroying the economic foundation of Jewish life.

In 1937, when my father finished law school, this end was not yet fully spelled out. Final plans remained to be laid, but the path toward the end had been charted. A November 1938 decree "to remove Jews from German economic life" marked the direction, and a December decree specified details. Issued jointly by the Reich Economic Ministry, the Reich Labor Ministry, and the Reich Interior Ministry, it declared that "Jews are no longer permitted to be managers of a company that they own ... Instead of a Jew, a manager is to be appointed who meets the bloodline requirements."[14] These decrees directly affected the Förster business, so provisions were put in place to protect it.

Walter was key to these provisions. As a German who met the "bloodline requirements," he could serve as an "Aryan shield" to step in as manager of the company. If need be, he could even be named owner. In case this contingency plan had to be enacted, my father prepared. After completing his law degree, he took courses in finance and management to learn how to run a business. To learn how to build a piano, he apprenticed in the Förster factory. "I learned everything about pianos except tuning," he laughed. "For that, I didn't have the ear."

In the end, these precautions proved superfluous, as the Nazis left the Förster firm alone. Perhaps the valuable revenue that their successful business regularly contributed to the Nazi coffers was protection enough. Whatever the reasons, Förster Piano Manufacturing survived both the war and Nazi years. So did its "Quarter-Jew" owners. Ineligible for military service because of their non-Aryan status, Manfred and Gerhard Förster stayed in Löbau and ran the company. Neither of them ever married, my father added. When I asked why, he speculated that their Jewish heritage might have been a factor. But Manfred adopted a son, he went on, who eventually took over the business.[15]

The historical irony to the Förster story is that the socialist state succeeded where the Nazis failed. It finally put the Försters out of business. In its zeal to eliminate private property, it imposed such crippling inheritance taxes on private companies that most just folded and sold to the state. In 1972, a little over a hundred years after Friedrich August Förster started a small piano manufacturing company in an old factory building in the Saxon town of Löbau, it was expropriated to become a People-Owned Firm (Volkseigener Betrieb, or VEB): the VEB Grand and Upright Piano Manufacturing Company Löbau.

Yet the vagaries of history are unpredictable. In 1991, when the two Germanies were reunited, the company became a family-owned business again under the original name of August Förster.

As I listened to my father, who had never evinced the slightest interest in business, describe his readiness to manage the company if Manfred needed him, I felt a sense of pride. It was a pride mixed with relief that I had felt before in relation to the question of Nazi membership. I knew that my father had never been a party member, a fact that he seemed quietly proud of too, but this trip added details to his decision. I learned that his father had made the same decision, refusing to join the party of what he called "uncultured thugs." Moreover, my grandfather didn't just refuse. He gave up privileges. When German industry was pressured to support the Nazi agenda, he resigned as director of the Association of German Industry in the Sudetenland and took a lesser job in the Association. And when the Nazi-controlled Bureau of Cultural Affairs that governed Prague after the German occupation offered him a leadership position in the music scene, he refused their offer. These weren't things to brag about, my father insisted. They were simply the right things to do.

But what do you do, I thought, when "right" is contravened by necessity, when the "wrong" side is in power and applying force? Sometimes principles can be luxuries that are hard to live by. Manfred and Gerhard Förster were a case in point. They had no interest in Nazi politics and abhorred what the party stood for. Yet party membership offered protection and they were vulnerable. So when their Jewish heritage disqualified them for membership in the Nazi party, they chose the next best thing: party affiliation. Manfred joined the National Socialist People's Welfare Association (National Sozialistische Volkswohlfahrt, NSV) and wore his NSV pin whenever he went out. His brother, Gerhard, joined the Nazi-affiliated Automobile Club (Der Deutsche Automobil Club, DDAC) and displayed the DDAC decal on the windshield of his Mercedes roadster.

My father (left) after graduation from the Military Academy in Olmütz, Czechoslovakia with Manfred Förster (right) in Bratislava, 1937.

By now, my father and I were the only guests left in the restaurant. We had finished our wine. But we hadn't yet finished the story of Walter and Manfred.

"What happened after the war with you and Manfred?" I asked my father. He was silent so long that I no longer expected him to respond.

"We never saw each other again," he finally answered. "When I stayed in the West and didn't return east to join him in the company, he felt betrayed by me."

My father fell silent again and looked at me, stricken. When he resumed, his voice was tense and his tone defensive. "But there was nothing for me to return to there. I had met Ursula. I was starting a new life. The life I had imagined before the war was no longer possible."

I didn't know what to say and put my hand on his. His eyes filled with tears. "But for Manfred that was a betrayal."

Walking to Buchenwald

Germany after unification wasn't a new Germany, exactly—the East was still the East and the West the West. But something had changed, something fundamental. The horizon of expectations had shifted.

I was curious how this shift would affect not just the future but also the past, particularly the legacy of Nazi Germany. Claiming anti-fascist resistance as its historical foundation, East Germany had traditionally disclaimed responsibility for Nazi crimes, leaving them, like an original sin, to West Germany. Could this specious distinction between two different Germanys—one guilty, one innocent—be maintained in a unified state?

With this question in mind, I planned a trip to the east in 1992, two years after unification. At the heart of my trip was a visit to Weimar and Buchenwald, two of the most iconic sites of German history: Weimar, the celebrated center of German classical culture, and Buchenwald, site of the largest Nazi concentration camp on German soil.

My mother was coming with me. She proposed November. It was off season and there would be no crowds. We booked a room in a former Weimar convent that was now a guesthouse. It was simple, practical, no frills. Two narrow beds, a basin for washing, and two straight-backed chairs put us in the mood of pilgrims.

We played tourist first, starting with the historic German National Theater in Weimar. This was where Germany's first democratically elected parliament convened in 1919 to draft Germany's first democratic constitution. But this theater in Weimar wasn't just where German democracy was born. It was the place where, a century before a German state existed, the idea of Germany as a cultural nation was shaped.

Two Weimar residents played a critical role in that process. In a creative collaboration that spanned more than six intense, productive years, Johann Wolfgang von Goethe and Friedrich Schiller—writers, playwrights, and politically engaged intellectuals—developed the idea of a German nation based on Enlightenment ideals: a belief in the common good supported by a culture that served it. Between 1799 and 1805, during which Goethe as the theater's director produced Schiller's canonical late plays, they elevated an erstwhile provincial theater to the level of a national stage.[1] A statue of the two men in front of the building—side by side, their gaze directed forward—celebrates the German cultural ideal they stood for.

The playbill for that day was Brecht's *Threepenny Opera*. Beethoven's *Fidelio* was the next day. I checked at the box office for tickets.

"For *Fidelio*, any tickets left?"

"Two in orchestra, mid-row."

"Orchestra is perfect. We'll take them."

The next day, my mother and I found a local bus with a stop marked "Buchenwald." As the bus meandered through various Weimar neighborhoods, I saw an ordinary city with ordinary people going about their business: schoolchildren on a class excursion, women with groceries in recycled bags, an old man with a cane walking his dachshund. Fifty years earlier, under Nazi rule, it would have been no different. Then, as now, people went to work and school, shopped for groceries, met with friends and walked their dogs. The fact that, just 6 miles up the road, in a camp in the Ettersberg Forest, thousands of people were suffering and dying each day, would not have changed the daily life of Weimar citizens any more than our daily lives are changed by the fact that people are suffering and dying each day in our own communities—from poverty, from neglect, from violence.

If putting a giant concentration camp right by a major German city seemed brazen, putting it next to a cultural center like Weimar seemed outright perverse. Yet its location had many obvious benefits. For Nazi administrators and SS officers, it probably made for a desirable posting. They could live in Weimar and partake of its cultural offerings: they could go to the theater or opera, have dinner in one of the fine restaurants, and be at work in the camp the next morning. Those who were housed in the camp and couldn't live in town were periodically entertained by members of the National Theater in the casino on the Buchenwald grounds.

The practical benefits of the location were equally obvious. The camp could easily be accessed and supplied with labor and goods from the surrounding area. Local masons could lay the bricks, local electricians do the wiring, and local plumbers the plumbing. Local carpenters could build the wooden barracks that housed the prisoners and the three-tiered shelves that served as beds. Local farmers could supply the produce. The wrought-iron entrance gate with its elegant Bauhaus lettering, JEDEM DAS SEINE (To Each His Own), was probably forged in a local smithy.[2]

People knew the camp was there. Did they wonder—or know—what went on there? Were they ashamed—or afraid—to know? Or were the people of Weimar, like most of us, simply busy with their own lives, concerned with private cares that avert our gaze from public violence? Perhaps, they reasoned, what was happening "over there" in Buchenwald was not their business. Perhaps their callousness was just the casual sin of indifference.

By the time our bus reached the Buchenwald stop, it was raining. The morning fog had turned to drizzle and the drizzle had condensed to rain. We turned our collars up and started walking. No one else was around. The road to the camp was deserted. We seemed alone in a world of dripping beech trees, soggy ground, and a chilling rain. A lone car passed us, slinging water, the windows fogged from the warmth within. I considered flagging it down and begging a ride, but was too miserable to even try. We trudged on through the woods in silence.

My shoes were sodden, my hands and feet were stiff from cold, and water was running down my upturned collar. My mother's raincoat was soaked. We had been walking for thirty minutes, but it seemed like hours and we had no idea how far we still had to go.

"I thought you would at least take your umbrella," I snapped. I was angry and wanted to blame her.

Her response collapsed my anger into guilt. "It feels like a kind of penance," she said softly.

Glancing over at her, I thought with a pang, how old she looked. In less than a month, my mother would turn seventy. Her hair was plastered against her skull like an old-time bathing cap and underneath her bold, red lipstick her lips looked pinched. "I'm sorry," I relented. "This is all my fault. We should have taken the car, like you suggested. I thought the bus would take us straight to the camp ... I didn't realize we had to walk."

My anger turned on myself. "I wasn't thinking."

But I *was* thinking, just not clearly. Her word *penance* unintentionally got it right. Going to Buchenwald, once one of the most notorious Nazi concentration camps, was not a tourist visit. It felt more like a pilgrimage. Driving comfortably in a Volvo didn't feel right. Real penitents walked on blistering pebbles in their shoes or wore hair shirts that rubbed their flesh raw. They beat their bare backs with whips. They crawled on their hands and knees, praying for forgiveness. All we did was take a bus instead of our car.

Going the last part of the way on foot, even in a cold November rain, was no great hardship. Instead of grumbling, I should have gone barefoot.

I learned about penance as a Catholic girl. Confession of sins was a sacred ritual of contrition and forgiveness. On my knees in the confessional, I said to the priest, "I have sinned, *mea culpa*, and want to make amends." For penance, he assigned me a set of prayers—five Hail Marys, say, or even a whole rosary. Then he blessed me and absolved me of my sins. "*Ego te absolvo*," he murmured, making the sign of the cross as I bowed my head, *Go, you are free, your guilt is taken from you.* This state of absolution was called grace.

Being German always felt much like being Catholic. You could be guilty of things you hadn't done. You were even born guilty. Original sin, the Catholic Church called it. In the religious sphere, baptism washed the soul's original sin away and later sins were removed through confession. But the guilt that came from being German seemed irredeemable. I couldn't escape it by leaving Germany. I couldn't shed it by becoming American. No hair shirt, no Hail Marys, no walk to Buchenwald in the rain offered absolution.

During the almost eight years that Buchenwald was in operation, some 280,000 prisoners were interned in the camp.[3] The majority were Jews, but there were also political prisoners, deserters, prisoners of war, homosexuals, so-called "work-shy" people who didn't "earn their keep," Roma and Sinti, and Jehovah's Witnesses. Some 56,000 people were murdered or died there.[4] They were worked to death in the stone quarry or one of the 139 Buchenwald subcamps that provided slave labor to the armaments industry. They were shot, hanged, injected with phenol, and killed in "medical" experiments. They died of exhaustion and malnutrition, neglect and abuse. They died of diseases. They died of despair.

In 1937, when this camp was built, my mother was a fifteen-year-old schoolgirl and my father a recently minted lawyer. During the years of the camp's operation, they met, fell in love, got married, and planned their future. My parents' romance, where my own life started, and the horror of Buchenwald where countless lives were destroyed—these perverse convergences of history are my original sin.

At some point along the way, a sign directed us to a memorial to "victims of fascism" ("the first of its kind on German soil," my guidebook claimed). It was a large bronze sculpture on a bluff overlooking Weimar. Eleven figures gazed out across the horizon. A bell tower stood guard at their back. The colossal scale of the memorial—the larger-than-life figures, the high tower, the panoramic view—made our human size feel insignificant. "Revolt of the Prisoners," as the artist, Fritz Cremer, had named his work, commemorated the revolt of Buchenwald prisoners on April 11, 1945, when, just hours before the arrival of the Ninth Armored Infantry Battalion of the US Third Army, a group of desperate and determined prisoners seized control of the camp. When the liberators arrived, the prisoners had already achieved their own liberation.

Cremer's figures are wounded and weak, their gaunt bodies close to starvation. Yet he presents them not as victims but as victors. They stand tall. They raise their arms in defiance. They turn their backs on the camp and face the world they will rebuild in the image of their socialist worldview.

To see a memorial celebrating history's victims as victors was inspiring. Yet I found its triumphalist stance troubling, as it risked distorting the history of the camp. To remember the "victims of fascism" as architects of a new socialist Germany, as the description of the memorial explained, was to ignore the vast majority of prisoners who didn't build a new Germany, but were murdered here on racial grounds.

Commissioned by the East German government in the early 1950s and installed in 1958, Cremer's memorial reflects the Stalinist mindset of East Germany at a time when the crimes of others were readily remembered and its own murderous history ignored. The resulting historical amnesia allowed East Germany to declare itself innocent, as if anti-Semitism and the Holocaust occurred elsewhere.

When my mother and I resumed our walk to the camp, the wind picked up and the rain grew heavier. Another sign directed us to another memorial on a side road, where a double set of train tracks led into the woods. A plaque explained that this had been the site of a munitions plant, where prisoners made weapons for the German army. It was a model of engineering efficiency. Trains on one track brought in prisoners to work in the factory. Trains on the other track carried the munitions out. When the prisoners planned their revolt in April 1945, they staged it here, blowing up the factory and the train tracks that serviced it.

Shortly after that, we reached the main camp entrance. Before us lay the infamous Appellplatz that Imre Kertész, once a prisoner here himself, described as "an enormously large plaza lighted by reflectors."[5] Only the swish of wind and the spatter of rain broke the silence. This was where prisoners assembled for roll call. This was where their days began and ended. This was where they stood, in sun and rain, summer, winter, spring, and fall, arrayed in rows, hands at their side, silent and motionless, until the commandant's whistle gave permission for them to move. Sometimes the roll call was used to torture or punish the assembled prisoners for someone's alleged misdeed. At such times they had to stand for hours, sometimes into the night, until they dropped or the whistle released them.

Some of the prisoners, like Imre Kertész and Elie Wiesel, were boys when they arrived at Buchenwald. Some, like Jean Améry, Bruno Bettelheim, or Dietrich Bonhoeffer, were men in their prime. Some, like Maurice Halbwachs and Léon Blum, came as old men.[6] We remember them because they wrote books, held public positions, or were given awards. The hundreds of thousands of others who stood here remain nameless. Over the years of the camp's operation, as many as 280,000 prisoners assembled on this square.

The day of our visit, the Appellplatz was a vacant wasteland. The square was empty except for a flagpole without a flag. On closer look, I realized it wasn't made to hang flags. It was made to hang people. It was an instrument devised for torture. Prisoners were strung up with their hands tied behind their backs until their backwards-twisted arms dislocated. A former Buchenwald inmate, Jean Améry, tried to describe the mind-numbing pain. Every sensation in his body—his entire will to live and not die—gathered in his shoulder joints, until his body, in helpless agony, surrendered. He felt a "crackling and splintering" in his shoulders as "the balls sprang out of their sockets." And then, he writes, "I fell into the void." It was over. He had survived. But, he goes on, it is never over: "Twenty-two years later, I am still dangling above the ground from dislocated arms, panting."[7]

This horrifying image made me want to flee the Appellplatz, but the horror followed us throughout the camp. There was the building where Nazi doctors conducted so-called medical experiments on prisoners and amused themselves with such occupations as shrinking heads for souvenirs. There was the former horse stable, where Soviet prisoners of war were executed through close-range pistol shots to the back of the neck. SS men, dressed as physicians, pretended to measure the prisoner's height, while the prisoner stood with his back against the wall aligned with the measuring bar. Concealed on the other side of the wall was the executioner, who shot the prisoner through a vertical slot in the measuring bar. A secret record by a survivor counted 8,483 Soviet prisoners executed this way.

I had brought a small photograph of my children on this trip with the vague idea of leaving it at Buchenwald. I hadn't worked out the details ... it wasn't a thought-through plan, more a symbolic gesture of reckoning. As a kind of penance, I would offer what was most precious to me. The photograph showed two blonde five-year-olds. On the back, I had written their names and birth date—*Bettina and Nicolas Bammer-Whitaker, September 26, 1985*—and underneath, to explain the single date, *born two minutes apart.*

But now that I was there, my plan seemed absurd. Where in Buchenwald would I leave such a picture? And for what purpose? The very idea felt perverse and sentimental to me now, a maudlin gesture of atonement. I no longer wanted to leave anything of myself in this place of death, least of all my children. I left the photograph in my pocket where I had put it. Weeks later, when I wore my coat back home, I found it again, creased and bent on the edges. They smiled at me. Their trust that the world would be safe for them weighed on my heart.

Before we left that morning, I had grabbed my camera, but I hadn't taken any pictures. Tourists take pictures, and being a tourist here felt unseemly. But my visit was also a kind of witnessing, and it was to witness that I took my camera out. Yet as I looked through the viewfinder, adjusted my aperture, and captured images of the camp on film, I barely seemed to know what I was seeing. I relegated it instead to film. I let the camera do my witnessing for me. When the film was developed and I got the prints, I filed them away.

When I retrieved them years later the photos showed me what I had seen. More importantly, they showed how I had been looking. Every photograph I had taken was a close-up: the geometry of bricks in the crematorium where human bodies were burned to ash, the iron handle of the oven that sealed the doors, the grainy gravel of the Appellplatz. It was as if I had only taken Buchenwald in measured doses, isolated fragments to be assembled one at a time. Abstracting parts made the whole more bearable. And the abstractions rendered violence aesthetic. Function was reduced to form. Objects of torture became patterns of line and color. In my rendering, the Buchenwald crematorium was a pattern of different shades of brick.

But the close-ups had another purpose. They were a way for me to draw close to the experience of torture and suffering. Shielded by the camera, I could virtually touch it with my eyes.

One photograph in particular holds me captive. Each time I see it, it's as if for the first time, as if my mind won't absorb the memory. I scan it slowly, taking in every small detail. It looks like a kitchen table with a white tile surface. Practical. Smooth and shiny. Easy to wipe off. I remember running my hand over the table edge, the cool, clean feel of ceramic tile on my fingers. A few of the tiles are cracked. There is a faucet at one end of the table. The table isn't level. It slants toward the middle from both sides. I see the shadow formed by the shallow trough on the photograph.

With that shadow, the memory of that room returns with a wave of nausea. I remember looking down and seeing that the floor was tiled too, and there was another trough on the floor, straight across the room. A white-tiled channel ran from the table to the outside wall. Through the exit hole I could see a patch of daylight.

Purpose and form were in precise alignment. Every part of the room design was practical. The table was perfectly shaped to hold a human body, laid down flat. Fluids, like blood or urine, could drain into the table trough and be channeled out through the trough on the floor. Solids, like excrement or body tissue, could be rinsed from the table with the faucet and the tile floor could be easily hosed down. Within minutes, the room could be clean and white again. A dumpster on tracks outside carried off the refuse. Cleanliness, as they say, is a German virtue.

Every cliché has a grain of truth and so does this one. An American friend once confessed to me that he always wanted a German wife because "she would keep the house clean." My mother kept such a house. Leftovers were eaten, clothes hung on the line to dry, and every day, after the dishes were done, she swept the kitchen. When I had a house of my own, people often commented on how orderly and neat it looked. I felt embarrassed, as if some shameful German trait had been exposed. As if my own—or my mother's—clean kitchen floors somehow led to the gleaming white torture room of Buchenwald.

They don't, of course. Keeping things orderly and clean doesn't lead to Buchenwald. Nor do Germans have a particular claim on cleanliness. Yet the memory of my mother's daily sweeping invariably triggers another memory from Nazi history: an elderly Jewish man forced to scrub the stones of a Vienna street on his hands and knees. The two scenes are unrelated, yet they feel connected.

However, my response to the tidy torture room had another side. It was darker and more atavistic. I felt horror, but also fascination. I didn't want to avert my eyes. I was curious. I wanted to know exactly what had been done there. The perverse intricacy of how cruelty is enacted attracted me in some way. I wanted to grasp how the machinery of destruction functioned.

I touched the deep and murky bottom of human existence in that room, where the question of what "human" means overwhelmed me. It had to include all that was suffered and all that was done at Buchenwald. We call a gruesome crime "inhuman" as a way of distancing ourselves, seeking safety in the separation between "us" and "them." That day in Buchenwald, I resisted the separation. I went the other way. I drew in closer. Part of the horror I felt was sensing that the distinction did not hold: "we" and "they," torturers and tortured, are not that far apart.

This uncertainty about what the human encompasses (how it can account for the white-tiled table at Buchenwald) might partly explain why we are drawn to the suffering of others, even the perverse pleasure we can take from witnessing their pain. It made me think about my parents' bedroom. Over the bed, where they shared the intimacies of their nights, was a large, black crucifix with a tortured man. His mouth was twisted and his fingers splayed, his muscles tensed in spasms of agony. My parents slept and made love in his shadow.

This room always felt taboo to me. I was drawn to it, but avoided entering. When my parents went out, I sometimes opened the door and peered in. The bed, always neatly made, was covered with a bedspread, and above it hung a dying man on a cross. The two together, marriage bed and crucifix, made my stomach tingle. The stark proximity of pain and pleasure was seductive. And it felt shameful.

Our last stop in Buchenwald was the camp museum. As we walked across the Appellplatz an icy wind stung my face and I felt the presence of those who had once stood there, cold cutting through their rags, as they waited for the commandant's whistle. In the shelter of the museum, the ghosts receded, but the sense of hauntedness remained. I gripped the photograph of my children in my pocket, like a talisman, and joined my mother.

She was standing by a display case with documents and artifacts from the camp's history. One was a letter by a German woman to a Nazi state agency. Neatly typed, it requested that the ashes of her late husband (she included the "Israel" that Nazi ordinance required be inserted before the surname of all Jewish males) be sent, as promised, to her home address, "in return for payment, already submitted in full, for the cremation." A copy of the receipt for payment, *submitted in full*, was enclosed with the letter.

This is how murder is done bureaucratically, I thought: efficient, cost-effective, orderly. A Jewish man is murdered, his body cremated, the ashes pre-paid by his widow, who politely requests that his remains be sent to her for proper burial. History tells us that she would not have received the promised ashes that she had paid for. She probably never even received a reply. What remains is a crime unpunished and a grief denied.

The letter left me shaken and speechless. I had always valued complexity and nuance, yet as I read this letter by a German wife about her Jewish husband, they seemed irrelevant, if not misplaced. Nothing, I thought, could justify what had been done there. Sometimes, things are simple and clear. You help or you hurt. You care or are indifferent. You harm or are harmed.

As we left the museum, we passed through a new wing, still under construction, that documented the history of Buchenwald after the war. After the camp was liberated, we learned, it was reactivated by the Soviet military as a concentration camp for German prisoners of war, and after the Soviet occupation ended, it was used to house East German political prisoners.

Holocaust histories of the camps typically end with their liberation by Allied forces, but that wasn't always the end. Many camps, including Theresienstadt, Buchenwald, and Auschwitz, "never went out of business."[8] They were used by groups across the political spectrum. The transition was sometimes almost seamless.

I was reminded of this again a few years after my visit to Theresienstadt. I was in Berlin visiting family friends and we were exchanging stories about the war years. Heide was the daughter of my father's Rumburg friend, Heinz Vatter. She and her family lost their home in the east after the war when ethnic Germans were expelled from Czechoslovakia. Heide's husband, Peter, had spent the Nazi years in China with his Jewish mother and returned to Germany after the war. On one level, the lines of their stories diverged radically: hers was part of the history of Germans in the Sudetenland, his was part of the history of Jews in Nazi Germany. But at one unexpected point they converged. Both Heide's and Peter's grandparents, I learned, were murdered in Theresienstadt: his during the war by the Nazis, hers after the war by the Czechs. His were killed by the Germans because they were Jewish, hers were killed by the Czechs because they were German.

Like the stories of Heide and Peter, the displays in the Buchenwald museum reminded me that crimes against humanity aren't uniquely German crimes. There are other genocides. But Germans committed the genocide we know as the Holocaust. And that is the history I reckon with.

Many aspects of that reckoning, though, confound me. The questions are too general, too broad. Is there something about Germans, or German history, that led to Auschwitz or the torture room at Buchenwald? Did Germans murder in a particularly German way? And if efficiency and order are German virtues, is anti-Semitism a German crime? I don't know how to answer such questions. They exceed what I can understand and know. I try to scale them down to a small, personal level where answers are possible: what I experienced, what I remember, what I was told.

We had spent the better part of the day at Buchenwald and I was emotionally spent. My mother also looked exhausted. It was time to go.

Just before exiting the new museum wing, I stopped at one last display. Another letter caught my attention. Like the letter by the woman requesting her husband's ashes for burial, this one was also neatly typed and business-like. It was written by a German mother whose son had been imprisoned by the Soviets at Buchenwald on suspicion of membership in the fascist partisan organization, Werwolf. At the time of his arrest, he was just fifteen. He was sixteen when she wrote her letter. Her request for his release was accompanied by notarized copies of testimonials by "respected citizens of Weimar" attesting that her son was "a good boy, industrious, and hard-working."

The terms of these testimonials unsettled me. What did it mean for a member of a fascist organization to be called "a good boy"? Who adjudicates "good" and "bad" in changing contexts? We set "good" and "innocent" against "bad" and "culpable," yet betray our uncertainty about this pairing by commonly reinforcing "victim" with supplements like "innocent." If a victim isn't always innocent, could a perpetrator also be good?

Ready-made pairings—"innocent" and "victim," sometimes "German" and "Nazi"—offer the illusion that we reckoned with history. They suggest that justice was done. Yet what most struck me about the letters on display at Buchenwald was that all the parties involved in them were German—the good and the bad, the innocent as well as the guilty. The man killed by Nazis because he was Jewish was German. So was the boy who joined the fascist partisans. The wife who requested her Jewish husband's ashes was German. So was the mother who requested release of her Werwolf son. The bureaucrats who received and answered—or ignored—their requests were also German.

On the map of good and evil, there is no particular place for "German." Most of the SS camp personnel who managed the machinery of death at Buchenwald were probably German. So were the Jews they persecuted and killed. The Weimar actors who entertained the SS in the Buchenwald casino, the workers who built and serviced the camp, the people who ran the trains that delivered the prisoners—most of them were German. The killers and the killed, the guilty and the innocent, the traitors and the betrayed—they were all German. So were those who just went on with their lives, shopping for groceries, going to work, or walking their dogs, while they kept their heads down and their eyes averted. There were Germans, good and bad, in every group.

By the time we returned to our guesthouse, both my mother and I needed time alone. She rested and I went walking. I didn't have a goal or destination; I didn't have a plan or a map. I wanted to walk down random streets and exhaust myself, walk until I was too spent to think. I wanted to get lost. However, instead of getting lost, I found a building that said NIETZSCHE-ARCHIV. It was Villa Silberblick,[9] the house where Nietzsche spent the last years of his life, now maintained as a Nietzsche museum. The stately building and manicured grounds reflected the bourgeois culture of nineteenth-century Germany that marked Nietzsche, the man, even as the philosopher rebelled against it. It was imperious, with pretensions to grandeur, and built to last. The Art Nouveau entrance added a decorative flourish.

The museum was open and I went in.

As I walked through the rooms where an invalid Nietzsche spent his last three years in his sister's care, I pondered the ambivalent German legacy he represented. Growing up, I was taught that Nietzsche was a Nazi thinker. His fascination with the "magnificent *blond beast* ... at the centre of every noble race," a beast whose power, when unleashed, was fearsome;[10] his celebration of the "will to power" on which a people's greatness was based; and his vision of an *Übermensch* existence beyond ordinary human limitations sounded proto-Nazi. And since he was claimed as one of theirs by Nazi ideologues, including his sister and her Nazi friends, I dismissed him as a thinker to engage with. By the same token, I dismissed Nietzsche's friend and compatriot, the composer Richard Wagner, whose grandiose spectacles and Germanic mythologies became a celebrated part of Nazi culture. However, in my adolescent rush to judgment I ignored the fact that Nietzsche ultimately rejected Wagner himself. I didn't know at the time that he ended their friendship over Wagner's anti-Semitism and ethnic nationalism and broke with his editor for the same reason. Nor did I know that, rather than be a German subject, Nietzsche had his German citizenship annulled and became stateless.

But there in the Nietzsche house, where a late photograph of the philosopher showed a frail and ailing man, it was neither his politics nor his philosophy that moved me. It was his silence. At age forty-five, Nietzsche had a breakdown that left him silent for the next twelve years. More than silent, it left him wordless. He supposedly never spoke or wrote again. As the German phrase so hauntingly puts it, he was enveloped by spiritual night (*geistige Umnachtung*).

As I gazed at his image, a lone visitor in a silent house, I realized that this was the one place in Weimar I wanted to be. After Buchenwald, this was the only place that felt tolerable. After Buchenwald, madness and silence made sense to me in ways that reason and speaking didn't. I thought of Nietzsche, who braved the force of reason's encounter with unreason, for it only to destroy him. Reason succumbed. When spiritual night came, reason couldn't protect him. Madness won.

In the wake of crimes as horrifying as the Holocaust we often distinguish between two different kinds of silence. We call the silence of the victims trauma. We call the silence of the perpetrators guilt. But something fundamental gets lost in this opposition. Silence can be a defeat, a failure of language. But it can also be a choice, a refusal to speak falsely. When words stop explaining things or providing comfort, forgoing them can provide relief.

After Buchenwald, I didn't pity Nietzsche for his silence; I envied him. I didn't want to think or try to figure things out. I didn't want explanations for how Buchenwald happened. I wanted to let go of language and submit to the confusion I felt. Perhaps, I thought, even Nietzsche surrendered willingly to his sister and her Nazi friends when they spoke for him after he fell silent. Perhaps he was relieved to finally let reason go.

When I returned to the guesthouse, my mother was reading. "How was your walk?" she smiled.

"Fine."

I didn't feel like talking. I felt ungenerous, petty, mean. Polite formalities had become unbearable. I wanted to break through the formal surfaces, cause trouble, and inflict pain. I wanted to counter my inner torment by being violent. I was tired of the protocols pretending we were civilized. I didn't feel civilized. I felt savage.

That evening, we went to the theater to see *Fidelio*. Well-dressed people, Weimar citizens and tourists, filled the foyer, chatting, laughing, meeting up with friends. Some sipped a pre-performance cognac, others were still in line to check their coats. We had good seats in a middle row. I perused the program.

"Did you know that *Fidelio* was the first complete opera to be broadcast on radio?" I asked my mother. "Toscanini directed. In December 1944."

December 1944, I thought. My father was in Belgium, in the Ardennes Offensive. My mother was in Rumburg, as the Russians approached. Buchenwald had between 60,000 and 70,000 prisoners. The machinery of destruction was going strong.

I looked at the elegant, well-bred people around me. My mother had our opera glasses on her lap. How could I connect this world of culture with the world of Buchenwald? When the actors from the National Theater entertained the SS in the camp casino, I wondered, were their performances different there than here? I thought of Goethe and Schiller, proud symbols of German classical culture, outside the theater. Then the lights went down. As the orchestra struck up the overture, music filled the room and my consciousness of Buchenwald receded.

It returned, full force and shockingly, at the end of the first act. First one by one, then in a shuffling, stumbling line, a group of prisoners, guarded by Fidelio, emerge from their cells for a respite in the prison garden. As they move from the dark of imprisonment to the light of day, they sing the achingly beautiful ode to freedom. I watch, transfixed, as the stage slowly fills with men and women in striped, gray uniforms, numbers tattooed on their arms. They shuffle into the light of the theater, where I am sitting. At first, their voices are little more than a whisper and I strain to hear. Confused and dazed, unable to fathom what freedom might mean anymore when the freedom they had known was taken away, they search for language. Even their own voices, slowly joining in chorus with other voices, sound foreign to them at first. I am listening with my whole body. I sit in my plush orchestra seat, next to my mother. I am listening to the chorus of prisoners singing and I am crying.

Music often makes me cry, especially a multivoiced chorus in harmony, underscored by strings. But my tears that day in Weimar felt different. It wasn't just the beauty of the music or the fragility of a human voice rising up in darkness. It was the power of people's voices joined in song. And it was the tension and confusion, grief and shame, that had been strangling me for the past two days. The sound of the prisoners singing released me. For all I knew, every person in the audience was crying. But I didn't look to see what others were doing. I didn't care. My tears were my own truth. They spoke of what I didn't know how to say.

After the performance, my mother and I walked to our hotel in silence. She didn't say a word. Nor did I. There was no lack of things to say. There was a surfeit. But perhaps we both feared that if we started talking, all the words in the world wouldn't be enough.

Back in our room, we undressed without speaking. I heard her slip into her nightgown and turn the faucet on. I heard her brush her teeth, rinse, spit, then rinse and spit again. I heard her get into bed and adjust the covers.

"Are you going to bed ... will you read a bit ... or would you like to talk?" My mother's question was an invitation, but I refused it.

"Good night," I said and turned my light off.

"Good night."

We lay awake in darkness.

The next morning, we headed back to Bonn. Our trip was over. We didn't talk about Buchenwald or Weimar.

I don't know if I thought we would talk about it some other time, when I was less angry and she less hesitant, or whenever we could summon the courage or trust that failed us then. But there was no other time. Later came too late. The next November, my mother was diagnosed with terminal cancer, renal cell carcinoma. She died the following spring.

I missed my chance to ask why she went to Buchenwald with me and what our visit there had meant to her. Perhaps her reasons were the same as mine: to face the past we feared by literally putting ourselves in the place where the violence happened. Perhaps, as she put it at the time, her trip to Buchenwald was a kind of penance, an act of contrition for German crimes. Or perhaps she went on this trip to be with me as I searched for answers to questions that haunted me. Was it guilt or shame or love that took my mother to Buchenwald? All or none of these? I didn't ask and she didn't tell.

The Quiet Dignity of Being True

May 1995 was the first anniversary of my mother's death. I wanted to remember her in a place where she had spent some of her happiest and most formative years and decided I would go to Münster. She had lived there from the start of secondary school through graduation from high school; she had formed some of her deepest and most abiding friendships there; and she had once confided to me that if my father died before her (which she expected, since she was ten years younger), she might move there to share a house with her beloved friend from her Münster days, Gisela.

My mother's roots in this city ran deep. Her mother, Maria Thoma, had grown up in a family of eight in the city's medieval heart, the Ludgeri Quarter. To make ends meet (her mother was widowed young and a widow's pension didn't go far with seven children), they took in boarders, and one of them—a young law clerk named Hans Bushoff—fell in love with dark-eyed Maria, the eldest daughter. They were married on August 3, 1914, the day that World War I broke out.

Some twenty years later (by then, Maria and Hans Bushoff had moved to Velen, where Hans had been hired by the Count of Landsberg-Velen to manage his estate), their daughter, Ursula, moved back to the city her parents had left. She went to get an education. Velen was just a village with a primary school. For anything beyond that, you had to go to a city and Münster, the regional capital of Westfalia, was the closest one.

So, in 1936, when Ursula was thirteen, her parents enrolled her in a private secondary school in Münster, the Annette School. Founded as a Catholic girls' school in the late seventeenth century and named after the revered Westphalian poet, Annette von Droste-Hülshoff,[1] it was the school of choice in the region for families of means. Since Ursula had to get there by train (Münster was 35 miles from Velen and her family didn't own a car), she roomed with a Münster family, the Wolters, during the school year. The arrangement suited her. It was just a short walk to school from their place and their daughter, Gisela, was Ursula's age. "She was the sister I had always wanted," my mother said.

On my first day in Münster, I wanted to visit the Annette School. I had an appointment with the school director for two that afternoon, but I took time to look around. I was early.

From the photograph in my mother's album, I wouldn't have recognized the school. The building that my mother knew had been destroyed during World War II and the school was rebuilt in the functional postwar style of the 1950s. It was also no longer a girls' school. Girls and boys of all ages mingled in the halls, a swirl of color, noise, and youthful energy.

To get a sense of the school during the time my mother had been here, I had researched some of its history. Its reputation as the best secondary school for girls in this part of Westphalia seemed undisputed, so I was not surprised to find that, despite its official identification as a Catholic school, the Annette School had historically also been the school of first choice for Münster's Jewish community.

However, over the course of the 1930s a series of anti-Semitic measures targeting Jewish students first isolated and finally removed them. The first cut came in April 1933 when the "Law Against the Overcrowding of German Schools and Secondary Schools" specified that, in a given school, "non-Aryans" could make up no more than 5 percent of the student body.[2] Two years later, the distinction between "Jews" and "citizens of German and related blood" established by the Nuremberg Laws, and the resulting requirement that "Jews" and "Germans" be kept separate, led to a wholesale exodus of Jewish students from German schools. The Annette School was no exception. By 1936, the year that my mother started at the school, most of the Jewish students had already left. The last two Jewish students admitted to the school enrolled the same year as my mother, but they never graduated. Before they could finish their third year, they were gone.

Their departure was effected by a directive issued by the Reich Ministry for Science and Education on November 15, 1938, in the wake of the orchestrated assault against Jews and Jewish property across Germany known as Kristallnacht. It was no longer tolerable, it declared, for German teachers to be expected to teach Jewish students. Likewise, it was "intolerable for German students to be seated in the same classroom as Jews." Effective immediately, therefore, "Jews are not permitted to attend German schools."[3] They either left "voluntarily" or were expelled.

As I planned my trip to Münster, I wondered what my mother had witnessed of these events. Had any of the girls in her class been Jewish? Had she known the two Jewish girls who enrolled in 1936 along with her? We had never talked about any of this, so I could only speculate. In 1936, when my mother started at the school, she was a thirteen-year-old girl from the country, new to the city and living with a family she still barely knew. She would have been absorbed by the challenge of adjusting to her new environment: a new school, a new city, a new family, and the work of making new friends. The two new Jewish students were not only younger than her, but at home in this city where they had grown up. They would have been in different classes and had different friends. In a student body of over 600 students, their meeting doesn't seem likely. And two years later, when the two Jewish students left the school, it seems equally unlikely that she would have noticed. She was almost sixteen by then and, like the girls I had seen in the hallway earlier, laughing and talking and tossing their hair, she would have been preoccupied with girlish things.

By the time my mother graduated in 1941, there had been no Jewish students at the school for over two and a half years.

Since I could no longer ask my mother, I had sent my questions to the school. What could they tell me about these last two Jewish girls at the Annette School? Who were they and what became of them after they left? And what could they tell me about my mother's homeroom teacher, Fräulein Büchner, whom she had so often talked about? "I would be grateful for any information," I wrote in my email.

For weeks, I had no response. Then, just as I was about to leave for Germany, I got an email from the director of the school himself, a Herr Arnold Hermans. After apologizing for the delay (he had been busy with final exams and graduation), he answered my questions. The last two Jewish students at the school were Ingeborg Saul and Ursula Meyer. Both were from Münster. In 1936, when they joined the school, Ingeborg Saul was eleven and Ursula Meyer twelve. My mother's homeroom teacher, Anna Margarethe Büchner, taught at the Annette School until she retired in 1956. When she died in 1968, the school honored her memory. Should I come to Münster, Herr Hermans added, he would be happy to meet and talk more.

We met in his office, his assistant served tea, and we chatted about the school and its history. We looked at photographs of the 1909 remodeling of the school that resulted in an imposing four-story structure; we reflected on the addition of home economics to the curriculum in 1939 for which another new wing was added; we registered the destruction of the school during World War II that left just part of the front façade standing.

When Herr Hermans wondered what my mother remembered about the school and how she spoke about her time there as a student, I told him that Fräulein Büchner, her homeroom teacher for the last three years, was the only person that my mother ever called heroic. She didn't look the part. With her swollen ankles, heavy-lidded eyes, and wiry grey hair that always seemed disheveled, she was the very stereotype of a spinster. But to my mother and the other young women entrusted to her care, this matronly woman with the thickened torso of advancing middle age was a mentor they relied on and looked up to. Her subjects were modern literature and history, but what she taught, more than subjects, was a way of being: how to act with integrity in a world that rewards conformity. Her heroism wasn't the kind that draws attention to itself, the grand, dramatic gesture that makes headlines. Fräulein Büchner's heroism took a modest form: it was a small, daily act of courage. At a time when the mandated greeting in Germany for civil servants was *Heil Hitler*, she refused and simply said, *Good morning.*[4]

"When she entered the classroom," my mother recounted, "Fräulein Büchner would say, *Good morning, girls,* and we answered, *Good morning, Fräulein Büchner. All right, then,* she would say, *let's get started.*"

The urgency in my mother's voice as she shared the memory of this schoolroom ritual betrayed her uncertainty over how to convey its import. How could something as ordinary and routine as a plain "good morning" be significant, much less heroic? How could she explain to me, who had grown up with the luxury of postwar freedom, that in repressive times ordinary words can be dangerous. When everything you say is surveilled and monitored, saying the wrong thing—or not saying the right thing—can get you in trouble. This was the world of my mother's youth. When criticizing, doubting, or mocking the government was considered criminal, refusing to declare allegiance to the state through the Hitler salute was an act of resistance.

To explain this to me would have required the ability to bridge the world of Nazi Germany my mother grew up in and the world of postwar democracies that I knew. The enormity of such a bridging was daunting, so my mother just repeated her account.

"I never heard Fräulein Büchner say *Heil Hitler*, and I never saw her give the Hitler salute. She just smiled and simply said, *Good morning.*" She paused. "Fräulein Büchner lived by her principles," she said. "She was the person I most wanted to be like."

My mother studied literature with Fräulein Büchner, but the lesson she took to heart was ethical: hold to your principles, even when they go against prevailing norms. She found the words for this lesson in her final year of high school English. It was June 1940 and they were reading *Hamlet*, when she came across Polonius' famous counsel to his son Laertes:

This above all—to thine own self be true
And it must follow, as the night the day
That thou canst not be false to any man.

She copied the words into her diary and added: "This is what I believe too."

I often wondered what these words meant to my mother at the time, a seventeen-year-old young woman in Nazi Germany. What was the core of that self to which she vowed to be true: the small-town Catholic girl, the dutiful daughter, the diligent student, the young woman in love with a soldier on his way to war? In a compromised time, what was the true north of her moral compass?

While I was looking through materials that Herr Hermans had laid out, he excused himself and opened a file drawer. When he returned, he handed me pictures from Fräulein Büchner's retirement and a thumb drive with historical photographs of the school for me to keep.

Then we finally got to the subject I had written him about: the fate of the Jewish students in the Nazi years. My questions spilled out. When Ursula Meyer and Ingeborg Saul left the school in 1938, how did it happen? Were they told to leave? Did they leave on their own? How was their leaving registered? Did the school—their teachers or the principal—acknowledge their departure? Was there a farewell? What were their classmates told and how did they respond? Or did the two little girls just leave without any acknowledgment?

My mother, outside Velen, *c.* 1940.

Herr Hermans had no answers to this swirl of questions. We sat in silence and drank our tea. Then, instead of answers, he volunteered an anecdote. In the 1990s, a girl from a refugee family (from Lithuania, he believed) had to leave the school when her temporary visa expired. The school tried to intervene, but was unsuccessful. "We were concerned," Herr Hermans explained, "and wanted to do something, but we had no leverage … We were all very sad when she left." After a brief pause, he added, "And we still miss her."

My questions about 1938 hung between us, unanswered.

On my way home that evening, I thought about the Lithuanian refugee and what Herr Hermans had meant to convey. Did he want to tell me that in the Germany of today things were different than they were back then? That even though foreigners were still expelled, Germans weren't indifferent? That they tried to intervene, and when they failed they responded with sadness? Or did he want to suggest that, while things had changed and Jews were no longer expelled from Germany, others—non-German foreigners— were still at risk?

The day after my visit to the Annette School, I went to the neighborhood where Ingeborg Saul had lived. I was looking for traces of the past in the present, and Herr Hermans had mentioned a small memorial plaque that remembered Ingeborg and her family's fate.

A bus took me to a plain, somewhat down-on-its-luck working-class neighborhood—grey cement row houses with chipped, moss-stained walls. The front garden strips needed weeding. In front of the house on Schleswiger Street where the Sauls had lived, four bronze plaques, each the size of a cobblestone, were arranged in a square set in the sidewalk.[5] Like miniature gravestones in the middle of the urban landscape, they remembered the four members of the Saul family killed in the Holocaust: Ingeborg, her mother and father, and her younger sister. The inscription on Ingeborg's plaque condensed her life into four terse lines: "Here lived Ingeborg Saul. Born 1925. Deported 1942. Died in Trawniki."

I mapped these dates onto the dates of my mother's life. Ingeborg Saul and Ursula Bushoff were born three years apart. They grew up in the same Westphalian culture. They enrolled at the same school in the same year and for a while were students together. Then the lines of their lives diverged. The one had to leave the school because she was Jewish. Because she was Aryan, the other could stay and get her Abitur. When Ingeborg Saul was seventeen years old, she was murdered. When Ursula Bushoff was that same age, she fell in love. And by the time Ursula's family celebrated her wedding, all the members of Ingeborg's family were dead.

As I stood in front of the house in Münster where Ingeborg Saul had lived, watching people from the neighborhood pass by, I recalled the words in my mother's diary, "to thine own self be true." It was the principle her teacher had impressed on her; it defined the integrity that my mother called heroic. But under pressure, I wondered, how did this principle hold up? As the noose of anti-Semitism tightened around the last two Jewish students at her school, what did "staying true" mean to Fräulein Büchner? Did she protest their threatened departure? Did she speak to the girls or their parents to offer help? When they left, did she say goodbye, either directly or in a note to their families? Or did she say nothing and perhaps, alone one night, weep to face the truth of her limited courage? Did replacing "Heil Hitler" with "Good morning" matter when the lives of two little Jewish girls were at stake?

Perhaps the sadness I sensed in Fräulein Büchner's postwar photographs held an answer. I would never know.

Later that summer, when I returned to the United States, I ordered a history of Jewish life in Münster to get more information on the fate of this community.[6] I learned that Ursula Meyer came from a prominent Münster family that had not identified as Jewish in her lifetime. Her father, Max Meyer, had been born to a Jewish family, but became a Protestant as a young man in the 1900s. When he married, he and his wife raised their children as Christians. Although he had served as a cavalry officer in the German army during World War I and been decorated for valiant service, Nazi race laws stripped him of his German citizenship. When Max Meyer, as a non-Aryan lawyer in private practice, was barred from practicing law, he considered emigrating, but his wife's poor health made emigration difficult. To at least safeguard their children, the Meyers finally sent fifteen-year-old Ursula and her nineteen-year-old brother Fritz to England on a Kindertransport in 1939. For the parents, there was no escape. Both were deported: Herr Meyer to Theresienstadt and Frau Meyer to Auschwitz, where they were both killed.

A picture of Ursula and Fritz Meyer from 1934, two years before she joined the Annette School, shows the siblings with their arms around each other,

A young family walks by the small Stolperstein memorial to the Saul family—Friedrich Saul, Hedwig Saul (née Hurwitz), Ingeborg Saul, and Ruth Saul—embedded in the sidewalk in front of their former home on Schleswigerstrasse 25 in Münster. (Photograph by author, 1995).

smiling. Ursula has two long pigtails and a starched white apron over her dress. She looks more stereotypically German than my dark-haired mother ever did.

Ingeborg Saul's fate was even more tragic than that of her classmate, Ursula. For although Ursula Meyer lost both her parents and the country where she was born, she survived and made a life for herself in England. She finished school, became a nurse, married, and had a family.[7] Ingeborg Saul and her whole family were killed.

According to the historical account, Ingeborg Saul left the school "voluntarily" at the end of the school year in April 1938. The official reason for her departure was "relocation to a new school in Berlin," but the so-called relocation was merely a step in her family's increasingly desperate attempt to survive in the face of growing anti-Semitic threats. Ingeborg's father (like Ursula Meyer's father a decorated World War I veteran), had already lost his job as a postal inspector in 1935, when Nazi ordinances barred Jews from civil service positions. With no source of income, the Meyers left Münster to live with relatives in northern Germany, then tried to go underground in Berlin. They were finally caught, and on March 28, 1942, the Sauls were deported to the slave labor camp of Trawniki. From Trawniki, they were sent to another camp. Neither the place nor the date of their deaths are recorded.

The entry on the Sauls in the history of Münster Jews includes a small black and white photograph of Ingeborg from 1934. The date suggests that it is cropped from a group picture of the League of German-Jewish Youth taken the year that Ingeborg joined as one of its youngest members. She is a beautiful child: dark hair frames her face in a mass of curls, full lips bend in a smile. Big, dark eyes look straight at me and hold my gaze.

I had saved my last day in Münster to explore the neighborhood in the Ludgeri Quarter where my mother had lived for five years, starting with Von Kluck Street, where she had roomed with the Wolters. I decided to start by reconstructing her daily walk to school: down Von Kluck Street, at the southern edge of the Quarter, across the tree-lined promenade that marked the border of the old medieval city, through a warren of narrow streets to the school.

The Ludgeri Quarter had changed radically since my mother's time. Entire streets had disappeared, erased from the map by the war. Von Kluck Street was still there, but none of the buildings from the prewar period still existed. What hadn't been destroyed by bombs had been torn down and replaced in the 1950s by the drab apartment blocks of Germany's postwar urban reconstruction. Only one structure from my mother's time remained: the Von Kluck bunker. It was on the same block as the Wolters' former apartment.

A giant, five-story, windowless hulk, it filled the parking lot of the local public school. Once designed to shelter over 2,000 people during air raids, it was now a useless relic of the past that loomed over the school and playground. Since tearing it down would be too expensive—its reinforced concrete walls were 2 meters thick—it just stood there, its thick steel doors padlocked shut and its rusted outside staircase choked with ivy.

As I headed down Von Kluck Street, following the path my mother would have taken on her way to school, I imagined her there during wartime. By the time the bunker was built, she was no longer in Münster (she left after her Abitur in March 1941 and construction on the bunker didn't start until September 1942), but the air war was already well underway during her time there. On May 16, 1940, just weeks after Ursula started her last year of high school, the RAF launched a midnight attack on the city to retaliate for the bombing of Rotterdam by the Luftwaffe two days earlier, giving Münster the dubious distinction of being the first German city to be bombed. The bombing continued throughout that summer, averaging five to six alarms per week. An attack on July 2 ignited such a massive blaze that the entire Münster fire brigade couldn't control it, and over five hundred firemen from neighboring townships had to be summoned.

Even though air raids were becoming more frequent, the war could still feel distant for many Germans. They could still tell themselves it was happening elsewhere, in someone else's country. For Germans, things still seemed to be going well. In May 1940, Münster citizens cheered the defeat of the Netherlands with a victory parade, and two months later they celebrated the recent victory in France by greeting the returning 79th Regiment with a sea of swastikas.

By 1941, however, the war was drawing closer, spreading its shadow over places and people that Ursula knew. Early that year, Velen had mourned its first war dead: the first in February, the second in May, and two that June. That summer, Münster was bombed again, with a new ferocity that made the previous year's attacks seem like target practice. Around midnight on July 5, 1941, sixty-five Wellington bombers dropped around 400 massive pressure bombs and 6,000 light incendiary bombs on a woefully unprepared city. Astonishingly, given its position as headquarters of the Wehrmacht's 6th Military District, responsible for protecting major industrial cities of the Ruhr, Münster's anti-aircraft defense was not yet in place. Over four successive nights in July 1941, RAF bombers rained devastation on a more or less defenseless city. As water supplies were soon depleted, fires were left to burn themselves out. When it was over, entire neighborhoods had been reduced to rubble and the old part of the city, including the Ludgeri Quarter, lay in ruins. Already imperiled supplies, including food, were critically depleted: "2500 crates of tomatoes destroyed by bombs," a shocked eyewitness recorded in her diary.[8] And even though Ursula had moved away by then, the news from Münster must have made her heart ache with worry.

I had gone to Münster to retrace my mother's steps there in the years preceding and during the war. But two days of immersion in memories of violence—bunkers, air raids, burning cities, families deported and murdered—had left me emotionally drained. I longed for a place away from it all that felt calm and peaceful. An old habit from my Catholic girlhood solved the problem: I looked for a church.

I didn't have to go far. Just blocks away, in the heart of the Ludgeri Quarter, was the renowned Ludgeri Church, one of the oldest religious buildings in Westphalia, dating back to the late twelfth century. My grandmother had gone to mass there with her mother and siblings.

I pushed the massive oak door open and entered. For a while I just sat and inhaled the quiet, letting my eyes adjust to the shadowed light from the stained glass windows that created patterns of color on the floor. Behind the thick stone walls, the outside world was kept at bay. Time itself seemed suspended, insubstantial.

Yet this moment of grace didn't last long. My respite from the pull of historical time was cut short by an image that ineluctably drew me back to that history. It was a painting of a man and a woman in religious garb. He wore the vestments of a bishop: a purple cassock with a scarlet cincture and a purple silk biretta on his head. She wore the habit of a Carmelite nun: a simple, floor-length dark brown tunic and a long brown veil. Her face was framed by a white wimpled headpiece.[9] But something didn't fit: the bright "Jewish star" affixed to her tunic.[10] What was she? A Jewish Catholic? A Catholic Jew? Both, as the painting suggested? The categories spun in my head. Their alignment made no sense, religiously. An information plaque gave an explanation. The woman in the painting was Edith Stein.

I knew that name. I had first heard it from Sister Walburgis, my eleventh-grade religion teacher at the Liebfrauen School in Bonn. She had been a great admirer of this woman in the painting and proudly called her "our Edith Stein." At the time, I couldn't explain my feelings, but the pride in Sister Walburgis' devotion—the "our" in front of "Edith Stein"—embarrassed me and made me angry. It wasn't just the appropriation that bothered me; it was the guilt that it covered up. Edith Stein was sent to Auschwitz, not as a Catholic, but as a Jew, and German Catholics neither protected nor defended her. What right did we have to claim her in the aftermath, we in whose name she was murdered? The excuse of postwar hindsight didn't seem enough.

In her own time, when the stakes were high and her life hung in the balance, we didn't call her "ours." Not in 1933, when she was dismissed from the University of Münster as a "non-Aryan." Not in 1938, when she had to flee Germany because she had been classified as a Jew although she had been Catholic for two decades and consecrated as a Carmelite nun. And not in 1942, when she was deported and murdered in Auschwitz. She didn't count as "ours" then. When the Nazis came, neither the German nor the Catholic community claimed her as "ours." Those who claimed her as "our Edith Stein" at the time were her killers.

Later that summer, after I returned to the United States, I searched for more information. I wanted to connect the haunting image I had seen in Münster—the Catholic nun with the Jewish star—to the story of this woman and her history.

When I learned that Emory University, where I taught, had Stein's collected works, I went to the Theology Library to get them. I appeared to be the first person to have ever asked for them. The bindings were tight and the pages crisp. They didn't look to have ever been opened. I read her autobiography, *Life in a Jewish Family*, first. Written in the anxious aftermath of the 1933 electoral victory of Hitler's National Socialist Party, it described the events of that year as nothing less than a "national revolution," presaging what Stein predicted would be a "catastrophe" for Jews. "The battle on Judaism in Germany" has begun, she announced, and her first sentence sounded the alarm: "German Jews have been catapulted ... out of the peaceful existence they had come to take for granted."

In this moment of historical crisis, Stein offered her autobiography as an intervention. By describing the everyday life of an ordinary German Jewish family from the perspective of her own experience, she hoped to provide a counterweight to prevailing anti-Semitic images. Genuine knowledge of a people beyond their stereotype, she wrote, "is rarely found in outsiders."[11]

Born 1891 to an assimilated bourgeois Jewish family in what was then the Prussian city of Breslau (today's Polish Wrocław), Edith Stein was of my grandmother's generation. Surrounded by a large family that valued learning ("reading ... played a large role," Stein recalled), the discipline of work, and the communal rituals of their Jewish faith, Edith grew up assured of her place in her family and community. The youngest of seven children, small of stature and of delicate health ("I was always rather pale and anemic"), she was "spoiled by affection," as she freely notes.[12]

What Edith loved—more than family, more than romance, more than travel and seeing the world—was philosophy. It was the passion that shaped her life and that compelled her to leave her home and family in Breslau and move halfway across the European world, first to Göttingen and then to Freiburg. She wanted to study with the renowned phenomenologist, Edmund Husserl, whom she called the Master. "I educate my students to be systematic philosophers,"[13] Husserl claimed, and his claim matched his student's ambition. When she began her doctorate, Edith Stein announced, "I want to see if I can accomplish something of my own in philosophy."[14]

She did. When Stein submitted her dissertation to the philosophical faculty of the Freiburg Albert-Ludwigs University in 1917,[15] it was awarded the rare distinction of *summa cum laude*. At a time when there were a mere seventy-nine women among a thousand students at German universities (and hardly any at all in philosophy), this young Jewish woman whom the Master once praised as "a very talented little girl" (*ein sehr begabtes kleines Mädchen*) earned her doctoral degree with distinction.[16]

Her topic was empathy. Once we realize that "our encounter with subjects other-than-ourselves (*fremde Subjekte*) and their ways of experiencing things is a given,"[17] Stein explained, the "underlying problem" becomes how to understand someone other than ourselves. Empathy was the solution she proposed: our ability—and willingness—to engage an Other by feeling our way into (*ein-fühlen*) the particulars of their condition.

Stein wasn't interested in abstractions—what empathy *was*. She was interested in the phenomena of human experience. What does empathy *feel* like? How do I feel my way into the subjectivity of another person? For Stein, empathy was an affective, not a cognitive, process. To highlight this fact, she chose an embodied term—*Einfühlung* (literally, a "feeling-into")—over the Latinate abstraction, *Empathie*.

Pondering these questions for her doctoral work against the backdrop of World War I, Stein spent five months in a field hospital tending to wounded, ill, or dying soldiers, and studying Greek for her written exams on the side. This visceral encounter with suffering taught her the power of empathy in ways that became foundational to her thinking. She discovered that empathy was transformative. It had the power to heal emotionally, spiritually, and sometimes even physically.

In light of this power, she concluded, its absence in the modern world, in what a later historian would describe as an Age of Catastrophe,[18] would have disastrous effects. For what made this age catastrophic, Stein believed, was not only that "The best lack all conviction, while the worst/Are full of passionate intensity," as Yeats lamented in 1919, but also that people saw one another's differences as threatening. Instead of wanting to understand—much less try to relate to—one another across differences, they segregated themselves into groups. Sometimes they even staked the survival of their own group on the destruction of those they had marked as Other.

Stein's case for empathy as a response to otherness had political and ethical implications that she couldn't foresee as a 26-year-old doctoral candidate in 1917. Her work was nonetheless prescient. In our own time, as ethno-nationalist forces are on the rise and the world splinters into ever more contentious face-offs between warring groups, the acuity of Stein's insight could not be more evident.

It is her tragedy and our loss that her insights have gone unheeded. The Nazi genocide didn't just kill her. It undermined and blocked her work. To destroy a people, you destroy their culture; to destroy a person, you destroy their work. Nazi anti-Semitism succeeded on both counts. During her lifetime, most of Stein's work was either lost, destroyed, or barred from circulation. As a result, her contribution to modern philosophy, both in phenomenology and ethics, has gone unrecognized.

No manuscript copies of her dissertation, either hand- or typewritten, survived. They were lost to war when large holdings of the Freiburg University library burned in air raids; they were lost to anti-Semitism when works by Jewish authors were destroyed under the aegis of the University Rector, Martin Heidegger;[19] they were lost to the vagaries of fate when Nazis confiscated the Stein family's property and the copy that Edith had given her mother was scattered to the winds. All that remains of her doctoral study are three of the original seven sections that were published separately as a philosophical treatise on "The Problem of Empathy" (*Zum Problem der Einfühlung*).[20] And in 1936, when Stein presented what she considered her most important philosophical work, *Endliches und ewiges Sein* (Finite and Eternal Being), it was rejected for publication because its author was a Jew.[21]

One of the lessons I draw from the story of Edith Stein is that discrimination works. If its aim is to keep someone out of a place they might otherwise enter or presume to occupy by banning or removing them or relegating them to the margins, it was successful in Edith Stein's case. A brilliant scholar who had promised to "contribute work to the field of philosophy that would stand on its own," she fulfilled that promise with original and important work. Yet in the wake of Nazi anti-Semitic politics, aggravated by the gender bias of her field, she remains all but unknown as a philosopher, her work reduced to little more than a footnote.[22]

Stein never ceased being actively engaged professionally—publishing, lecturing, teaching—but her life-long ambition for a university appointment was consistently foiled. It briefly seemed within reach in 1932 when she was hired as a lecturer at the University of Münster. But the appointment didn't last a year. In April 1933, twelve days after the Law for the Restoration of a Professional Civil Service that banned Jews from civil service jobs in Germany was passed,[23] her position at the German Institute for Educational Studies (Deutsches Institut für wissenschaftliche Pädagogik) was terminated.

Yet just as her dream of an academic career ended, another long-deferred wish was fulfilled. Within a year of her dismissal as a lecturer, Stein joined the Order of the Discalced Carmelites as a novitiate. It was the final step in a lifelong spiritual journey. It began in Judaism, moved through a loss of faith when she was young, and continued in her thirties when she returned to faith, but as a Christian. A chance encounter with the autobiography of the sixteenth-century mystic Teresa of Avila occasioned her conversion. In St. Teresa, Stein discovered what she saw as Truth.[24] Inspired by this Truth, she converted to Catholicism and was baptized on New Year's Day, 1922. The fact that her conversion marked a parting of ways from her Jewish family was a consequence that she faced directly. Immediately after her baptism, she took a train to Breslau to tell her mother in person. "Mother," she reportedly said when she arrived in Breslau, "I am now Catholic."

Stein longed for the contemplative life of a Carmelite convent, but the Church asked her to defer her wish. It was a time of social unrest and the Church thought Christian intellectuals like Stein had a critical role to play in public. Allowing her to retreat to a convent was a luxury it couldn't afford. Stein willingly complied. For the next ten years, through the 1920s and early 1930s, she traveled across Europe in service to the Church. She gave seminars and public lectures and published articles on matters from education and women's rights to social justice and the ethics of responsibility.

However, when the Nazi Party came to power in 1933, Stein's public presence and Jewish background put her at risk. Entering a convent would afford protection. In October 1933, after a last trip to Breslau to say goodbye to her family, she entered the cloistered life behind the walls of the Carmelite convent in Cologne. The following spring, after her investiture, she adopted her new spiritual name: *Teresa Benedicta a Cruce*, Sister Teresa Benedicta of the Cross.

Five years later, it was no longer safe for Sister Teresa Benedicta to stay in Germany. In the eyes of the Nazis even a Catholic nun could be a Jew, and Jews were being hunted. The Kristallnacht pogrom that November marked the tipping point. Even a convent could not guarantee shelter. Stein had to flee. On New Year's Eve 1938, she was smuggled across the border to the Netherlands, where she found refuge in the Carmelite convent in Echt.

For a while, she seemed to be safe there, but the German occupation of Holland renewed the risk. By 1941, when all "non-Aryan" German residents in Holland were declared stateless and ordered to report for deportation,[25] her situation had become desperate. The protest of Dutch Christian churches against the genocide of European Jews was ineffective. The attempt to evacuate Stein to Switzerland was blocked by red tape. There was no place for her to go, no place to hide. Like game at the end of a hunt, she was cornered.

On August 2, 1942, in the stillness of evening meditation, the Gestapo arrested Edith Stein. Her sister, Rosa, who had joined her in Echt, was arrested with her and, together with 985 other Jews from Holland, they were deported. Five days later, they arrived in Auschwitz. The serenity of cloistered seclusion was replaced by the maelstrom of organized destruction that was "planet Auschwitz."[26] Stein entered this miasma of violence and despair, of stench and smoke and suffering, in the robes of a Carmelite, complete with a crisply starched white wimple.

Soon after her arrival, she was stripped of everything that had defined her until then: her clothes, her name, her cultural identity, her very status as a

Sister Teresa Benedicta a Cruce. Detail of painting *Nils Stensen and Edith Stein* by Gerhard van der Grinten, Ludgeri Church, Münster, 1990. (Photograph by author, 2012)

legal person. On "planet Auschwitz" she was no longer Sister Teresa Benedicta a Cruce. She was no longer even Edith Stein. She was just a Jew who had been assigned a number. It was as a number that she was sent to be gassed.[27]

Did her faith hold? Give her soul comfort? Or did she feel forsaken like Christ in the face of death? I try to imagine her end, but fail. I can only imagine dread. Then silence.

The last word we have of Edith Stein is Dossier No. 108796, compiled by the Bureau of Information of the Netherlands Red Cross. In the neutral tone of a bureaucratic record it declares that Edith Teresa Hedwig Stein, born in Breslau, last residing in the Monastery of the Carmelite Nuns in Echt, is "to be considered as having died on 9 August, 1942 … for reasons of race, and specifically because of Jewish descent."

I had sought refuge from wartime memories in the Ludgeri Church. Instead of finding respite, I had been summoned. "Who am I to you?" a woman in a painting had asked me.

I sat in the empty church and pondered her question. She was a thread in the web of my past, tied to this place where my mother and grandmother had once lived. For a while, they had each called this city home. They had believed in the same God, worshipped in the same faith, and lived through the same dark time that destroyed her. But she was the loss my mother and grandmother failed to register.

Before I left, I stopped to see the statue for which the Ludgeri Church was known: the Christ with the hole where his heart should be. I had read that when the church was bombed in September 1944, along with the surrounding Quarter, this wood sculpture survived. It seemed a miracle. The Savior had himself been saved. He had not escaped unharmed, however: a grenade splinter had pierced his left side. After the war, when the church was rebuilt and damaged artifacts repaired, the hole was left as a memory trace of Münster's history.

I bought a votive candle and placed it in the row of candles by the crucified Christ. The first hesitant sputter soon grew to a strong, upright flame. The flicker and glow of the candles and the smell of melting wax evoked memories of my Catholic childhood. I was partaking in an ancient ritual: offering fire to the gods. This is what prayer is, I thought: memories of the past and hopes for the future, entwined. I watched my candle burn.

It burned for my mother, who came of age here during the Nazi years. It burned for my grandmother, who was married the day that war broke out. It burned for Edith Stein, who believed that truth and empathy could transform hate and lies. And it burned for the people who believed in the power of the man who hung suspended on the cross above me: a god whose heart was torn out by his people's violence.

In Love and on Trains

Around the time of my birthday in 1996, a small package came in the mail for me from my father. When I opened it, I found a rectangular object wrapped in tissue paper. It was a cassette tape. The label on the case identified its contents with formal precision: *Notes on the encounters of the years 1940 to 1943, made as a Christmas gift 1943, recorded in August 1996.*

The words blurred through my sudden tears. I knew what this was. It was a record of my parents' life from when they met through the year they married, and my father was sharing this part of their history with me.

In 1943, for their first Christmas as a married couple, my mother had made a booklet for her husband chronicling their relationship. She was living with Walter's parents in Rumburg at the time, where she had moved after their wedding that January. Walter's mother was ailing and Ursula had gone to help, but far from home and with Walter off at war, she was sometimes homesick and often lonely. Recalling times with Walter made her feel closer to him and gave her comfort.

She got a slim, lined notebook of the kind that children use in elementary school and wrote in the form of a journal addressed to Walter. It began in September 1943, when she started writing, and went back to January 1940, when they first met. But she didn't organize the journal chronologically. She organized it like a calendar, by month, recalling all of their Januaries, all of their Februaries, all of their Aprils, Mays, and Junes, as if the months were chapters in a story that never ended. Like time itself, the form of her chronicle implied, their life as a couple would go on forever, month after month, year after year, season following season.

I had known that this booklet existed. My parents had shown it to me before, and I had even tried to read it several times. But my mother's careless penmanship, combined with the old-fashioned *Sütterlin* script she used, made it indecipherable.[1] I even consulted a book on German scripts, but it didn't help. Her swishes and zigzags didn't become words I recognized. "Some day you're going to have to read it aloud to me," I once told her jokingly, and, in the end, that's just what my father did. The tape he sent me was his recording of my mother's chronicle. Instead of reading it, I could listen as he read it to me.

I was thrilled, but also apprehensive. My parents' intimate past was unknown terrain for me. Did I really want to go there? Unsure, I put the tape aside. But that evening, I found my old tape recorder, piled pillows on the bed, and got the tape out.

Both sides of the ninety-minute tape had been recorded. I slipped the A side into the recorder, snapped the cover shut, and pressed "Play." A faint hiss as the tape began unspooling. I heard my father clear his throat. A pause (I pictured him adjusting his glasses). Then I heard him read: *Rumburg, 11 September 1943, My beloved Walter.*

Although my father was in his eighties, his voice was still strong and clear, just as I had always known it. And having him read aloud was a familiar pastime. He had read many a book to me when I was a child. What felt strange was that the words he was speaking were my mother's words. Even more strangely, they were words she had addressed to him. He was the "beloved Walter" she was writing to. These were her memories recalled for me by him.

This displacement—my mother's thoughts in my father's voice—increased my disquiet. I hit "Pause" to collect myself and think. What did I hope to discover on this journey into the past? Where—into which part of the past— would it take me?

I soon had an answer to the "where." For while my mother's chronicle covered all four years of my parents' relationship up to that point, it focused on a particular period: fall 1941 to spring 1942. During that half year, they had spent an unusual amount of time together, some of it fated, some of it by choice.

It began with fate. On September 8, 1941, in the offensive known as Operation Barbarossa, Walter was shot and almost killed by a Russian sniper in a forest near Leningrad. After weeks of intensive care, first in a field hospital, then a German clinic, he was transferred to a sanatorium in Rumburg to convalesce. Meanwhile, Ursula, who had just completed the compulsory six months Reich Labor Service that followed her Abitur that Easter, volunteered for another six months of War Relief Service.[2] The assignment she volunteered for was in Berlin. That's where choice came in.

Berlin was just three hours by train from Dresden, and Dresden was an hour and a half from Rumburg by car. With Ursula in Berlin and Walter in Rumburg they were close enough to be together frequently and they took every opportunity they could. Sometimes Manfred Förster took Walter to Dresden where he had business, and Walter went on to Berlin by train. Often, Walter and Ursula met in Dresden. For Ursula, it was a welcome respite from the nervous tension that had gripped the capital. The war kept expanding (as of December 1941, the United States had joined the Allies and Japan the Axis), but rumors swirled that it wasn't going well, and nightly deportations were spreading terror through an anxious city. For Walter, meeting in Dresden was a chance to share his beloved city with his bride. They went to concerts. They went to the theater. They went to the movies. They had dinner at Walter's favorite restaurant in the old part of town. But their favorite place was the Zwinger, Dresden's famous art museum, with its renowned collection of Renaissance and Baroque art. Perhaps that winter, after Walter's brush with death in a Russian forest, my parents realized that, even in wartime, they needed art for survival too. Art feeds the soul. It anticipates a future. It holds the promise that "against the daily death it does not die."[3]

That winter, on Christmas Eve 1941, two weeks after Ursula's nineteenth birthday, Walter and Ursula got engaged. Their families gathered in Velen for the occasion. Walter's parents came from Rumburg; Walter's brother from Marienbad in Czechoslovakia, where he was stationed as an army doctor; and Ursula's brother, an army medic, came from Berlin.

After the engagement, they all went east again, including Walter and Ursula. Walter, still on medical leave, returned to Rumburg, and Ursula resumed her work in Berlin. Before separating, they spent New Year's Eve in Löbau with Manfred Förster, who had organized a party to celebrate his friend's engagement and introduce Ursula to the Förster circle. "I was so nervous," my mother once confessed to me, recalling that evening. "What would they think of me … a girl from a Westphalian village." As I listened to my father read my mother's recollection of that evening, I recalled his account of that same evening to me years earlier. It had been hard for Ursula, he had acknowledged. The Försters were a sophisticated and worldly bunch. And Ursula? My father hesitated, as he searched for words. "Your mother," he finally finished, "was very young."

The tape stopped. Side A had ended. I adjusted my pillows, switched to the B side, and settled the tape recorder on my lap. As my father's voice returned, I watched the slim, brown ribbon of the tape spool around the spindle and my mind wandered to the image of my parents at their engagement. Walter looked official in his Wehrmacht officer uniform, his two Iron Crosses and recent Wound Badge prominently displayed. Ursula was equally formal in a taffeta dress. The silvery shimmer deepened the shale grey of her eyes.

Suddenly the lights went out and I was in darkness. In old neighborhoods like ours, when air-conditioners are on, power failures are a common nuisance. But the tape recorder was on battery and unaffected. The electrical appliances fell still and the silence deepened. The only sounds were my father's voice and the hiss of the tape. I sat in the dark, my senses attuned to the past, listening to my mother tell the story of my parents' romance.

"My beloved Walter," her first entry began, "In the past few days many thoughts have moved me deeply and I have longed to be able to share them with you. Today, a September day with fall in the air, I will start writing them. I am writing them for you, my Walter." She wrote of their passion and her sexual hunger that his touch awakened. "Do you remember?" she asked, remembering the evening he took her to his room and she stayed the night. "I carry that evening and night in my heart. Every word. Every moment. Every touch."

My earlier discomfort resurfaced. These words weren't meant for me. I was entering the forbidden zone of my parents' passion and felt hot and flustered. The image of my parents' naked bodies, in bed, having sex, was unsettling. *Every moment ... Every touch.* I didn't want to imagine my parents' lovemaking. But I also didn't want to stop the tape. I had wanted to enter their past and here was an opening. If I was intruding, it was with permission.

The tape played on and I continued listening. "Happy days!" my mother wrote, "Do you remember Magdeburg? Oh, happy days!"

I closed my eyes and let my mind time travel. At that point in my mother's account, it was January, then February, 1942. Walter was still on medical leave and Ursula still in Berlin with the War Relief Service. They were together almost every week. A week after the Försters' New Year's party, they met in Dresden for Walter's birthday. Two weeks later, Walter spent a weekend with Ursula in Berlin, and two weeks after that, February 7–8, they met again in Dresden. Before the month was up, Walter returned to Berlin for a five-day stay, and in early March he was back for another visit.

All this traveling back and forth seemed astonishing. Germany, after all, was at war. But they were young, in love, and wanted to be together. Ursula's refrain, *Do you remember* charted their story. One afternoon, she recalled, when Walter was napping, she wrapped him in a sheet like a mummy and covered his face with kisses through the shroud. Then she unwrapped him and covered his eyes, nose, chin, and lips with fresh kisses.

By now it was 2 a.m. and I was exhausted. The tape was still going, but I had to stop. I turned the recorder off and felt the silence. Yet I was restless and uneasy and couldn't sleep. Something was troubling me that I couldn't identify. Was it the sex? The image of my parents on the bed playing kissing games? I tried to focus, but couldn't.

I went over in my mind what I had heard thus far. The engagement in Velen, the regular trips between Berlin and Dresden, the rendezvous in Magdeburg. They were going back and forth, between east and west, a weekend here, a weekend there, in the midst of wartime. How was this possible? How did this work? I found my flashlight (the electricity was not yet back) and got my atlas out. With the beam of my light I traced their routes.

Then I realized what was making me uneasy. It wasn't the sex. It was the trains. Suddenly the trains were all I could think of.

For this was the period—fall 1941, spring 1942—when the Nazi plan to rid Europe of Jews was set in motion. In the fall of 1941, Hitler expressed the wish that Germany and the territories it controlled "be cleared of and freed from Jews from west to east as soon as possible."[4] His wish was his staff's command, and deportations of Jews to the east began immediately. Plans to "deport them even farther eastward next spring," as Hitler had requested, were also put in motion. Adding urgency to these plans was the continued bombing of German cities. As entire neighborhoods were destroyed and countless people rendered homeless, removing Jews to clear space for "Germans" was a partial solution to the housing crisis.

To implement these plans, trains were critical. They offered the means to transport large numbers of people "from west to east ... [and] even farther eastward," as Hitler had ordered, quickly and efficiently. The infrastructure was already in place. The Reich Security Main Office (Reichssicherheitshauptamt, RSHA), with its combined state police and security forces, was operational and specific duties had been assigned. The Gestapo and SS were responsible for arresting, detaining, and killing people. The Reich Transportation Ministry was responsible for getting them where they were supposed to go. The organizational structure for managing a genocide had been charted. Adolf Eichmann, since March 1941 director of section IV B4 (the so-called Jewish Department) of the RSHA, was in charge of transportation, and by October 1941, deportation trains had started rolling.

The machinery for murder was oiled and ready, the engines primed. All that was needed was the full-steam-ahead order. It came on January 20, 1942, after a top secret meeting of key Nazi Party members, government officials, and SS officers, who decided it was time to implement the "Final Solution of the Jewish Question." With this decision, the eliminationist anti-Semitism that a later historian would divine in the deepest recesses of the German psyche was unleashed. Official euphemisms didn't fool anyone who paid attention. "Evacuation to the East" meant extermination.[5] A February 25 headline in a Hannover paper made it explicit. "The Jew is being exterminated" (*Der Jude wird ausgerottet*), it announced.[6]

Plans had been laid and structures put in place, yet the logistical challenges were considerable. It fell to Adolf Eichmann to make it work. There had to be enough trains and they had to run on time to get everyone to their destination: soldiers to the front, prisoners of war to prison camps, and Jews to concentration camps and killing centers. By 1942, the Reich railway was running an average of 30,000 trains a day. The number of Jews to be deported was staggering. In 1941, around 4 million Jews, about half the Jewish population of Europe, lived in Germany and German-occupied territories. Moving millions of people was a challenge in itself. Where to put them was another problem. For the other half of Europe's Jewish population—some 4.5 million eastern Jews—lived in Russia or Russian-occupied territories, the very areas where the western Jews were supposed to go.[7]

An ingenious solution was devised to address the problem. Russians were removed from Russia and sent to Germany, while Jews were removed from Germany and sent east. Another problem was addressed in the process.

With German men off at war and Jews being deported, Germany had a labor shortage. The so-called Russian trains (*Russenzüge*) provided replacements, bringing Russian prisoners of war and slave laborers to work in German factories, till German fields, and rebuild German cities. The transportation logistics were resolved economically. Trains brought Russians from the east to the west, where they were unloaded. Then the trains were reloaded with Jews from the west going east.

Many of these trains traveled the same routes as Walter and Ursula on their lovers' circuit. Berlin and Dresden were major thoroughfares on the east–west route. From Berlin to Auschwitz, an average train took ten and a half hours. To Majdanek eleven. To Sobibor twelve. To Treblinka, it was seven hours and forty-one minutes, if the train was punctual. And in thirty-five hours, with at least one stop (perhaps Minsk or Warsaw) to service the engine, a train could take you across Europe all the way to Riga.

The first Jews to be deported from Velen—Abraham Frank and his wife Helene—were put on just such a train. In December 1941, along with some 400 Jews from the surrounding area, they were sent to Riga. It was the first deportation of Münsterland Jews.

The very same week that trains heading east carried Münsterland Jews to a camp in Latvia, trains heading west carried Walter's parents to Velen for their son's engagement. The routes intersect. The ends are incongruent. Some travelers are joyous as they anticipate seeing loved ones. Others are heavy with dread as they envisage death.

I imagine my parents traveling to see each other. Ursula boards the train, knowing that Walter will meet her when she arrives, and before she leaves they will plan their next visit. I try to imagine the men, women, and children boarding a deportation train. They don't know where they are going or how long they'll be traveling. They are met by armed guards when they arrive. Whatever future they might have envisioned is shattered. This is the endpoint. They will not return.

Images of Jews on trains are stock-in-trade of Holocaust history. People herded into cattle cars, SS guards with whips, snarling German shepherd dogs, the train tracks that end at Birkenau.[8] I grew up with these images. They are familiar. What was new to me—and strange—was imagining my parents in this context: their mummy kisses, their "happy days." In February 1942, when Ursula and Walter were in Berlin playing kissing games, the first gassing of Jews took place in Auschwitz.

These convergences feel unbearable. I need distance and stop the tape. There will be time to revisit this past later.

That time came in June 1998 on a visit to Berlin. A new memorial commemorating the deportation of Jews from Berlin had recently been

19 APRIL 1943	688 JUDEN NACH AUSCHWITZ
17 MAI 1943	395 JUDEN NACH AUSCHWITZ
28 JUNI 1943	297 JUDEN NACH AUSCHWITZ
4 AUGUST 1943	99 JUDEN NACH AUSCHWITZ
9 SEPTEMBER 1943	53 JUDEN NACH AUSCHWITZ
8 SEPTEMBER 1943	74 JUDEN NACH AUSCHWITZ
14 OKTOBER 1943	74 JUDEN NACH AUSCHWITZ
29 OKTOBER 1943	50 JUDEN NACH AUSCHWITZ
8 NOVEMBER 1943	50 JUDEN NACH AUSCHWITZ
7 DEZEMBER 1943	55 JUDEN NACH AUSCHWITZ
20 JANUAR 1944	48 JUDEN NACH AUSCHWITZ
2 FEBRUAR 1944	32 JUDEN NACH AUSCHWITZ
9 MARZ 1944	32 JUDEN NACH AUSCHWITZ
'44	36 JUDEN NACH AUSCHWITZ

Memorial wall commemorating deportations from the former Levetzow synagogue, Berlin. In 1941, the Levetzow synagogue, one of the largest synagogues in Berlin, located in the working class district of Moabit, was designated a central assembly site for deportations. Deportation trains departed from the nearby Grunewald freight train station. In 1988, architects Theseus Bappert and Jürgen Wenzel and sculptor Peter Herbrich created the Levetzow Synagogue Memorial. One part of the memorial features a steel wall the height of the former synagogue with cut-outs listing the dates and size of deportations from here to Auschwitz. Glimpses of sky are visible through the cut-outs. (Photograph by author, 1998)

installed and I went to see it. Named after its location on track (*Gleis*) 17 of the suburban Berlin–Grunewald station, the Track 17 Memorial was sponsored by the Deutsche Bundesbahn, the state railway that succeeded the Deutsche Reichsbahn of the Hitler era.[9]

Track 17 was located in the former freight section of the Grunewald train station. This had once been a busy place. Between October 1941 and March 1945, 183 transports carried over 50,000 Berlin Jews from here to camps and ghettos throughout Eastern Europe. Of the 50,000 Jews deported, only some 1,900 survived. But the tracks had clearly not been used for some time. Deportation trains stopped running over half a century ago and when a new station was built for an urban train line that ran parallel to the old tracks, the old station, with its once bustling freight section, was abandoned. Neither trains nor passengers came through anymore, just tourists and pilgrims of memory. Weeds pushed up through the tracks.

On the day I visited the memorial, I was there alone. The platform was empty. The sun shone. Birds sang. I didn't hear any city noises. It was a warm summer day and the air was fragrant. The length of the platform along track 17, from which most of the deportation trains had departed, was edged with yellow bricks, each inscribed with a date, a number, and a place name: Riga, Warsaw, Łódź, Theresienstadt, Auschwitz. The inscriptions reduced the story of genocide to simple data points: when each transport left, how many people it carried, and where it went.

The first deportation was massive. On October 18, 1941, 1,251 people were sent to Łódź. Within the space of two weeks—on October 21, October 27, and November 1—three additional transports followed, again to Łódź. They too were huge: 896 people, then 1,034, then 1,002. The next three transports also went to Łódź. Soon after that, the destination changed, perhaps in response to Hitler's wish to "deport them even farther eastward." Starting in late November 1941 and continuing through January 1942, deportations from track 17 went to Riga—over 760 miles, two days' travel—northeast of Berlin. The size of the Riga transports was staggering: 1,035, 1,026, 1,005, and 1,014 people. To accommodate these numbers, so-called *Sonderzüge* ("special trains") had to be provided.

Then, abruptly and dramatically, the pattern changed. Starting in June 1942, mass deportations were replaced by much smaller transports. Instead of deporting over 1,000 people at weekly intervals, fifty to a hundred people were deported on a daily basis. This shift from large but infrequent to small but regular transports puzzled me. It was at odds with the conventional image of freight trains with Jews herded into cattle cars.

The Track 17 Memorial challenged this conventional image. It wasn't wrong, just only partly true. Freight trains and cattle cars weren't the only kinds of trains used for deportations. As the numbers on the bricks along track 17 revealed, during the time that Jews were deported from this station *Sonderzüge* carrying masses of people were the exception, not yet the rule. The Holocaust historian, Saul Friedlander, underscores this fact. In the "overall daily traffic of 30,000 trains operated by the Reichsbahn in 1942," he notes, "only two *Sonderzüge* per day carried Jews to their death during this period."[10] As I later learned, in the initial phase of deportations from Germany, regular trains were a common means of transportation.

Instead of being put on "special trains," groups of fifty or a hundred deportees were put on regular trains carrying regular passengers. A special car (generally a passenger car but occasionally a boxcar) was merely added for the "special" passengers. It was a practical solution to the logistical problem of transporting large numbers of people efficiently and cheaply. Attaching one or two additional cars to a regular passenger train allowed up to a hundred people to be deported each time at virtually no cost.[11] The train ran anyway, and since Jewish communities had to cover the travel costs for deported members (4 pfennigs per kilometer for adults and 2 pfennigs for children four and younger), the Reichsbahn could even net a profit.

The shift from mass transports to small group deportations had first puzzled me. But this new information shocked me. Learning that, in this early phase, Jews were commonly deported on regular passenger trains and merely segregated in separate cars changed my perspective on how deportations happened. They didn't happen secretly, under cover of darkness, when people were asleep. Trains weren't routed through a separate network of tracks or stations. They used the same tracks and stations that regular Germans used as they went about their regular business.

The first deportation of Berlin Jews for Łódź on October 18, 1941 took place in the open and in broad daylight. As over a thousand people were gathered up and deported from a crowded neighborhood in a busy city, in the heart of Berlin's working-class district, Moabit, no attempt was made to hide what was happening. The Gestapo had designated the Levetzow synagogue, one of the largest synagogues in Berlin at the time, as the assembly place for deportations.

Two days before the scheduled departure date, deportees were instructed when to assemble at the synagogue. Local police and SS personnel were on site to supervise the process. They checked each person off by name and number and made sure that the numbers were clearly visible on clothes and bags. They recorded the valuables that deportees were required to hand over: foreign currency, bank certificates, jewelry (everything but wedding rings), cash in carefully sealed envelopes. They took roll and stamped identity cards, "Evacuated."

For the deportees, it was a terrifying and exhausting process. The previous two days had probably gone by in a frantic blur. Not only were they overwhelmed by conditions beyond their comprehension, they had also been given a detailed list of tasks to complete. The Gestapo had issued clear instructions. All bills pertaining to housing—rent, mortgage, gas, electricity, and water—had to be paid in full and receipts submitted. The gas was to be turned off, the front door locked, and the key handed over. A key ring for this purpose was provided with the departure instructions.

But these administrative tasks aside, there were wrenching personal matters to deal with. How do you say goodbye to people you love and will never see again? What do you do with a beloved pet? Or the things you have accumulated over a lifetime? Fifty kilograms was the luggage limit for deportees. How do you decide what to take when you can't know what you will need where you are going? Most probably took warm clothes, some bedding, food for the journey, and, if they could afford it, the permitted 200 Reichsmark in cash. Some stuffed extra bedding into a pillowcase and hid jewelry and additional cash in their clothes. Many a child clutched a favorite toy.

There is no record of how they spent their last night in the synagogue. Dignity demands privacy at such times. Only those who shared the experience have the right to see what we, who were not there, avert our eyes from. Primo Levi was such a privileged witness. Remembering his last night in an Italian detention camp before he and his fellow Jews were sent to Auschwitz, Primo Levi describes "what men do when they know they have to die."[12] "Some prayed," he recalls, "some drank to excess, others became intoxicated by a final unseemly lust." One group, however, spent its last night differently. "The mothers," Levi writes,

> stayed up to prepare food for the journey with tender care, and washed their children and packed the luggage … Nor did they forget the diapers, the toys, the pillows, and the hundred other small things that mothers remember and children always need.

While others drank, prayed, or had sex, the mothers cared for their children. Levi closes this tribute to the mothers by asking what we would do in a similar situation. "Would you not do the same?" he asks. "If you and your child were going to be killed tomorrow, would you not feed him today?" He expects no answer. It is not a question. It is a plea for compassion and love.

After a last night in the city that had been their home, the men, women, and children in the Levetzow synagogue were assembled for deportation. October 18, 1941 was a Saturday. They left in the early morning. It was raining. The very young, the very old, and those too ill or infirm to walk were piled onto open trucks and driven. The others, flanked by police and SS guards, went the 6 kilometers to the Grunewald station on foot.

In my imagination, these deportations and my parents' travels intersect. They were on the same routes. Their trains took the same tracks. They could even have stopped at the same stations. An encounter would not have been impossible. It could have been something like this:

Ursula is waiting in Berlin for her train. She is meeting Walter in Dresden for the weekend. She has pinned her hair back the way he loves it. My little Madonna, he will say and smile. He will be waiting on the platform when she gets there. He is always early. On the rare occasions when the train is late, he waits.

It is January or February and probably freezing. An icy wind might be blowing through. Walter warms his leather-gloved hands in the pockets of his uniform greatcoat, but beneath his officer's cap his ears are numb from cold. His high boots keep his feet and legs warm. He checks his watch.

Ursula checks her watch too. She is on the train and has found a window seat. They should depart shortly. She gets out the thermos that her father gave her the previous spring when she started her Reich Labor Service and pours herself a cup of hot tea. She cradles the cup in her hands. The warmth feels good. She looks out the window and checks her watch again. Already two minutes late. She wonders what the reason is for the holdup. The window has fogged up. She wipes a space to look out and sees a group of people (maybe fifty or so) on the opposite platform. They stand close together. Men in uniform stand around them, holding dogs on leashes. The steam from Ursula's tea fogs the window and she wipes it again.

Now she sees that they are Jews. She sees the yellow stars on their coats marked Jude.[13] *She wonders about the number tags pinned to their coats next to the yellow star and sees that their baggage is marked with the same numbers. They are stenciled on suitcases, taped to backpacks, and inked on cloth bundles. Some people are wearing more than one coat and some of the younger children are holding a toy or doll. There is something strange about this group: the number tags, the uncommon assortment of baggage, the double layers of clothes. Why are they gathered here and where are they going? Despite the size of the crowd, it is strangely quiet on the other platform. The guards aren't shouting, the dogs aren't barking, the children are unusually restrained. The adults are still as they stand together, and watchful parents keep their children close.*

Then—there must have been a signal that Ursula couldn't see or hear—the group starts moving. They pick up their bags, take their children's hands, and walk to a train that has been waiting on the track for them. They board the last car.

As they board, Ursula loses sight of them. She doesn't see the guards lock the doors from the outside or the signal for the train to depart. She watches it move out of the station, just as her train starts moving too. They briefly run side by side on adjacent tracks. Then hers veers off and the other train with its yellow-starred passengers disappears from view. Ursula is still holding her cup of tea, but it is cold. When she drinks it, the taste is bitter.

I wonder how my mother or father would have responded in such a situation. Would they have been shocked or moved to action? Would they have been distressed? Would they have dismissed it and turned their attention to other things? My imagined scenario is troubled by Ian Kershaw's observation that "the road to Auschwitz was built by hate, but paved with indifference."[14] The antithesis of love is not hate, but indifference, Freud famously noted. In its lack of caring, it is no less deadly.

Later that summer, visiting my father after my time in Berlin, I decided to raise some of my questions with him. We were lingering after a late afternoon coffee. He was on the couch and I was in the chair across from him. In the waning light, he had become a silhouette against the window and I couldn't see his features anymore. Perhaps the fact that his face was obscured from view, like a person on television when their identity has to be hidden, would enable me to speak more freely.

He took his glasses off and rubbed his eyes. He seemed tired and I felt sluggish myself, but there were things I had been waiting to say to him and this seemed a good time. I drained my coffee and tried to focus.

The last thing I recalled him saying had to do with trains. "We spent a lot of time on trains," he had said, "your mother and I. She would come where I was; I would go where she was. Whenever we could, we would be together."

It was the trains that I wanted to get back to. "How did that work," I asked, "all those trips on trains? How could you travel around like that with … with everything else that was going on?" My questions crumbled, as I stumbled over words I avoided using around him. "Deportation" felt too blunt, too aggressive. The indirect vagueness of "everything else that was going on" felt more safe. Over a lifetime of practice I had perfected the art of communicating indirectly.

Yet he ignored the indirection and took my question literally. As a soldier, he said, he could travel anytime, anywhere. No ticket needed, just a soldier's pass.

"I could take any train I wanted. My uniform gave me the right."

That wasn't what I had meant to ask about. It wasn't what I wanted to know. What I wanted to know was what did you see, what did you hear, what did you do? At a time when German newspapers carried headlines like "The Jew is being exterminated," how did you live with that fact?

Yet I didn't know how to ask these questions. The rule of silence is a hard rule to break. I swallowed and tried again. "Were the trains that you took to see Ursula the same trains that carried troops to the front?"

Another deflection. Why am I talking about troops when I am thinking about deportations? Why can't I get the right words out? My lack of courage felt shameful. I took a deep breath and plunged into the vortex I had been avoiding.

"Were the trains that you and my mother took ever the same trains that deported Jews?"

It was as if a dam had broken. The words I had been holding back poured out. *Did you ever see any trains like that, did they stop at the same station where you stopped, what did they look like, were they marked, what did you see?* I felt dizzy and literally breathless.

My father waited for me to finish. But I wasn't finished yet.

"What did you know?" I blurted out. It was the question I had lacked the courage to ask earlier. I sounded hoarse and my voice was scratchy. "What did you know about the Holocaust at the time?" I looked at him.

Frontispiece and first page of my father's *Soldbuch.* Originally designed to record pay (*Sold*) information for men serving in the German military, the *Soldbuch* issued by the Wehrmacht doubled as a personal identification document. Issued to "Dr. Walter Bammer" on October 1, 1939, my father's *Soldbuch* identified him by rank (with promotions recorded by date), ID tag number (144), blood group (0), gas mask size (2). His military service registration number is given as Bautzen 13/241/131/3.

Soldbuch record of my father's military awards (left) and partial list of furloughed travel (right).

He averted his eyes and his answer was another evasion. "I was lucky," he said, incongruously. "The war took me out of all that. It took me out of what was happening in Germany."

I waited. He said nothing more. The word *lucky* rang in my ears.

I felt completely drained and exhausted. The little courage I had earlier had been spent. I had neither the energy nor the will to continue talking. We were done, at least for that evening. The room was in darkness and my father was just a shape I could barely see. I wanted light and got up to turn the lamp on.

"Just about time for the evening news," my father said and I handed him the remote.

Once Upon a Wartime

When we went swimming and my father took his shirt off, the sight of his exposed body always made me cringe. It wasn't his nakedness that bothered me—his pale skin and thin shoulders, his wispy chest hair. It was the scar. A ragged ridge that ran diagonally from his left collarbone across his chest, it stopped just above his heart. Like a bandolier carved into his body, it was a brand-mark left behind by war.

He never talked about the circumstances of his injury. Only once did he volunteer information. It came in quick staccato bursts. "September 8, outside Schlüsselburg. We were in the forest ... Heavy artillery. I was in charge ... So close to the Russian line, we could see their faces." He paused before his final comment. "There were Russians in the trees. Russian snipers ... They were shooting us, but I couldn't see them." It was the 1941 German siege of Leningrad. A Red Army sniper's bullet entered his chest just below the shoulder.

The German invasion of the Soviet Union, code-named Operation Barbarossa, began on June 23, 1941. Before the summer was over, more than 3 million German soldiers—a full three-quarters of the German ground force—were marching eastwards.

It wasn't just another military campaign. It was a plan of epic proportions, aiming to make Germany the dominant power in Europe. The name of the campaign signaled this ambition. It invoked the memory of the medieval emperor, Frederick I (dubbed Barbarossa for his red beard), whose reign as ruler of the Holy Roman Empire of German Nations extended across the entire European continent.

But territorial expansion was just one aspect of Hitler's plan. The war in the east was a war of annihilation. The land would be cleared of Russians to provide more *Lebensraum* for Germans: land to settle and land to cultivate for food. The means to this end was a double strategy: military conquest and organized mass starvation.

The assault on Leningrad was part of this plan. The city wouldn't just be conquered; it would be destroyed. A hunger blockade was the tactic: encircle the city, trap people inside, and cut off all outside access. Key to this plan was Schlüsselburg, a garrison town that controlled access to the city from the Neva River.

On September 8, 1941, the day my father was shot, German ground forces took control of Schlüsselburg. For his leadership in this campaign, Colonel Harry Hoppe, commander of the 126th infantry division, was awarded the Ritterkreuz, the highest military honor bestowed in Nazi Germany. The siege of Leningrad had been successful. It had taken a staggering toll. Over a million people in Leningrad lost their lives to hunger, cold, and air attacks by the German Luftwaffe. Those who survived resorted to desperate means, eating dogs, cats, rats, sparrows, crows; and, in extremis, even resorted to cannibalism.

For the Germans, it was a Pyrrhic victory. By the time Operation Barbarossa was over, the historian Ian Kershaw reports, "almost three-quarters of a million [German soldiers]—nearly a quarter of the eastern army—were dead, wounded or missing."[1] It had been a catastrophe for the German forces. In the heralded march toward German domination, Operation Barbarossa was a crippling step toward the Reich's downfall. Not only was it famous as "the most gigantic ... armed struggle in history," it was infamous as "the most deadly."[2]

The only photograph of my father in a war zone dates from sometime after his injury. Tall and upright, framed against an empty sky, he is in uniform but his head is bare. His right hand holds his officer's field cap; his left arm is in a sling.[3] There are no identifiable landscape markers, no other human beings around. Just a high, flat sky and flat, bare land stretching to the horizon.

The desolation of this scene evokes Walter Benjamin's reflections on World War I and the way it shaped a generation. The experience was so shattering, he suggests, that it made men mute, turning what they couldn't say into silence. If there were words to convey their experience—what they suffered, what they did, and what they witnessed—they didn't have those words. If they found them, they didn't know what do with them. They no longer trusted that anyone would listen or that, if they listened, they would understand. The world and the people in it had become unfamiliar, even to themselves. What remained was a fearsome aloneness. "A generation that had gone to school on horse-drawn streetcars," Walter Benjamin wrote,

> now stood under the open sky in a landscape where nothing remained
> unchanged except the clouds and, beneath those clouds, in a force field
> of destructive torrents and explosions, the tiny, fragile human body.[4]

In 1936, when Benjamin wrote these words, World War II had not yet taken shape. But its contours were becoming visible. It was a darkening cloud that would soon engulf another generation.

By the time the war ended, my father once noted, he had been a soldier for a quarter of his life. When he was drafted in 1937, he was twenty-five years old. When it was over in 1945, he was thirty-three.

Walter was drafted into the Czechoslovak army on October 1, 1937 and immediately applied to the Officer's Academy in Olmütz, Moravia. He graduated in June 1938 as a lieutenant, one of 170 newly commissioned officers in his class. In photographs he cuts a stylish figure: fitted jacket,

My father in late 1941, recovering from a shoulder wound sustained during Operation Barbarossa.

jodhpurs flared at the knee, and high boots made of soft brown leather. He had hoped to join the equestrian infantry, but was assigned to an artillery regiment in Pressburg (today's Bratislava). His assignment was cut short, but not for reasons of his own choosing. The part of Czechoslovakia he was from was incorporated into Germany, and Walter's citizenship changed from Czech to German.

On October 1, 1938, German troops crossed into northern Bohemia to claim the region for the German Reich. It would henceforth be the "Reichsgau Sudetenland." As members of the "citizenry of German blood" (*Staatsangehörige deutschen Blutes*), all ethnic Germans in the new Reichsgau were designated Reich citizens (*Reichsbürger*), with all the rights and responsibilities of their new status.[5]

For Walter this meant that, along with his citizenship, he changed armies: within a week of the Sudetenland annexation, he was transferred from the Czechoslovak to the German army. A year after graduating from the Officers' Academy in Olmütz, he graduated as an officer a second time, now in the German Wehrmacht. His immunizations were updated for smallpox and typhus, his personal data verified and checked, and on August 28, 1939, two days before Germany invaded Poland and World War II officially began, he was issued his German military papers, the *Soldbuch*.[6] This condensed the information about his person to the essentials needed in warfare, with the critical identifying data on the opening page: name, rank, serial number. Height: 173 cm. Face shape: oval. Stature: slender. Eye color: grey blue. And in bold print: blood type (O) and gas mask size (2), followed by the name and address of his next of kin.

He was assigned to Heavy Artillery Regiment No. 255. This meant tanks, he clarified when I asked him, or, as he preferred, "coffins on wheels." His position was forward observer. "My job," he explained, "was to spot the enemy and make sure I wasn't spotted first. We were the eyes of the artillery." Military histories I consulted define this position as "the most dangerous job in the field artillery."[7] They say the forward observer is often the first person hit.

Over the course of six years as a German soldier, Walter fought on almost every European front. In May 1940, he was among the ground troops invading the Netherlands; that June, he was in Paris for the German occupation; the following spring, he went to Yugoslavia as part of the Balkan campaign; and that fall, he was deployed to Russia. In June 1944, he fought in Normandy; in November, he was in West Prussia; and before the end of the month, he returned west again for the Ardennes Offensive. In March 1943, he was on his way to Kharkov in the Ukraine to participate in what has been called the largest armored battle of all time, with over 5,000 German and Red Army tanks involved and some 146,000 German casualties, when he was pulled from the train with a life-threatening case of jaundice. Finally, sometime in early 1945, somewhere in the Ardennes Forest, he ran out of ammunition. Combat over, he decided to head for home. In the town of Butzbach, north of Frankfurt, he surrendered to American soldiers and became prisoner 3115 3109 721 in the Cherbourg POW camp in northern France.

Along the way, he collected his share of medals. "Over time," he explained, "I collected most of the medals you could get as a combat soldier. Medals for bravery, medals for injury, medals for doing what a soldier does. The irony is that all I was doing was trying not to get killed."

"Do you still have them?"

He directed me to the bottom shelf of a cabinet, where a small, scuffed 3 in. × 5 in. cardboard box was wedged between a box of chocolates and the safe where he kept personal documents, reserve cash, and old family jewelry.

"That's it," he nodded.

I got it out. Inside, nestled on a bed of cotton wool and carefully wrapped in several layers of tissue paper, was a set of medals attached to a ribbon bar. Two Iron Crosses "for bravery in battle," one from the Balkans and the other from Russia. An Artillery Assault Badge for participation in a front-line attack. A Silver Wound Badge for the severity of his injury.[8] Four miniature medals in an orderly row, each the size of a button on a dress shirt.

"I never wore them again," he offered, "After the war, I mean. But I couldn't quite throw them away, either."

"So, in the end, what were they really for?" I said. It was not a question, more a comment on the madness of war. But my father answered.

"For not running away," he shrugged.

"He must have seen terrible things," a friend remarked, when we were talking about our fathers' wartime experiences. She hesitated, as if unsure whether to continue. "And also done them," she finally added, her voice low.

Yet when my father talked about war, it wasn't about combat. It was about love. His war began and ended with Ursula. He fell in love with her on the way to his first deployment and the war was over for him when he returned home to her arms. When they met, he was twenty-seven and a German officer. She was a seventeen-year-old schoolgirl. But they didn't just meet during the war; they met because of the war. Walter's unit was on its way to invade the Netherlands. Quartered in Velen, they awaited orders. Ursula was home on a war-related break from school.

Velen was a strategic location for the German army. It was close to the Dutch border—the city of Winterswijk was just 15 miles away—and the flat terrain was perfect for a ground invasion. But the weather caused problems The winter of 1939/40 was the coldest winter in Europe in over a century. As temperatures plummeted to −30 °C, military maneuvers stalled. Road- and waterways froze and ships on the Rhine were crushed by floating ice packs. The Netherlands invasion was postponed and Walter's unit stayed in Velen, waiting.

The civilian population felt the bite of winter too. As the coal shortage across Germany reached crisis levels, emergency conservation measures ordered all "non-essential" spaces closed. In Westphalia, a so-called "coal break" was announced until further notice and schools were closed. Instead of returning to Münster for classes after the Christmas break, Ursula remained in Velen on coal break.

And so Walter and Ursula met in a village pub, the Velen Dorfschänke. It was New Year's Eve, 1940. Walter had come for the festivities with men from his unit; Ursula was with her mother and a senior officer who had been quartered in the Bushoffs' home. For Walter their meeting was epic. Not just a new year and a new decade; a whole new measurement of time began for him that day. On his way to war he had found his love, his destiny.

They met again in early February at the start of Carnival. Schools had not yet reopened, and the invasion of the Netherlands was still postponed.

Walter and Ursula again were in the Dorfschänke to celebrate Carnival. This time they danced, and Ursula's mother invited the young lieutenant over for coffee. Two days later, Walter's unit received orders to move on, but before he left, Walter and Ursula agreed to write each other. A relationship that would define the rest of their lives had begun.

For the next six years, they were only rarely together physically. They saw each other when he was on furlough, usually only a few days at a time, with months and up to a year between visits. They wrote instead, creating an intimacy made of words and sustained by longing. They got engaged in 1941 and were married in 1943, when Ursula was twenty and Walter thirty. But the war continued and they kept writing.

Not until the end of the war, when Germany's infrastructure failed and all lines of communication were disrupted, did they lose touch. They last saw each other in November 1944, before Walter left for the Ardennes Offensive. "Wait for me, Ursula," he had said to her. "Wait, I will come back to you." Then silence for over a year. Letters weren't coming through anymore. Ursula's search request through Radio Hamburg, the last official German radio station still on the air, went unanswered. A psychic she consulted assured her that Walter would return, but by November 1945 she still had no word.

In the meantime, Ursula had left Rumburg and returned to Velen. Taking only what she could stuff into a baby carriage, including vodka and aquavit that she could use for bribes, she fled from the Soviet Occupied Zone (where Rumburg now was) to the British Occupied Zone (where Münster and Velen were). When the border was closed and she didn't have proper transit papers, the bottles of vodka and aquavit cleared the way. "*Bystro, bystro,*" she recalled the young Russian border guard saying, "quickly, quickly." Then she ran across the militarized no-man's land in the darkness, pulling her baby carriage behind her until a wheel came off, and she half-carried, half-dragged it across the stubble. She ran toward a light in the distance. It was a farmhouse in the British zone. She was safe.

Ursula left Rumburg on August 27 and arrived in Velen on September 3. She had traveled some 600 miles, across the landscape of postwar Europe, by truck and farm cart, on passenger and freight trains overflowing with refugees, the last part on foot. "I—am—home!" she wrote in her first diary entry from Velen.

A few months later, Walter headed home too. Officially discharged from the German army on October 27, and given a medical examination to assess his physical condition (he had "restricted mobility" in his arm, but was "not disabled," the report concluded), he was released from American custody on November 9, given 80 Reichsmark to cover travel expenses, and provided with transit papers from Cherbourg to Velen. The last he knew, Ursula had been in Rumburg. Yet he decided—it was a wager based on hope—to first try Velen. Perhaps he would find his beloved there.

In Münster, the British military authorities stamped and signed Walter's Certificate of Discharge. He was free to go. No longer a soldier, he was again a civilian.

The sight of war-ravaged Münster must have been a shock. Over 90 percent of the city had been destroyed and a population of some 143,000 had shrunk to around 76,000. Smells of offal, wood smoke, and death hung in the air. This was what German cities looked like after the war, the writer W.G. Sebald recalled. "Nothing," he wrote, "was so unambiguously linked to the word *city* as the presence of heaps of rubble, fire-scorched walls, and the gaps of windows through which one could see the vacant air."[9] Walter later confided to his diary, "I made my way toward Velen with an anxious heart."

From Münster, he caught a train, but he didn't take it all the way to Velen. He got off two stops early in Coesfeld. "My heart and mind were filled with dread," he wrote in his diary, "and I tried to postpone the moment of truth as long as possible." What if Ursula wasn't in Velen but still in Rumburg? What if his worst fears were confirmed and she was gone? To postpone the moment of truth, he decided to take the slow way home. Walter went the last 10 miles to Velen on foot.

The final stretch took him through the High Moor outside Velen. Once the greatest expanse of moorland in all of Westphalia, it was a dense thicket of low-lying shrubs. Only the trill of swallows, the croak of moor frogs, and the rustle of dry grasses in the breeze would have broken the stillness. There would probably have been no cars, just the rustle and creak of horse-drawn farm carts. In Velen alone, the number of cars in use had gone from thirty-seven before the war to just five in the immediate postwar period.

When Walter reached Velen, he saw that the Archive building, where the Bushoffs lived, was undamaged. But his wild joy was tempered with caution. "Only a miracle could have brought Ursula to me here," he later confessed thinking. Yet the moment of truth could no longer be postponed. Passing the Union Jack on the flagpole in the courtyard and the British military vehicles parked to the side, he walked up to the front door and rang the doorbell.

Then the miracle he had hoped for happened. The door opened. It was Ursula's friend from Münster, Gisela Wolters. For a moment, she just stood there and stared. Then she shouted, "Ursula … it's your Walter! Walter is here!"

A lifetime later, when my father recounted this story, the emotional force of that moment was still palpable. The shock of survival, of finding his Ursula, of having returned safely.

"I heard footsteps and I knew it was Ursula." The memory quivered in his voice. "Then I saw her face and my war was over. I felt her arms around me ... I was home."

That Christmas, Walter made a star for the tree that he and Ursula decorated with homemade ornaments. He gilded it with gold foil scored at the edges. For the first time in their life together, the promise of *peace on earth* rang true. Every year of my childhood that star shone on top of our Christmas tree. I was conceived in the light of its promise and born in the first year of postwar peace.

The day after my parents' wedding in January 1943, they went on a short honeymoon to Dresden. An air raid stopped the train en route. "We just prayed that we wouldn't be hit," my mother recalled later. "There was no place to hide or escape to."

Since the Luftwaffe bombing of Warsaw in September 1939, followed by the bombing of Rotterdam in May 1940, the air war had escalated exponentially. Between 1943 and 1945, the tonnage of bombs dropped by the Allies on Germany increased more than fivefold each year, reaching an annual total of 1,202,000 tons in 1944. The word "carpet bombing" was added to the English language to describe a new form of warfare: "terror from the skies."[10]

The limits of this terror strategy were first tested in July 1943 during Operation Gomorrah, when Allied bombers dropped 9,400 tons of bombs—around 3 million of them fire bombs—on Hamburg. The resulting firestorm turned the city into an inferno, liquefying asphalt and setting canals ablaze. By the time the fires abated, around 40,000 people were dead and "the Reich's second-largest city lay in ruins."[11] Later that year, it was Münster's turn, as massive aerial bombardments on October 10 and 12 reduced the old part of the city to rubble.

However, even as the air war intensified, Dresden—cherished for its cultural treasures—was declared a protected zone. This German city, the Allies promised, would be spared. On his way to Dresden as a German prisoner of war, Kurt Vonnegut's Billy Pilgrim is reassured: "You needn't worry about bombs ... Dresden is an open city." When he arrives Billy sees why it has been afforded this special status. It is "the loveliest city" he has ever seen, "like a Sunday school picture of Heaven."[12]

When my parents arrived in Dresden for their honeymoon, they could easily have been equally enchanted. The mere fact that the city was still intact was itself astonishing. At a time when cities across Germany were being attacked, the very normalcy of daily life in Dresden must have made it seem as if some magic spell were shielding this city. In Dresden, Billy Pilgrim marveled, you could almost forget that there was a war:

Steam radiators still whistled cheerily in Dresden. Streetcars clanged. Telephones rang and were answered. Lights went on and off when switches were clicked. There were theaters and restaurants. There was a zoo.[13]

On their honeymoon in Dresden in January 1943, Ursula and Walter would have gone to the theaters and restaurants that Billy mentioned. Perhaps they even visited Billy's zoo. One day they went to the Zwinger and Walter photographed his bride in the courtyard. She smiles at her husband and tilts the brim of her hat against the sun.

Two years later, Dresden was destroyed. The beautiful city that some hailed as "Florence on the Elbe" was reduced to "ashes and dollops of melted glass."[14]

On February 13, two hours before midnight, 773 British Lancaster bombers attacked a sleeping city swollen to capacity by thousands of refugees fleeing from the eastern war zones. They first dropped 4,500 explosive bombs, then 400,000 incendiary bombs. Hundreds of American B-17 Flying Fortresses finished the job. The bombing continued, unabated, for two nights and two days. When it was over, on February 15, Dresden was gone. Likened by some to the Biblical Armageddon, by others to the incineration of Pompeii, the destruction of Dresden was the apotheosis of "terror bombing."

Flak: "Defensive Fire Over a German City, 1940."
(Photographer unknown. Courtesy of ullstein bild)

In the burning city, buildings glowed crimson; their burned-out skeletons shimmered ghostly white. As news of the disaster spread, horrified witnesses provided details. The ferocious firestorm had sucked everything into its vortex. "People by the thousands," a Berlin reporter wrote, "ran through the streets like flaming torches, got mired in red-hot asphalt, [and] leapt into the waters of the river Elbe."[15] For days afterwards, an ashen pall blocked the sunlight, while the stench of rotting bodies filled the air. Charred corpses and parts of bodies lay scattered like debris after a storm. Small children had often simply been vaporized. Some 35,000–40,000 people had perished.[16] Billy Pilgrim's "loveliest city" was "a city of the dead."[17]

The shock of Dresden caused the strategy of aerial bombing to be reviewed. The goal of sowing terror had been effective and it seemed just retribution for Germany's crimes. "Terror bombing," some argued, could be justified as "moral bombing." Germany had sowed the wind when it bombed Warsaw, Rotterdam, and Coventry. It reaped the whirlwind in Hamburg and Dresden. Yet in the wake of Dresden this righteous sense of retribution faltered. An ethical line had been crossed. On March 28, 1945, Churchill ordered a halt to the bombing of German cities. The Allied air war was officially ended.

The specter of Dresden—images of my parents' honeymoon mixed with the horror of the firebombing—came back to haunt me when my children were in their teens. A friend had invited us to a Passover Seder and, while there were other non-Jewish guests, we were the only Germans. Toward the end of the evening, after pieces of the *afikomen* had been distributed, we were sitting around the table, chatting. Coffee had been poured, sweets were being passed. My son, Nicolas, sat across the table from me.

"Dresden," I suddenly heard someone say. It was the woman sitting next to Nicolas. Somehow the conversation had turned to World War II and the firebombing.

"It served them right," I heard her say. "The Germans got what they deserved." For a moment the conversation halted. Everyone seemed to hold their breath. Into the silence she added, calmly, "More of them should have been killed."

I looked at my son and saw my parents' features: my father's lips and hazel eyes, my mother's chin line. This was their grandson. Their history was partly his history too. A rush of emotions pressed my thoughts into words, and I addressed the woman who had made the Dresden comment.

"What you said is your opinion. I understand that. But as my parents' daughter and my children's mother, I can't agree."

My parents on their wedding day, January 21, 1943, in Velen.

No one responded. Even if they had, I might not have heard them. The sound of my heart pounding was too loud.

On October 29, 1998, the South African Truth and Reconciliation Commission presented its official Report to President Nelson Mandela. Recognizing that "the past refuses to lie down quietly. It has an uncanny habit of returning to haunt," the Report insisted that only by facing the full truth of the past directly can we stop it from "returning to haunt."[18] As the implications of this insight reverberated throughout communities across the world, it encouraged—and emboldened—many a conversation that might previously have seemed too difficult or painful to risk. That fall, I had one of those difficult conversations with a colleague.

"What did your father do during the war?" she had asked me. "He was on the Eastern Front ... Do you know what he was involved in?" When I didn't have a ready answer, she pressed on, "Can you be sure that he is innocent of war crimes?"

"No," I had to be honest, "I can't be sure." I felt a doubled shame for my answer. Once, for doubting him. And twice, for not knowing what he might have done.

By the late 1990s, the actions of the Wehrmacht, particularly on the Eastern Front, had become an explosive topic. An exhibition on *Crimes of the Wehrmacht, 1941–1944*, sponsored by the Hamburg Institute for Social Research, had shattered the myth of an "unblemished Wehrmacht" —soldiers focused on the business of waging war—and replaced it with the charge of war crimes.[19] In its view, the German war in the east was never just a war of military combat. It was always a genocidal war: a "war of annihilation," as the title of the exhibition defined it. Members of the Wehrmacht were not just soldiers. They were accessories to genocide.

As the exhibition traveled across West Germany and Austria over a period of four and a half years, with stops in thirty-three cities, it sparked a national debate that marked a watershed in Germany's struggle with an unresolved history. It was not the first crisis of the German social body in relation to its Nazi past. Like fevers caused by a lingering infection, such crises recurred. But this became the most convulsive.

An early crisis was triggered in January 1979 by the West German screening of the American television mini-series *Holocaust*. When ARD, one of the three major German television networks, aired the series during prime time over five successive days, between 10 and 15 million Germans watched it. As households across Germany tuned in to the same program at the same time on the same day, the shared experience of this collective viewing led to a national soul-searching about German complicity in Nazi crimes. Confronted with the horrors of a past they had largely closed their eyes to, Germans experienced a sense of collective shame, and the word "Holocaust" became part of the German language.

A decade later, the so-called Historians' Debate (*Historikerstreit*) revisited the question of Nazi crimes and German complicity.[20] Over the three-year period from 1986 to 1989, German historians argued—often heatedly and quite uncivilly for what was ostensibly a scholarly debate—about the proper place of the Holocaust in historiography: Did it occupy a unique—and uniquely German—place as an evil that stood alone? Or was it one among a set of comparable events: a genocide in a history of genocides, a war crime in a history of war crimes? How, in short, should one remember the Holocaust?

By the mid-1990s, what the Historians' Debate had framed as an argument among intellectuals reentered the German public sphere as a general discussion. The occasion was the screening in German movie theaters of Steven Spielberg's film *Schindler's List*. By the time it premiered in Frankfurt in 1994 under the patronage of German president Richard von Weizsäcker,[21] it was evident that the popular mood had shifted from a largely passive sense of guilt and shame to a much more active—even activist—sense of political responsibility. As evidenced by the proliferation of Holocaust monuments and memorials across Germany, a new sensibility had emerged that remembered the past in relation to the future that Germans were engaged in shaping. Healing the wounds of history, as the South African TRC Report had cautioned, meant "not to be obsessed with the past ... [but] to take care that the past is properly dealt with *for the sake of the future*."[22]

Daniel Goldhagen's 1996 polemic, *Hitler's Willing Executioners: Ordinary Germans and the Holocaust*, brought this debate about the relationship between past, present, and future to a head.[23] Responses to his work among Holocaust scholars ranged from ambivalent to sharply critical.[24] The German public, however, was wildly enthusiastic. As the American historian toured Germany for book signings, interviews, and public forums, sold-out crowds treated him like a rock star. Far from rejecting his claim that German anti-Semitism was marked by something uniquely German and particularly sinister—what Goldhagen called its "eliminationist" quality—Germans embraced it.

Two decades earlier, watching *Holocaust* in the privacy of their living rooms, Germans responded to the accusation of historical guilt with a sense of shame. Now, they accepted the accusation of collective guilt with a strange, almost grateful sense of pride, as if it were a kind of expiation.

In this volatile context the Wehrmacht exhibition, like flint to tinder, struck sparks. The material on display was shocking. Reams of documents and stacks of photographs gave evidence of war crimes committed by the Wehrmacht—in Russia, in the Ukraine, across Central and Eastern Europe. Countless military orders and administrative directives (some labeled "secret," many undisguised) evidenced the blatant violation of international laws regulating warfare, while diary entries and letters by German soldiers revealed their willing collusion. As civilians were massacred, POWs executed, and villages pillaged, torched, and burned to the ground, orders to kill—and reports of killings—were conveyed in bureaucratic terms, with language precise and carefully purged of affect. This was murder and genocide in the passive mode, as if neither the actors nor the acted-upon were human. The following report stands for many:

> 1.) Due to heavy losses, 2.) due to the complete destruction of all villages and numerous storehouses, and 3.) due to the evacuation of the population, by which he has lost his workers especially for the fall and spring field work, our opponent has ... had taken from him ... his means of existence.[25]

The instrumental language is chilling; but it is the pictures in the exhibition that sear your soul. They accuse you. They question you. They make you witness. They haunt you and don't let you go. POWs, some of them mere boys, look anxiously at the camera. Villages are ablaze in flame. Bodies hang from makeshift gallows like fish on a trotline. And on picture after numbing picture you see corpses: in crumpled heaps like rag dolls, stacked in piles like firewood, sometimes dismembered with limbs or heads missing. In some images, soldiers preen for the camera. "Look where I am," their pose suggests. "Look what we did." A photograph shows a group of grinning soldiers with their pilfered livestock: one has a chicken, another two geese, and a third is cradling a lamb in his arms like a baby.

Some of the photographs were enlarged to poster size, but most were so small that to see them you had to move in close. This intimate distance magnified their impact. The brutality of the violence, the callousness of the added comments was harrowing ("They didn't want to work for Germany," a soldier captioned three photographs of Russians hanged).[26] But what shocked Germans most about this exhibition was another matter, one that previous debates about the Nazi years hadn't touched: it attacked the honor and integrity of German soldiers. It exposed the painful truth that, under a criminal regime, honor is compromised by the regime's demand for allegiance. In Hitler's army, being a good soldier—serving your country, doing your duty, and obeying orders—could mean moral compromise.

For many Germans—particularly men—of the war generation, this was too painful a truth to take. Or at least too painful to take without protest. Coming on the heels of the debates around Daniel Goldhagen's claim that Germans were guilty of a particularly virulent anti-Semitism (a claim that Germans at the time seemed to have largely accepted), the Wehrmacht exhibition, for some, took the matter of guilt too far.

The war it depicted wasn't the war many former soldiers remembered fighting. They didn't recognize themselves in the words and images of the soldiers shown. Most of them had gone to war when they were drafted, taking up arms when they were called to serve. They hadn't fought for Hitler or the Nazi Party, but for their homeland at a time of war, and to protect their families, comrades, and their own lives. Some of them believed in Nazi ideology; some of them were actively opposed; most of them had never evinced much interest in politics. As soldiers, none of them had been members of the Nazi Party.[27]

By the end of the war, all illusions of a glorious outcome were shattered. Many soldiers didn't know what they had fought for anymore. Many had never grasped the goal in the first place. What they knew was they had lost: not just lives and the land they had fought for, but their very honor and dignity as a people. Germany had become a pariah among nations. For many former soldiers, the war was not past. They lived with it in their memory. They reckoned with the outcome by trying to salvage a sense of personal integrity from the wreckage of history. They had at least, they told themselves, tried to be good soldiers, good citizens, and good men.

The exhibition challenged these assumptions and the image of a "clean" Wehrmacht by leveling the charge of war crimes. The effect was immediate and intense. Public displays of emotion escalated into collective hysteria. Opposing sides squared off—left against right, old against young, nationalists against anti-nationalists, pacifists against militarists—in a storm of rage, resentment, shame, and wounded pride. At times emotions ran so high that some venues offered on-site counseling. And in a defiant act of self-affirmation that had no precedent in German history, men of the war generation—by then old men in their seventies and eighties—gathered to protest what they felt was a skewed rendering of the history they had lived through.

By early 1997, responses to the exhibition were garnering more attention than the exhibition itself. Wherever it went, protests and demonstrations followed. Property was damaged and people were injured. As fire bombings, death threats, arrests, and lawsuits trailed the exhibition, costs mounted.

After a demonstration of around 15,000 people in Munich turned the inner city into a virtual war zone, the government decided it had to address the growing crisis. In March 1997, a special session of the German parliament discussed the Wehrmacht exhibition: the issues it raised, and the political costs and gains of raising them. The debate was emotionally charged with comments that were deeply personal. Social Democratic Party representative Otto Schily, for example, remembered his Luftwaffe officer uncle, who committed suicide when he realized that the government he had pledged to serve was committing genocide.

In October 1998, the Wehrmacht exhibition came to Bonn and my father was planning to see it. Even before it came, it sparked tensions in this city that, for decades, had been the West German capital and, even after unification, still housed key federal ministries, including Defense. The Bundeswehr (the German armed forces and their civilian administration) and one of the major governing parties, the Christian Democratic Union, had publicly disavowed the exhibition. It was finally sponsored by a broad coalition of local groups comprising historians, peace activists, labor representatives, ecumenical religious groups, the German-Israeli Society, and the local Green Party affiliate. Despite this broad coalition in support of the exhibition, the controversy surrounding it remained heated. The Bonn affiliate of the far-right, ultra-nationalist National Democratic Party had scheduled a protest march, boasting an expected crowd of some 3,000 marchers.

The venue had already proven controversial. To prevent it from being housed in the Haus der Geschichte, the renowned local museum of contemporary history, the Chancellor himself had intervened. A politically neutral space was finally agreed on: the Beethoven Hall. My father was happy with this decision. Not only was he familiar with the Beethoven Hall (he had been a concert subscriber there for decades), but it was an easy bus ride from where he lived.

As in other cities that had hosted the exhibition, organizers in Bonn had scheduled several public events aimed to foster dialogue. A self-styled Working Group of Historians and Former Soldiers held a public forum on "Truth for Wehrmacht Soldiers" that included former soldiers, historians, and representatives from the media. My father had selected a forum scheduled for one of the big lecture rooms at the university. One of the participants was a man he admired and respected: Johannes Rau, a leading Social Democratic politician. Within a year, Rau would be elected German President with the campaign promise "Reconciliation, not Division."[28] However, at the time of the Wehrmacht exhibition, public sentiment did not yet echo Rau's aspirational motto. In the heat of the controversy over how to view the war and Nazi past, reconciliation seemed elusive. Division ruled.

Long queues had been predicted for the forum with Johannes Rau. For some events, people stood in line for hours. "Go early," I had urged my father. "Go early, and make sure you get a seat." He was eighty-five years old and unsteady on his feet. His balance was shaky. A recent fall, when the bus lurched forward before he reached his seat, had scared him into finally getting a walker. "I'll look old," he had initially objected, when I pressured him to take precautions. But fear eventually conquered vanity and he got the walker.

I called him the day after he saw the exhibition and attended the forum at the university. I wanted to hear his reaction. The lines had indeed been long, he confirmed, and the auditorium had been packed, as expected. But, he reassured me, he had found a seat. "It was a mix of generations like I've never seen," he said. "Old people like me, including men who had been Wehrmacht soldiers. People your age, of the postwar generation. And young people your children's age, who learn about the war from school books."

When I asked about the exhibition, "What did you think of it?" my father hesitated. "Before I can answer you, I need time to think." He paused. "It still feels too fresh."

I got my answer a few weeks later when a letter came in the mail. Instead of writing by hand, as he usually did, this time he had typed it. His handwriting was getting shaky, he explained. I quickly skimmed the part about the panelists' contributions. His response to the exhibition was what interested me. It came toward the end of the letter. A new paragraph. "I want to add from my own perspective," it started.

My reading slowed. This—his "own perspective"—is what I wanted.

"I want to add from my own perspective," my father wrote, "that the degree of participation or non-participation in war crimes was often attributable to fate or chance." The distancing abstraction of his diction, the impersonal syntax, felt like a barrier between him and me.

I continued reading. "In my case," he went on, "I didn't happen to become involved, simply because I was never deployed to the so-called *Etappe*, behind the front lines, but was always, when I was deployed, at the front line, where there was no room for such *Schweinereien* to happen."[29]

The structure of the sentence was tortured, but the tone was that of a report. The language was dry and factual. The personal dimension— what he did or didn't do, what his options were and how he chose among them, what and how he felt—was missing. He wrote that participation in war crimes was "often attributable to fate or chance," to whether one was deployed at the front or "behind the front lines." He was lucky, he implied: his "fate" was the latter, "where there was no room for such *Schweinereien* to happen." The word "happen" jarred me. The war crimes revealed by the Wehrmacht exhibition didn't "happen," I wanted to counter. They weren't acts of nature like fires or floods. They were human acts committed by people.

This wasn't what I had hoped to hear from him. I had asked him what he thought of the exhibition, but what I really wanted to know was what he felt. What was it like to have been involved in a war that was not just a war, but an orchestrated program of genocide? How did he live with the memories of the things he had done and seen: the suffering, the violence, the evil? I had thought that the exhibition might pierce the protective screen of his postwar persona to reveal the man he had been when he went to war. But his words didn't provide that opening. They remained objective, factual, analytical. They shielded him—and barred me—from his feelings.

Then it hit me. All the feelings I had hoped to find in his letter and thought were missing—the shame and shock and horror his language concealed—were there, hidden in plain sight. He had compressed them into a single word: *Schweinereien*. This was the one word that escaped the emotional control of my father's diction. *Schweinereien* shocked. It was crude, uncontrolled, not measured. It was not a word my father normally used. It expressed disgust and was itself disgusting. It referred to dirty things that pigs, not people, do. Yet my father used it to refer to things that "happened" behind the frontlines, the war crimes that the Wehrmacht exhibition documented.

We call them "unspeakable acts," as if we have no words for them. If we speak of them, we use words like *Schweinereien* that relegate them to the sphere of beasts. Yet beasts don't rape and murder, torture for pleasure, or commit genocide.

Humans do.

A World in Letters

As my parents got older and the Nazi years grew more distant, I sometimes wondered where that time had gone in their memory. The killing, the dying, the world collapsing all around them—what did they remember and how did they remember it? They had always closed this part of their past off to me, like a room that only they could enter. They went in alone and shut the door behind them. They never invited me to come along.

But there were times when the door didn't close all the way, or perhaps they left it open intentionally. One of those times came the summer after I had gone to Buchenwald with my mother. I was visiting my parents in Bonn. The year had begun with their golden anniversary, fifty years of happy marriage. It ended with my mother in the hospital with the cancer that would kill her the following spring.

My parents were in the living room, reading. I had been upstairs and came down to join them. They were reading aloud to each other, as they often did, usually my father reading and my mother listening. One year, they had read Proust's entire *Remembrance of Things Past* this way, followed by Theodor Fontane's *Travels Through the Mark Brandenburg*.

Field post letter to my mother from my father on deployment to an unidentified site, January 16, 1945.

Another year, Heinrich Böll's *Irish Diary* inspired them to visit Ireland. When my father was assigned a new diplomatic post in Spain and they were both learning Spanish, they struggled through *Don Quixote* together in their stiff new language, carefully checking their pronunciation as they went.

I sometimes joined them on these occasions. Sitting on the couch next to my mother, I would catch a segment of whatever they were reading and enjoy the sense of intimacy that reading aloud creates. When he reached a good place to break, my father would stop. "That's it for tonight." Then we would talk until one of us decided it was bedtime.

It was no different on this occasion, or so it seemed. My father was in his armchair. The table lamp lit his book. My mother was on the couch, her legs warmed by a blanket. He was reading and she was listening, her hands in her lap. When I came in, they looked up briefly, but didn't let my intrusion interrupt them. I was about to sit down by my mother, as I usually did. But something felt different that evening. There was an awkwardness in the air. I wasn't sure what was going on and waited.

Then I noticed that my father wasn't reading from a book. He was reading from loose sheets of paper. "My dearest Ursula," I heard him say. In my confusion, I only caught fragments: "birthday … with you … our engagement … promise … forever and always, your Walter." This wasn't Proust or Heinrich Böll. This wasn't the kind of literature they used to read. This was a letter my father had written.

As I tried to orient myself, I remembered a letter from my mother a few months earlier. Among the usual chatty trivia—an Amnesty fundraiser they had hosted, the annual parish flea market she organized, a concert, a meal out, the weather—was a casual aside that I didn't think much about at the time. She had found "a bundle of old letters from the wartime," she wrote, that she hadn't known still existed. After her father's death, a few months earlier, she had discovered them among other things. They were in a box labeled "Letters, 1941–1944: Walter to Ursula," next to her father's stamp and coin collections. "After the war," she had written, "when your father got a job in Frankfurt, we left everything we didn't need behind. There was no room in our tiny apartment."

As my parents moved—first to Frankfurt and then abroad—their letters stayed behind in Velen. Postwar life moved on, and the letters were of a time that was over. Yet unbeknownst to my mother, her father, with his archivist's instincts, had saved them. These were the letters that my parents were reading that night.

A decade later, after my own father's death, I inherited the box with their letters. They were in five fat accordion folders stamped *Landsberg Archive* that my grandfather had brought from work: four folders with letters from

Walter to Ursula and one with letters from her to him. They spanned the war years from 1941 to 1945. The first year, 1940, much of 1944, and most of Ursula's letters were missing.

I knew that not all of their wartime letters had survived. Of those they were able to save, most were Walter's. When I asked what happened to Ursula's letters, my father explained that it had been impossible. There were just too many, he said. He was in the field. They were heavy and he had his gear. He said, "I kept her picture. The letters I carried with me in my heart."

Still, I was stunned by what was in the folders. The volume was astonishing in itself: there were hundreds and hundreds of letters. My parents had written almost every day. They had numbered each letter successively so that, if any letter was lost to the vagaries of war, they would know right away which one was missing. They began writing soon after they met in early 1940 and they kept writing throughout the entire war. At the beginning of their correspondence, my mother was just seventeen—"a mere girl," in my father's memory. By the end, she was twenty-one and his wife.

They carefully kept track of each number. "Yesterday, 4 and 5 arrived," Walter wrote to Ursula on January 10, 1943. "Number 2 is still missing." At the beginning of each year they started with number 1 again, and when they lost count, as they did in 1941 in the turmoil of Walter's deployment to Russia, they started a fresh count with new numbers. Only once, for a period of several months, did they interrupt their counting: when Walter was wounded in September 1941 and in hospital. As soon as a new year started, their counting resumed. Walter's first letter to Ursula on January 3, 1942 was number 1 of that year; his last letter on December 31 was number 204.

They wrote on whatever paper was available. Sometimes a scrap of paper had to do. Sometimes a postcard took the place of a letter. They wrote by hand, usually in pen. When they ran out of ink or didn't have a pen, they wrote in pencil. Many of Walter's letters from 1941, posted from a location he identified merely as "Eastern Front," were scribbled in a hand that spoke of haste and a nervous urgency.

They wrote even when they weren't sure where to send their letter (Was Ursula still in Rumburg or back in Velen? Where had Walter been deployed?), or whether the letters could even be delivered when they arrived. By the end of the war, in early 1945, Walter started putting two different addresses on each letter: First, "Ursula Bammer in Rumburg/Sudetenland," and underneath, "if undeliverable, send to Bushoff in Velen/Westphalia." His concern was justified. After he left for the Ardennes Offensive in November 1944, none of his letters reached Ursula anymore. They arrived in Rumburg, but in the chaotic last months of the war, in the transition from German to Czech rule and the period of Soviet occupation, letters piled up in depots, were left in unopened sacks, were deemed undeliverable or simply not delivered. Months after the war, a package arrived in Velen. Letters from Walter had been found and were being forwarded.

Through all of this, through the chaos and uncertainty of war, even when they got no response, Walter and Ursula kept writing.

They wrote about ordinary, everyday things: news about family and friends, a book they read, an outing, a memory, the weather. Over and over, they said how much they loved and missed each other and how they longed to be together again soon. Walter wrote to his "beloved Ursula bride" and ended with the promise to "love you forever and always, your Walter." On occasion, he addressed her playfully as his "dearest Bammerwife" and signed off with "a thousand kisses, your Bammerhusband." Each letter was a variation on this theme. Each day, in each new letter, over weeks and months and years, they repeated the same words of love, reassurance, and commitment. Their letters were a form of prayer, an affirmation of faith in each other.

As I read the umpteenth repetition of "Ursula, my beloved wife," it began to dawn on me that the answer to my question—how did my parents survive the war emotionally?—lay in these wartime letters. They survived by countering a public world of destruction and violence with a private world of tenderness and trust between themselves. With *I love you, I am thinking of you, I am here for you*, they built a refuge in which to remain intact.

My first encounter with these letters was that evening in Bonn, when I happened across my parents reading them. I knew they existed (my mother had mentioned them to me that spring), but I had been busy and had forgotten about them by summer. Coming across them like this caught me by surprise and the sudden appearance of my parents' wartime past was unsettling. I felt out of place, like an intruder into a space they kept private.

My first impulse was to leave. Yet I didn't want to leave. I wanted to hear what was in the letters. My mother must have sensed my hesitation, because she gestured for me to come and sit next to her.

"Do you mind if I stay?" I asked.

By way of answer, she patted my knee and spread her blanket so that it covered both of us. "We didn't think you'd be interested in these old letters." Her voice was soft. "But we are happy for you to stay and listen."

My father had taken his glasses off and was waiting. I adjusted the blanket and leaned back. My mother looked at my father and nodded. He put his glasses on and continued reading.

January 18, 1942

My dearest Ursula, a week ago was my twenty-ninth birthday and I spent it with you, my love. Today, I remembered our walk in the rain when we met (that wondrous day in Velen), our dreams of a future together and our own family. At our engagement, we made a promise to be together "forever and always." Our witnesses were your parents and mine. But God was our witness for all eternity. May he bless our union, keep you safe, and get me through this war alive.

Wherever He, in his wisdom, sends me, I feel you there with me.

Forever and always, your Walter.

I saw my mother's hands next to mine on the blanket. I heard the familiar sound of my father's voice. We had spent countless evenings together like this in this very room. Yet I felt disoriented. I felt caught in the breach between two epochs: their wartime and my postwar time. I didn't know how to bridge the gap. But I didn't know how to escape it either.

I tried to imagine what my parents had been like when they wrote these letters. A young woman with long hair in a summer dress, a slim young man in a Wehrmacht uniform. I knew them as images from old black and white photographs. My parents before they were my parents.

But as I registered the date of the letter they had just read, another set of images crowded in. For at the very time that my parents were writing about love and a life together, other lives—the lives of Jews across Europe—were being destroyed. On January 20, 1942, two days after my father wrote his "dearest Ursula," top-ranking members of Hitler's government held a secret meeting in the Berlin suburb of Wannsee. There was only one item on the agenda: the "Final Solution of the Jewish Question." To ensure complete confidentiality, not even a secretary was allowed in the room. One of the participants had to take minutes and type them up. That job fell to Adolf Eichmann.

This convergence of dates—my father's letter and, two days later, the Wannsee Conference—replaced the tender images of my parents in love with iconic images from Nazi history: Germans with arms extended, screaming *Heil*; women holding flowers out to Hitler; men in brown uniforms; men in black uniforms; blond Hitler Youth boys;[1] blonde girls in pigtails from the League of German Girls;[2] people marked with yellow stars; Jews rounded up for deportation; iron gates proclaiming *Arbeit macht frei*; skeletal bodies in camps; mounds of corpses and bodies strewn about like debris. The two sets of images seemed incompatible.

On occasion I had wondered what if my parents had Nazi pasts? What if the scar by my father's left armpit was the trace of an SS tattoo, not the wound he sustained in Russia at the hands of a sniper?[3] But I knew these were idle fantasies. My mother had served her required term in the Reich Labor Service. My father had served in the Wehrmacht when he was drafted. That was all. There was no dreadful secret to uncover. Yet was that all? They had been happy in the midst of terror and fallen in love in the midst of war. She had come of age in Nazi Germany and he had been a Wehrmacht soldier. They had been dutiful citizens who served their country. Under such conditions, what did "innocent" mean?

The meanings of "innocent" and "guilty" shift as the context changes. They carry judgments inflected by their time and place. We remember the Nazi years from the stability of our postwar position, the poet Philip Levine proposes, and "call [our] … time/innocent for lack of a better word." We assign guilt from the same subjective position, Levine continues: "we call/all the Germans the Nazis, because it suits/the vengeance we exact."[4]

There were times when I almost wished I could have said, "My parents were Nazis." Times when this confession would have spelled relief. Perhaps then I could finally reckon with my German past. Perhaps condemning my parents might even redeem me.

I grew up with cultural images of Germans as the bad guys. Eyes of ice and hearts of stone, they barked, *jawohl,* and spoke with harsh, guttural accents. They wore black leather boots, carried whips, and moved their arms and legs like mechanized robots. They weren't just bad, they embodied evil. Good Germans were almost non-existent. On the rare occasions when one appeared, it was an anomaly. But whether good or bad, Germans featured in popular culture were usually outsized: either a Josef Mengele or an Oskar Schindler. They didn't resemble the actual German people I knew.

I never knew how to measure my parents on such an outsize scale. In the grand scheme of things their lives were unexceptional. Yet they lived in exceptional times. And in such times, the measure of a life must be calibrated to fit. From the perspective of their time, their pardon would be *they didn't do anything.* From the perspective of our time, *they didn't do anything* would be their shame. Which of these perspectives did I apply?

That evening in Bonn, as I listened to my father read his wartime letters, the unseemliness of it all overwhelmed me. I had inherited a past shaped by the legacy of Nazi Germany and my parents' story. Yet I couldn't fit them comfortably within one frame.

The Walter and Ursula I encountered in these letters felt like people I didn't know. I was shocked to see my father so devoted to his fatherland, so committed to the country he had vowed to serve. That wasn't the man I knew as my father. It wasn't the father I wanted to have. I wanted to disavow and distance myself from him.

At the same time, these letters moved me. I saw my parents as they had once been: young and tender and hopeful. I saw the dreamer in my father before the cynic pushed him aside. I saw (dare I still call it that?) their innocence. For a moment that evening in Bonn, I saw the people they had dreamed of being. The breach between us vanished and I joined them in their past. In the rush of feelings that flooded over me that evening—love, shame, and a melancholic sense of loss—the moral certainties of postwar Germanness were suspended.

I was touched and unsettled by the nostalgia that crept in, past the censors of my postwar politics. I saw it softening my parents' faces with memories of their youth as they recalled the hopes and dreams of forgotten longing. As I listened to my father's words—*when the war is over ... my beloved Ursel ... I pray*—I found myself wanting for them the very things they had wanted too: an ordinary life they could spend together and a future shared.

A photograph of my parents from early in their relationship has this quality of innocent longing. It has no date, but must be from the summer before or after their engagement. Walter is in a light linen jacket, Ursula in a summer dress with short, puffed sleeves. They are sitting on a low stone wall in a garden. Their bodies are touching. Their hands are clasped. They are not facing us. Only for a moment, as the photographer intrudes with his camera, do they turn in our direction and smile.

From a black and white photograph slowly fading to grey, they look out at me. I look back at them, as if their silent images could tell me what being German had meant in their time.

It is 2004 and I am with my father in Bonn. He is over ninety. My mother has been dead for twenty years. We are talking about the past and I am asking about his wartime letters to Ursula. He suddenly gets up and braces his right arm against the bookcase to secure his balance.

"Do you want your cane?" I ask.

He shakes his head and slowly makes his way to the far end of the bookcase. Holding himself steady with one hand, he leans down and pulls a book from the bottom shelf. The plain black cover has no visible title; the edges and binding look worn. Book in hand, he shuffles back to the couch and sits down next to me. He puts the book on his lap and opens it. It's an old Bible. Taped to the inside cover with ragged strips of yellowed tape is a photograph of a young woman. Dark hair parted in the middle. A shy smile. She looks like a schoolgirl.

"This is the Bible I always carried in my soldier's rucksack," my father tells me. "Everywhere I went, it went too." His voice is soft. He isn't looking at me. It's as if he is speaking to the face in the photograph. "Six years of war and she was always with me. I would look at her face and think, this is the gift that I received from God." He looks up at me and, for a moment, seems startled to see me next to him. It's as if he were expecting someone else.

"This girl, Ursula Bushoff, she was my life."

The picture of my mother that my father carried in his Bible during the war.

Part Three

There Was a Butcher Here, Once

In the world of law ... retribution rules, but ...
in the moral universe ... forgiveness comes out to meet it.

—Walter Benjamin,
"The Meaning of Time in the Moral Universe" (1921)[1]

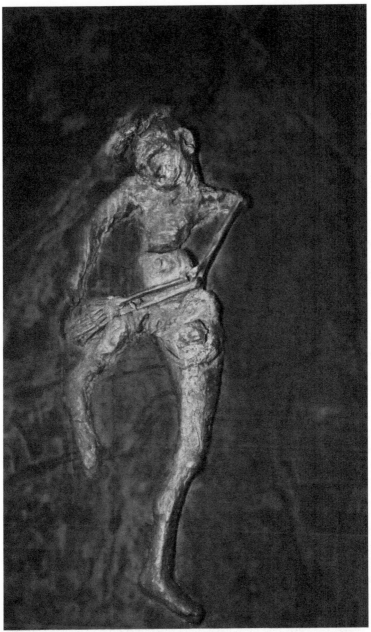

Relief sculpture of a charred female body. Detail from "Hamburg Firestorm" section of Alfred Hrdlicka's "Countermemorial," Hamburg, 1985.[2] (Photograph by author, 2004).

A Longing Called Home

Soon after the war, my father developed a curious habit: he photographed every corner of every room of whatever was home to us at a given moment. It began when we moved to Frankfurt for his first postwar job. He rented a room that served my parents and me as bedroom, living room, dining room, playroom, washroom, and kitchen. It was our first postwar home as a family. My father took pictures of that room from every angle: the bed, the table, the shelf with knick-knacks, the sink and stove, the basket I slept in, the pen I played in, the pictures on the wall. In every new place, he repeated this photographic ritual. The pictures were what he called his "record"—proof that we had made a home for ourselves for the time being.

The photographs were variations on a theme: our living room in Toronto was arranged in much the same way as our living rooms in Bonn or Bilbao. The same things were in the same places they had been in before. Fragments of home were assembled and reassembled in different settings. The objects were familiar, their order predictable. Home was the reassurance of this return.

When we looked through family photo albums, my father loved to discover familiar objects reappearing in new settings. It affirmed continuity through ruptures and linked our present to a family past. "That wooden candlestick came from your grandparents' home in Velen," he might say, pointing to a photograph. "That little aquarelle is your grandfather Bammer as a student in Prague." Even the things that were no longer there were preserved in memory. The massive oak desk with the carved wreaths of oak leaves that a Velen carpenter had made for him after the war didn't make it through the many moves. But there it is, preserved for all time, in a photograph. This repetition of familiar rooms maps the memory of home for me.

On my trip to Czechoslovakia with my father in 1990, I again pondered this relationship between the places we inhabit and the emotional weight of what we call home. As we walked around Rumburg, where my father had spent his childhood and youth, and where his parents lived until their postwar expulsion, I was struck by his sense of roots: the feeling that he came from here and had once been a familiar part of this community. His sense of loss was equally evident. He was no longer of this place. People there no longer knew him.

I was also struck by how differently my experience had shaped my feelings. The sense that I belonged somewhere, that I was of a place and part of a community, had never been more than a longing. As a feeling, it was all but unfamiliar. Wherever I had lived during the years that I grew up always felt provisional. It was my "for-now" home until we moved on. Growing roots always seemed too risky, an unwarranted presumption that I would be allowed to stay.

At the end of our trip, as we sped toward Bonn on the autobahn, I was overcome by a kind of melancholia. As I switched the headlights on and kept my eyes on the road ahead of me, I tried to put my feelings into words. "I've never really felt at home in the sense of belonging somewhere … of being rooted." I was groping for words, trying to understand a difference between my father and me that seemed critical. He had lost something he once had, but still preserved in memory. I had an absence. My loss was a sense of home I never had.

My father's response was swift and cutting. "I didn't know you were so attached to your Germanness," he observed curtly. Then he added, with a touch of sarcasm that silenced me, "I am so sorry that I failed you, Angelika. I suppose I should have been more nationalistic."

"It has nothing to do with nationalism," I wanted to say. But I had lost my hold on words. I no longer knew what I was trying to tell him.

I knew that nostalgia was just a variant of nationalism in his eyes, and that nationalism, as history had shown, was dangerous. I also knew that his citizenship history was fraught. My father had become a German citizen by fiat, not choice, when the Sudeten areas were annexed to Hitler's Germany. But at the end of the war, when the Sudeten areas returned to Czechoslovakia, he couldn't reclaim his former Czechoslovak citizenship. Ethnic Germans lost that right in the postwar settlement. A greater shock was his discovery that he had also lost his German citizenship, despite having served as a German soldier throughout the war. Since Sudeten Germans hadn't been incorporated into the German Reich as full state citizens (*Staatsangehörige*) but merely as members of the Greater German Reich (*Reichsangehörige*), he was officially stateless when that Reich ended. For a brief period after the war, my father was classified as a stateless refugee. When he was finally granted citizenship in the new Germany after the war, he recalled, "It was the second time I was made a German citizen."

In light of this fraught history, I understood his ambivalence toward national identification. Yet the vehemence with which he rejected anything that he construed as nationalism, and the sharpness of his rejoinder to me on our way back to Bonn from Rumburg, made me wonder if there were things he wasn't saying, and perhaps feelings that he couldn't express. There was grief, I sensed, underneath his anger.

Perhaps that day on our way back from the place he had once called home, the feelings of loss we were both experiencing were not that different. Perhaps we both recognized the longing for a sense of home as legitimate and the ways we expressed it just marked a break between our generations. Perhaps his sarcasm expressed a loss he didn't know how to mourn. And my melancholy expressed a never-felt possibility.

Later that fall, on a trip to London, I had an unexpected encounter with my father's way of recreating home. I was visiting the Freud Museum in the north of London on a cold November day. I was one of the only visitors. In the study, which doubled as Freud's treatment room, I was alone.

When Sigmund Freud moved to this light-filled house in the affluent London suburb of Hampstead, he was an 82-year-old refugee from Nazi-ruled Austria.[1] He had left the world he had known all his life: his native country; the city where he had lived since childhood; the neighborhood and house where he had lived with his family and worked for over four decades. The sense of loss must have been overwhelming. Yet when he arrived at 20 Maresfield Gardens in London in September 1938, it was as if the home he had left behind had come with him. His son, Ernst, and housekeeper, Paula Fichtl, had recreated Freud's study and treatment room on Berggasse 19 in Vienna.

The couch where his patients reclined during analysis, the angle of the chair where Freud sat, the objects on his desk and the pictures on his wall— including assorted photographs of family members and admired colleagues— had been placed just as they had been arranged in Vienna. Freud's familiar

"The Destroyed Südring," Coesfeld, 1945. (Photograph by Anton Wallerbusch. Courtesy of Collection Wallerbusch, City of Coesfeld)

Carriageway entrance to the Landsberg property where my grandparents lived in Velen, 1950s.

books—Goethe and Shakespeare, Flaubert and Dostoevsky—had been reassembled. It was as if the past he carried with him as a memory of loss had been recovered and recreated.

Alone in this room that served the ailing Freud as a refuge in exile, I was overcome by tears. I wept for the loss of home that he had suffered. I wept for the millions of people, both in his time and ours, who have been displaced from their homes and lack the means or will to recreate them. And I wept for my father and his family, implicated as Germans in the suffering of their time, yet unable to grieve their own losses.

We mitigate loss by working through grief and preserving memories. Yet as I surveyed Freud's reconstructed study and recalled the sequence of reconstructed rooms from my childhood and youth, I thought that the home we carry with us in memory can be as sustaining as the home we know as a physical place. Perhaps this very mutability is what redeems nostalgia's longing. We are displaced. We lose our homes. We leave our homeland. But in new places, with new people, we transplant our memories and recreate a version of home again.

I have followed my father's tradition of creating home as a collection of reassembled fragments. The Florentine glass paperweight that once sat on my grandparents' windowsill in Velen now sits on my windowsill in Atlanta. It faces east again and glows in the morning light just as I remember it from childhood. When I hold it in my hand, the shock of its heaviness evokes a childhood moment.

I reach for the paperweight. It is smooth and cool to the touch. It is heavy and I know that glass is fragile. If I drop it, it will break. Yet it draws me like a spell. I want to hold it. I want to hold its beauty. I see the light shine through it. I see a miniature world suspended in its depth.

Velen was a place of longing that my family called home. It was a physical place, a place of memory, and a place that we created in our minds.

My mother was born and grew up there. It was the first place my father called home again after the postwar shuffle of lands and peoples made him homeless. It was a web of connections to a community across generations. My mother's baptism and later mine, my parents' wedding and my grandparents' funeral, all took place in Velen. In Velen, I was Ursula Bushoff's daughter, the granddaughter of Hans and Maria Bushoff. I was part of the history of the village.

Yet we never really lived there. We stayed there for limited periods in times of transition: at the end of the war; when we returned from Canada; on breaks from boarding school, when my parents were in Africa. But those were visits. Where we lived was elsewhere. We even spoke a different language. My family spoke High German. Veleners spoke the regional dialect, *Platt*.[2]

We called Velen home, but it didn't feel that way. To a city girl like me, Velen was exotic. The rabbit hutch in the wood shed behind my grandparents' house, the pig sty under the same roof as our neighbor's kitchen, the frogs that spawned in the ditches along the road—these were like scenes from a storybook, while people from the village became characters in my Velen story.

One-legged Herr Kretschmer was a source of curiosity and fascination. He and Frau Brückner ("not his wife," village gossips whispered) lived above the carriage house on the property of the Landsberg estate, where my grandparents had the ground floor of the big house. Herr Kretschmer did odd jobs around the house and kept the grounds. Every Saturday evening, he raked the dirt carriageway from the road to the carriage house. As he hobbled along, the rake helped him keep his balance. But Herr Kretschmer didn't just rake the path to clean it. He turned it into an ephemeral work of art. With the tines of the rake, he made intricate patterns, creating a beautiful border along the entire length of the path. Unlike other Veleners, Herr Kretschmer didn't go to church on Sundays. He was Lutheran, and Velen had only one church: St. Andreas' Catholic church. His weekly ritual of creating something beautiful by raking the path to the house was his form of worship.

On weekday evenings, he and Frau Brückner often sat at their kitchen table, playing cards and getting drunk on Schnapps. In the summer, when their door was open to catch the breeze, I sometimes sat on their kitchen stoop and listened. They joked and drank and slapped the cards on the table. Sometimes they argued. Then they drank some more. Their rough tone and crude words, forbidden in our bourgeois household, were a glimpse into a world I didn't know much about, and their Silesian dialect heightened their aura of foreignness.

Only years later did I realize that Herr Kretschmer and Frau Brückner were no more foreign to Velen than my father when they first arrived. Like him, they came from the far side of Europe, where few Veleners had ever been. Like him, they were ethnic German refugees expelled from the east when Germany lost the war. The same history displaced them and him. My father came to Velen because of Ursula. Herr Kretschmer and Frau Brückner were repatriated there by the governing authorities.[3] When Frau Brückner lost her husband and Herr Kretschmer his wife during their expulsion, the surviving widow and widower decided to start their new life in Velen together.

The Velen I fashioned in my mind was a kind of utopia: a place where food was abundant and nourishing, life simple and work plain, and relationships grounded in community and kinship networks. Not until my grandparents died did I discover that my image of Velen was largely fantasy. It began with their house. The stately manor with the carriage house and spacious grounds, the towering blue firs and winding driveway lined with rhododendron— none of this belonged to them. Neither did the antique furniture, the large oil paintings on the walls—the Flemish still lives and portraits of noblemen—or even many of the precious objects displayed in their living room. They were the property of the Duke of Landsberg, on loan to my grandfather while he worked for the Landsberg estate.

Even my parents were surprised at the discrepancy between our imagined and the real-world Velen. The ledgers they found after my grandfather's death told a story of financial troubles that he had kept hidden. In the straitened economy of the postwar decades, the Duke of Landsberg had provided housing, but never adequately raised my grandfather's pay. So despite living frugally and working hard, my grandparents could not make ends meet. There were multiple receipts for borrowed money in their household records. Behind the façade of their manor-style living, it turned out that my grandparents were poor. The weekends of feasting we had taken for granted—the pork roasts, brandy puddings, and buttercream tortes—had come at a cost to them. After we left, we learned, they lived on lentils and potatoes and had meat just as a treat on Sundays.

Reality disturbed our Velen idyll. When the main thoroughfare through town was widened and a small supermarket replaced the family-owned convenience store where I got fresh rolls and Gouda cheese for Sunday breakfasts and the owner knew every customer by name, my parents were incensed. This wasn't Velen, they insisted, this modern business. Velen should remain untouched. They wanted it to be a refuge from history, not a site of history itself.

But as I grew up, the fantasy of a refuge from history lost its appeal for me. I no longer found it comforting. I found it threatening. Ghosts of the past lurked in the shadows and could emerge at any time. I had tried to shed them by leaving Germany, but they followed me. I couldn't escape them.

Now my parents were both dead and I had my own home and family. Instead of fleeing the ghosts of the past, I preferred to face them. There was no better place than Velen, where my life started.

I made plans to visit.

Memories of War

When my grandparents were still alive or on the few occasions, after their death, when I visited Velen, it always felt like a coming home, a return to a place of nostalgic memories. My trip in the summer of 2005 was different. I left nostalgia behind. I didn't want to see Velen through a personal or family lens. I wanted to see it in the light of history. I started in Münster with an old family friend from Velen.

As the train from Bonn passed through rural Westphalia, I thrilled to the familiar landscape of my early childhood. Lush green meadows were dotted with grazing dairy cows, picture-book perfect with their black and white spots. Small stands of oak trees or low-hanging willows offered shelter. Ripe grain fields alternated with pastureland in a checkerboard pattern. Sprawling farmsteads, with their solid brick buildings and steep tile roofs, set ruddy accents in a landscape of greens, browns, and yellows. They bespoke prosperity and pride of ownership. Many farms announced the date of their founding on a beam above the entrance threshold. They were built to last, to be passed along through generations. Everything looked orderly and cared for. It was a landscape that felt well loved. I recalled my mother, on walks, trying to teach me how to identify different grains—how to distinguish wheat from rye from barley—by the shape of the ears and their color.

My friend, Anna, was at the train station to meet me. Since I last saw her, her hair had turned white. She was in her seventies now, but her embrace, when she greeted me, was as strong as ever.

When we first met, I was twelve and Anna in her twenties. It was 1958 and my family had just returned to Germany after seven years abroad. While the government housing we had been promised in Bonn was still under construction, we lived in my grandparents' Velen house. Anna lived close by with her mother, grandfather, and an elderly aunt, and worked part time for my grandparents as a housekeeper. The job provided her with income, yet still allowed her to help run the household that she and her mother shared. For years this was the rhythm of Anna's life: two households, two gardens, two sets of elderly people to care for. After my grandmother's death, Anna became my grandfather's caretaker. She nursed him when he fell ill and was at his bedside when he died.

A year later, Anna met a widower with two children in Münster. When they married, she moved to be with him, and when her mother became infirm, Anna brought her to live with them in Münster. Since our last time together, both Anna's husband and mother had died, and she was living alone in the house with her stepson, Martin.

We took the bus out to the suburb where Anna and Martin lived. On our way, Anna linked her arm in mine and stroked my hand. "It's so nice to have you here," she said. The Westphalian accent, the restraint of her evident pleasure, the way her body felt next to mine, evoked such a physical memory of my mother that my voice caught.

I squeezed her arm and smiled. Our familiarity didn't depend on words. Over the lifetime we had known each other we had become family. But more importantly, Anna had been there for me when my own family couldn't offer reassurance. When we moved from Canada, where I had lived for the past seven years, to a Germany that I had left as a five-year-old, I was a confused adolescent. This place was supposed to be home to me, but it felt foreign. My mother was distracted; she had her own adjustments to a new life in yet another new city, Bonn, and a baby, my younger brother, to take care of. My father had rented a room in Bonn, where he had started his new job at the Foreign Ministry. The house we were going to live in wasn't built yet. I didn't know where I belonged. In the midst of this uncertainty, Anna helped me learn to feel at home.

We arrived in Velen in the middle of the school year, and the closest secondary school was in Coesfeld, a forty-minute train ride away. It was my first experience of German school. School got out at midday so that children could be home for the midday meal, but by the time I got back to Velen, it was early afternoon and mealtime was long since over. The house was still. Everyone was resting. Only Anna was up. She was waiting for me in the kitchen, cleaning up. She had put a lunch for me aside in the warming oven, covered with a plate so it wouldn't dry out. I sat at the kitchen table, eating the food she had made for me, telling her about school and my day in Coesfeld. While I talked, Anna washed the dishes, hung the dish towels on the rack to dry, and mopped the stone tiles with hot, soapy water.

There was no place I felt happier than in that kitchen. The smells of lye soap, boiled fish and potatoes, the scent of pine from the woods next to the house, the clatter of dishes and the swish of the mop, Anna's laughter in response to my stories—this was my first sense of what home in Germany might feel like.

Through the years, we had stayed in touch. Phone calls, letters, and occasional visits kept us connected. But I had come with a different purpose this time. Instead of talking about our present lives, as we usually did, I wanted to talk about the past. Armed with a notebook and a set of questions, I had come to ask her about the war and Nazi years in Velen.

When we got to her place, we walked through her small back yard. Anna showed me flowers and shrubs she had transplanted from Velen. A low hedge of boxwood bordered the path. I crushed one of the leaves between my fingers and inhaled the scent. It invoked a memory of my grandparent's yard in Velen. Anna got out two lawn chairs.

"Tell me about Velen during the war," I asked her after we had settled in. The first thing she told me was so strange that I started laughing.

"You remember the Hochmoor?" she asked, and I nodded, picturing the vast moorland terrain that stretched for miles between Velen and Coesfeld.

"Well," Anna went on, "they built a fake airport out there. Cleared away brush to make it look like runways and made dummy airplanes out of plywood and papier-mâché. They were perfect replicas, down to the swastikas painted on their tails. When they were finished, they were placed as decoys and camouflaged with brush and moorland grasses."

"The plan was to divert enemy bombers from the village," Anna continued. "For a while it worked. They actually bombed the papier-mâché airplanes. Twice! Then they figured out our ruse and moved on to more suitable targets."

We were silent for a while. Anna glanced at me. My initial laughter at the absurd tactics people try in war had faded. "It got real very quickly," she went on. "One day, it must have been around 1941 or '42, a British airplane was shot down right over the village … I was there." She fell silent again and I waited.

"The pilot parachuted out, but got tangled up in a tree. He hung there, like a rag doll, the cords of his parachute dangling. Occasionally, an arm or a leg would move. Like a leaf shifting in the breeze … you could barely see it."

I took a deep breath. The scent of boxwood from Anna's hedge was still on my fingers. Suddenly, Anna got up and went inside. She returned a few minutes later with an illustrated book on Velen history. She thumbed through it, searching for something. "Here," she finally said, her finger on a large, slightly blurry photograph of a towering crucifix in a grove of trees. *Am Großen Kreuz*, the caption said. By the Great Crucifix.

"Here," she said again. "This is where it was. At the crossroads, by the Great Crucifix. That's where he hung. Up in that tree, tied up in his parachute. He hung there until he died." The people of Velen, including nine-year-old Anna and her friends, stood and watched him.

I realized that Anna had stopped talking and looked over at her. Her hands were clasped, resting on the book. She was crying. I stared at the photograph of the crucifix and the grove of trees and imagined the dying man in the tree with the crowd beneath him. Were they silent, I wondered, as one is when death comes? Were they spectators or were they witnesses? Did the man dying in the tree remind them of the man dying on the cross right next to him? His death, too, was a spectacle to the people watching.

In the Biblical version of Christ's death, as recounted by his disciple, Matthew, some of the onlookers, moved by his suffering, felt pity. One of them, Matthew reports, "ran and got a sponge, filled it with sour wine, put it on a stick, and gave it to him to drink."[1] Were the good people of Velen, most of them raised on the story of Jesus' suffering and death, stirred by compassion too? Did any of them try to ease the dying man's torment? Or was he not a man to them, just an enemy?

Anna closed the book. She gazed out across her garden and, for a while, neither of us spoke. Day shaded into twilight. When she spoke again, I could barely hear her.

"One of the men even tugged at the parachute cords to increase his torment."

Later that evening we sat in Anna's living room, catching up on our present lives, and I realized that I hardly knew anything about her youth and childhood. This was the first time that I ever directly asked her.

"Tell me about when you were young."

The story she told was framed by the experience of war. In 1939, when World War II began with Germany's invasion of Poland, Anna was seven years old. By the time the war ended, she was an adolescent. "I'll always remember the day that war broke out," she started. "It was a festive day. I was a flower girl at my uncle's wedding and scattered petals down the aisle to the altar. *Engelchen*, they called us, little angels."

Her father, Bernhard Jägering, was a carpenter from a long line of carpenters. He was apprenticed in his father's shop and became a master carpenter who specialized in fine furniture. His masterpiece at the end of his apprenticeship was a dining room table and chairs. When war broke out, he was initially exempted from the draft, as carpenters were urgently needed on the home front. He stayed in Velen, doing his work and taking care of his family—his wife, two daughters, widowed father, and maiden aunt. However, his carpentry business soon started to have problems. Hardeweg and Röttger, the other two carpentry businesses in Velen, were getting the big jobs and official contracts.

"Both Herr Hardeweg and Herr Röttger were active members of the Nazi Party," Anna explained. "Herr Hardeweg was even *Ortsgruppenleiter*, local Party chair."

Bernhard Jägering's wife begged him to join the Party too. "To protect your family and yourself," she implored; but he refused on principle. "Those people are up to no good."

Retribution was swift and pitiless. His military exemption was lifted and the forty-year-old carpenter was conscripted into the Wehrmacht. It was the summer of 1941, Operation Barbarossa was underway, and he was deployed to the Eastern Front as a simple private, one of some 3 million German soldiers sent to acquire additional *Lebensraum* for the German people. However, things didn't go as planned. Instead of defeating the Soviet Army, the German army was beaten back by fierce resistance and the wrath of a Russian winter. By early December, it was clear that Operation Barbarossa had been a catastrophic failure.

Yet in his letters home, Bernhard Jägering tried to sound reassuring and make his daughters laugh. "We are doing military exercises in the snow," he wrote, adding a picture of himself spread-eagled on the ground in a field of snow, both arms extended. He is in uniform, his cap askew and his thick, woolen jacket tightly buttoned. "I couldn't stop looking at that picture," Anna remembered. "It was like he was looking right at me, laughing. I imagined him far off in Russia, making snow angels like me and my sister."

"After he left to go to war, I only saw him three more times," she resumed her story. "And the last time was so brief it barely counted. I remember my grandfather saying, *Just one day ... just one single, bloody day. They sent him home for just one day to say goodbye to us.*"

In the grip of her memory, Anna didn't realize she had switched to *Platt*, the language her grandfather always used at home with his family. Catching herself, she went back to standard German, but without translating what she had just said to me. "You understood that, didn't you?" she asked me. Her tight, thin voice begged me to spare her having to repeat the words.

"Yes," I nodded, "I understood you." I hadn't caught all the words, but I got the meaning.

Anna nodded too. "My Opa was sure he would never see his son alive again. He was right. He didn't. Neither did I. That was the last time that I saw my father."

They continued to get postcards, first from Russia and then from Poland. He was now stationed in Warsaw, Bernhard Jägering wrote, assigned to patrol duty along the borders of the Jewish ghetto. But when the Wehrmacht set up a carpentry shop, he was transferred there. His skills were needed and he was happy with his new assignment. "You can stop worrying now," he wrote his family on a postcard of historic Warsaw. "I am out of the danger zone. I no longer have to patrol the ghetto borders. We even sleep here in the workshop. For now, this is where I am living."

Then the ghetto erupted in armed rebellion, Anna continued, and the carpentry workshop was attacked. "August 1944," Anna recounted. "That date is seared into my memory. That's when my father died. On the day of the Warsaw Ghetto Uprising."

What happened to Anna's father was never solved. No report on how or when he died ever reached his family. Only months later did they hear from one of his surviving comrades that Bernhard Jägering had been gravely wounded in the attack. But there was no body to bury, no death certificate, no official closure. There were only memories and the fading hope that he might still be alive.

"The dead bodies were loaded on a truck and dumped into the craters made by the bombs." Anna was repeating the account she had heard as a girl from her father's comrade when he came to Velen to bring the Jägering family the news. Her voice sounded strange and I looked over at her. Was something wrong?

What I saw is hard to explain, much less rationalize, but it's what I witnessed. For a brief and startling moment, the years seemed to fall away and I saw the girl that she had been sixty years earlier. She was sitting on the couch, legs dangling, hands folded in her lap. Her face was smooth and unlined, her hair was brown, and the expression on her face was puzzled. She was hearing the words she was repeating to me, but she didn't seem to understand them. Not then and not now, sixty years later. There were no tears then and there are no tears now. There is no comprehension. Just the infinite puzzlement of love and loss.

For a while, we simply sat in silence. It was as if we had lost our hold on language. Like astronauts whose link to the mother ship has come undone, who are drifting into the infinite universe, we were adrift in the past, lost in a time warp of incomprehension.

Vague memories of what I knew about the Warsaw Ghetto and its fatal end floated through my mind. Around 56,000 Jews were said to have perished in the Ghetto Uprising. And while the exact number of dead remains disputed and will never be known, what we know is that the German occupation effectively extinguished Jewish life in Warsaw.

As I thought about the ghetto, I wondered what was going through Anna's mind. Perhaps she was searching for her father in distant memories. He loved *Schützenfest*, the annual marksmanship contest in Velen, she had once told me. And he couldn't stand being tickled. What else did she recall? What had her relationship to her father been like? When I asked her, she glanced at me as if this were a strange question to be asking.

"We all had our roles," she finally offered. It was a working-class life. Her father was at work by six, had breakfast at nine with his apprentices, and—with the exception of a break for the midday meal at home—spent his days in the workshop. Evenings were short and taken up with tasks, and everyone went to bed early. "Relationship" was not a word they used.

The next morning, I was driving to Velen and Anna decided to come along. "You can drive slowly," she suggested. "We can take our time." It was a warm and hazy June day and we left the windows open. We didn't talk much. We were content to enjoy the familiar countryside we both loved.

Wisps of fog were still drifting across the meadows, transforming bushes and grazing cows into phantom creatures. I thought of how people in this part of Westphalia were often referred to as *Spökenkieker*, people who see ghosts. In the low-lying marshland, barely above sea level in some areas, where things were shrouded in mist and fog, you couldn't tell real from unreal and your imagination conjured spirits from the elements. As a child, I loved to hear my mother recite some of the spooky ballads she had learned. Annette von Droste-Hülshoff's "The Boy on the Moor" was always my favorite. "*O, schaurig*," my mother would start, in a theatrical whisper,

> *O schaurig ist's übers Moor zu gehn,*
> *Wenn ...*
> *Sich wie Phantome die Dünste drehn ...*
> (How dreadful it is to go over the moor
> When ...
> mists are whirling like phantoms).[2]

As I listened, my heart pounding, I became the child in the poem, heading home across the moor at twilight. I felt the terror each time anew, as the ghosts of the dead and damned reached out to claim me, and each time anew I was relieved to know they were just phantoms. The feverish boy had fashioned ghosts out of whirling fog. I was safe at home with my mother.

Closer to Velen, foggy phantoms gave way to the sounds and smells of workaday farm life. A wagonload of sugar beet emitted the sickly odor of fruit beginning to ferment. A slow-moving spreader sprayed liquid manure across a freshly ploughed field and the loamy smell of earth mixed with the acrid stench of fecal matter. The sour smell of milk spills from the dairy at the edge of town told us that we had reached Velen.

I parked the car and we started our Velen day with a late breakfast at our favorite bakery. Over a second coffee, Anna picked up the story of her father's death that she had left unfinished the previous evening. After the news from Warsaw, she began, her father was presumed dead, but her mother, who still clung to the hope that her husband would return, was not officially a widow. Officially, Bernhard Jägering was just "missing," not dead. But with his status unresolved, his wife didn't qualify for a widow's pension and the family's situation grew increasingly precarious. Income from the carpentry shop had stopped when her husband was drafted, and now his soldier's pay had stopped as well. They were running out of money. Yet only when she wasn't able to pay the mortgage and risked losing her home did Frau Jägering face the bitter truth that her husband would not return and she was now responsible for the family: her daughters, her father-in-law, and her aunt. Declaring her husband dead was her only option.

It was the hardest thing she ever did, she later confided to Anna. "As long as I live," she vowed, "I will never drag myself up those stairs to the Velen town hall again." She kept her word. Decades later, when she sold her house and moved to Münster to live with Anna, she made her daughter walk up to the registrar to file the papers, while she waited at the foot of the stairs.

After our late breakfast, Anna and I decided to go for a walk. I asked her about daily life in the village during wartime. People didn't go hungry, she began. Not like in cities. Everyone had a garden and there was abundant livestock. Officially, meat was rationed. Every cow, pig, sheep, and goat had to be registered and you couldn't slaughter without prior permission. But, she shrugged, there were always ways. A pig would be slaughtered at night in the basement, and by morning all traces had disappeared. During an air raid, a cow would be injured in the field and immediately "emergency" slaughtered. People were inventive, Anna laughed. "Bed rice" was such an invention. When cooking fuel was rationed, you cooked rice in bed. In the morning, when your bed was still warm, you put rice in a pot of hot water in an insulated box. You set the box in the bed under the covers, piled on blankets, and by evening, the rice was done.

You adjusted. You made do. You improvised. Everyday life continued. Even so, Anna admitted, eventually everything and everyone was affected. A thirteen-year-old girl died from a simple cut on her lip. It got infected and she needed penicillin, but penicillin had been reserved for combat troops. Toward the end, no one could escape the grip of war. Old men and boys still in puberty were mobilized in the so-called *Volkssturm*, the people's militia.

"The irony," Anna recalled, "was that after the war, some of those same boys and men were arrested and charged with complicity. I saw our neighbor, a man in his sixties, dragged from his home in handcuffs."[3]

As we headed down a path next to my grandparents' former home, Anna asked if I knew about the one-man holes, the *Einmannlöcher*.

"Tell me." I was intrigued.

"It was toward the very end of the war," Anna recounted. "Only women, children, and old men were left. Schools were closed so we could 'support the war effort.' One day all of us school age children were told to go out to the roads leading into town and dig deep holes. We were to space them between the trees that lined the roads on either side. Each hole had to be big enough to hold a person."

I looked at the earth by the side of the road—hard-packed dirt reinforced with gravel—and tried to picture this operation. "Not just holes," Anna continued. "They had to be a certain shape: squared off on the sides so they wouldn't cave in."

"What on earth were they for?" I pictured the children of Velen, armed with man-sized shovels and spades, hacking and scraping and digging.

"Bomb shelters," Anna answered. "One man per hole. Roads were a primary target. If you saw an enemy plane, you could hide in the closest one-man hole." In the waning weeks of the war, she explained, between late February and early April 1945, five Veleners were killed in air raids or by strafing fighters.

With the toe of my boot, I pried a small clod of compacted earth from the side of the road. It was hard and solid and gritty.

We walked on for a while in silence. The stories of one-man holes had revived childhood memories of air raids for Anna. When she spoke again it was about that experience. "As soon as the siren howled, my mother took off with my sister. They were probably the first to arrive in the air raid shelter."

"And you?"

"I had to do things first. We had a woman and three little boys in our upstairs room. Women and children were evacuated to the countryside when the cities were bombed, and we had been assigned this family from Essen. My job was to help get the children down to the shelter." Anna paused. "They always seemed to come at night, the air raids. The boys were dazed with sleep when I rushed to wake them. When I tried to get them up, they pushed me away and cried for their mother. I'd have to drag them out of bed, and pull and carry them down the stairs, while they hung on me, like human sandbags. I wanted to just leave them there and save myself. But I couldn't do that. I had to get the boys to safety first."

As we walked, Anna had linked arms with me. Arm in arm like this, I was struck by her childlike size. Even in heels, she was under five feet and slight of build. She often shopped for clothes in the children's department. Both of her parents had been slight and small too. We walked for a while without talking. Suddenly, I heard her murmur into the silence, "I was just twelve years old." It wasn't me she seemed to be addressing. These seemed like words left unspoken in the past meant for her mother.

After a while, she resumed her story.

After I got the boys off, I had to go back and get my aunt Anna. She was old, her eyes were bad, and she had trouble walking. I took her arm and we stumbled off. You couldn't see where you were going ... all the lights were out because of the air raid. It was completely dark. There was just the sound of the sirens—that terrible, howling wail—and Aunt Anna gripping my arm so tight it hurt me. I saw the outlines of airplanes passing overhead and the crisscross beams of the air defense. I heard the drone of the airplane engines and the whine of the bombs and, right by my ear, Aunt Anna moaning. Any minute, I thought, a bomb will fall ... it will fall right on top of the two of us and I will be dead before I get to the shelter where my mother and sister are already safe.

I didn't know what to say. Anna stopped and looked at me. "I think my sister was my mother's favorite." Her voice carried no emotion. It was low and colorless and flat.

By then, we had reached the outskirts of Velen. Our path ended where fenced-in pastureland began. As we headed back toward town, Anna turned to other wartime memories.

"Every day of the war, we went to mass early in the morning. It was often still dark. But in the church, there were always people. Every day, I prayed for my father, asking God just to bring him back. Every day, the same prayer. Instead, we kept getting news of yet another death. There wasn't a family in Velen that remained untouched."

Even now, decades after the war, Anna's eyes still redden and swell at the memory. "Some families lost two, three ... even as many as four, sons. The Holzstegges, for example. You remember the Holzstegges? They made the *Klumpen*, the wooden clogs, that we all wore." Anna glanced at my leather clogs, the city version of *Klumpen*.

When you were little, you wore them yourself ... Well, none of the Holzstegges boys came home from the war. Every one of them died. The same with the Funkes. All of their sons died in the war too. Only the youngest survived. He stayed home to help run the farm, but after the war he wanted to devote his life to helping others and joined the priesthood.

He left Velen to work with peasants in South America. There was no one left to work the farm, so it was sold and the Funke family ended.

At the close of this day steeped in memories of war, I felt the need for some time alone. I decided to stop in at St. Andreas'. The doors were unlocked. The smell of candle wax, flowers, and incense welcomed me. I glanced around. The pews were empty. I was alone. I walked down the right-hand aisle, which in my childhood had been the women's side; the men sat on the left. I walked up the center aisle, where Anna had scattered petals at her uncle's wedding, a little angel on the first day of war. Then I walked down the left aisle, past the Stations of the Cross that traced the path of Jesus' torment and dying.

When my eyes had adjusted to the dappled light that filtered through the stained-glass windows, I returned to look more closely at a display near the front entrance. At the base of a life-size statue of the Pietà, a heavy oak case with a thick glass cover rested on a pedestal. Inside the case was a large ceremonial book that was opened to a list of names. By the light of the candles at the foot of the Pietà, I scanned the entries. They seemed to be in no particular order, just grouped under the heading "June."

Alfred Veit, missing since June 14, 1944 in Russia
Josef Klocke, died June 5, 1940 in France
Alois Rudde, missing since June 6, 1944 in Russia
Josef Goßling, missing since June 22, 1944 in Russia
Hubert Wolfert, died of the effects of war, June 21, 1950 in Wimbern
Fritz Eßling, fallen June 21, 1944 in Russia

In the month of June, through the duration of World War II, fourteen Velen men had died or gone missing. When I finished reading the entries for June, I carefully raised the heavy glass lid and turned to the next month. The list for July was shorter: just twelve names. Twenty in August, seventeen in September, sixteen in October, and fourteen in November. The winter months brought the heaviest losses: twenty-three in December, twenty-nine in January, twenty-seven in February, and twenty-three in March. The spring months—April, with twelve deaths, and May, with nine—were significantly lighter.

When I had read all the entries by month, I went over the list of names again, starting at the beginning by year. As the war progressed, the casualties mounted steadily. They began with four in 1940 and increased to ten the following year. In 1942, it was twenty-five, thirty-four in 1943, and in 1944 it went as high as sixty. The last few months were by far the most deadly; the war was lost, but the fighting slogged on. And the casualties didn't end with the end of the war: wounded soldiers succumbed to their

Honor Book (*Ehrenbuch*) in Velen's Catholic Church remembering the Velen men who died in both world wars. Dedicated November 1961 by the local affiliate of the Association of Returnees (*Heimkehrer*), here it is opened to the first December page. (Photograph by author, 2005)

injuries, prisoners of war were reported dead, and civilians were killed by land mines. The last World War II death recorded in Velen was in 1956, when a landmine left by the Wehrmacht exploded.

Kept in permanent twilight, occasional candlelight flickering across the page, this book was a memorial to the war dead.[4] It remembered the men who perished in the two world wars that Veleners know as the "World War" (*Weltkrieg*) and the "Hitler War" (*Hitlerkrieg*). They were killed in combat on war fronts all across Europe; they died "of the effects of war," from war-related injuries or illnesses; they died as prisoners of war. Some were just reported missing, their bodies never found.

The dates and places where they died were a virtual atlas of twentieth-century history. They mapped a geography of death, where men from towns and villages across Westphalia went to kill and be killed. They went west to Holland, Belgium, Luxemburg, France, and Italy. They went north to Denmark, Norway, Finland, Latvia, and Estonia. They went to Africa and to New Guinea. Most of them, like Anna's father, went east: to Czechoslovakia, Hungary, Romania, Poland, and Russia.

Above all, they went to Russia. Since the late eighteenth century, when Westphalia was part of Napoleon's vast empire, Westphalian men had been sent to fight in Russia. In Hitler's empire, they were sent there again. Of the twenty-five soldiers from Velen killed in 1942, twenty-three were killed in Russia. In 1943, it was twenty-eight out of thirty-four.

Most of them would have been men who either worked the land or had learned a trade—electricians, carpenters, machinists, tool and die makers. Many, if not most, of them had never traveled farther than the regional capital, Münster. Now they were traveling across the world to places they had never heard of.

What, I wondered, did this journey portend for them? It must have included apprehension, even dread. After all, this was wartime. But perhaps it also carried an element of excitement, the promise of a world beyond what they already knew. Was war an adventure they welcomed? Or did they just go as soldiers sent to either kill or die?

In the Velen inn, where I had booked a room for that night, I asked the woman cleaning the rooms where she came from. "You've heard of Kosovo?" she replied in broken German. "There was a war ..."

"Yes, I know," I said. "That war is how I learned about Kosovo."

"It's how I came to Velen," she said. "I am here because of that war."

Wars change the shape and scope of the worlds we live in. They can take us to places we hadn't even known existed. Sometimes we die there. Sometimes, in that new place, our life resumes.

But the men remembered in the book of the war dead didn't just die as individuals. They died as members of their families and their communities.

As I reviewed the names, I recalled Anna's account of Velen families who had lost all their men to war, and the family farms that were left abandoned when the men were gone. Against the backdrop of a global war with casualties in the millions, a casualty count of 184 might seem small. Yet in a village of Velen's size, in which no more than 250 men would have been of military age at a given time, the impact on the community was enormous.[5] Few families were left untouched. Eighteen families each lost two men; five families lost three; and three families registered four men dead. One family lost a staggering seven men to the war: six in combat and one in an air raid.

A 1931 photograph of Velen's combined third and fourth grade class provides yet another perspective. Forty-eight children between nine and ten years old sit in their pews, eyes on the camera, hands folded on their desks. The girls wear sweaters under their aprons; the boys wear their jackets buttoned up. Before the war was over, every sixth child in that photograph was dead.

Before I left the church, I lit two candles: one for the dead in the memorial book and one in memory of my parents. The war that brought my parents together and enabled my own life was the same war that took these other lives away. As the light outside the church darkened, I watched the candles burn.

For the remainder of the evening, the war dead were on my mind. I thought of where and how they died, in places far from home, for a cause that many of them weren't sure of or no longer believed in, and often never had. But as I reviewed the names in the memorial book, I realized that something critical was missing: the memory of Velen's Jews. How did they fit into this picture of wartime losses? Were they part of the war story or was theirs a separate story? I determined to ask Anna what she knew of their fate.

That night I dreamed of death and men in war.

A man lay stretched out on the ground, his arms and legs splayed wide. He seemed to be laughing, but could have been screaming. There was no sound. The ground was white. It looked like snow. He was a snow angel in a Wehrmacht uniform.

Then the ground and his aspect changed. He was lying in a pool of blood and no longer wearing a uniform. He was in civilian clothes now: suit jacket, shirt, and tie. His head was bare, his dark hair matted, his eyes open in a sightless stare. His neck had been twisted sideways.

Then the scene changed again. The body was gone, and where it had lain, spread-eagled on the sidewalk, I saw a massive, shattered slab of stone.

I awoke with a shock of recognition. I had seen this stone before. It was a memorial I had seen in Warsaw.

Weeks later, when I was back in Atlanta, I went through my notes and files to refresh my memory. It didn't take me long to find the scene from my dream. It was a memorial in the heart of Warsaw to Szmul Zygielbojm. He had been a member of the Bund, the independent Jewish Socialist Party in Poland, and he was the Bund's representative to the London-based Polish parliament in exile in the 1940s.[6] As he reported, with growing alarm, on the unfolding genocide that he was witnessing—not only were Jews being murdered, European Jewry was being destroyed—his despair that the world wasn't acting to stop it was growing too.

On May 12, 1943, Zygielbojm learned that his wife and son had been deported and that the final liquidation of the Warsaw Ghetto was underway. With this news, he lost all remaining hope. If the people he loved and the culture he cherished was to be destroyed, Zygielbojm didn't want to live. He chose to share the fate of his family, his comrades in the Warsaw Ghetto, and his fellow Jews. Jumping to his death from an upper story window, he committed suicide. Words from the letter he left behind, addressed "to the governments and peoples ... and to the conscience of the world," are inscribed at the base of his memorial. "I cannot remain silent," he wrote, "nor can I remain alive while the last remnants of the Jewish people perish in Poland." Choosing death was his last act, his final resistance. "By my death," he declared, "I wish to make the strongest possible protest against the passivity with which the world is looking on."

As I registered the date of Szmul Zygielbojm's death, four days before the Warsaw Ghetto was razed and its people massacred, Anna's description of her father's death came back to me. "August 1944," she had said. "That's when my father died. The day of the Warsaw Ghetto Uprising."

With a start, I realized that Anna had misremembered her father's death. Her account was wrong. The Warsaw Ghetto Uprising didn't happen in August 1944. It happened a year earlier, in 1943. It began on April 19, the first day of Passover, and lasted until May 16, when the Wehrmacht declared victory.

The date that Anna claimed was "seared" into her memory was off by a year. She had either got one of the dates wrong—her father's death or the Warsaw Ghetto Uprising—or she had wrongly conflated the two. Either way, I wondered, how could I explain her error?

As I searched for a plausible answer, another event came to mind that suggested a partial explanation. In August 1944, there had indeed been an uprising in Warsaw, separate and distinct from the Jewish Ghetto Uprising the previous year. The 1944 Warsaw Uprising was an armed rebellion of the Polish underground against the German occupation. It began on August 1 and ended on October 2, when Polish Home Army forces finally surrendered.[7] This must have been the uprising that Anna associated with the date of her father's death. So why had she insisted that his death coincided with the Uprising in the Warsaw Ghetto?

It could have been a simple error: "Warsaw Ghetto Uprising" instead of "Warsaw Uprising." Sometimes a word added or subtracted is just a word. Yet the words we add or subtract, deliberately or unconsciously, can contain meanings that we hadn't intended. Perhaps meanings we didn't even know we meant.

But Anna's misalignment of events and dates offered yet another, more consequential, explanation. It allowed her to free her father's memory from guilt for German crimes in Poland. If Bernhard Jägering was killed in 1943, when Anna said the carpentry shop was attacked during the Warsaw Ghetto Uprising, he would have died as a simple carpenter at work in his shop, not as a participant in a genocidal massacre. Instead of being identified as a perpetrator in one of the most heinous acts of this war—the destruction of the Warsaw Ghetto and its inhabitants—he could be cast as a victim of a war that he himself had unwillingly been forced into.

But if he was killed a year later, in August 1944, at the time of the Warsaw Uprising, his death would hold a different meaning. By that time, he would have lived through the events of the preceding year: the death and deportation of tens of thousands of Warsaw Jews and the annihilation of the Warsaw Ghetto.[8] Not only would he have lived through these events, he would have participated in them as a Wehrmacht soldier. His death would inevitably be tainted by guilt for crimes that he had by then been part of.

The next time I was in Velen, I checked the memorial book in St. Andreas' church. Anna had correctly remembered the date and place of her father's death. The record confirmed that Bernhard Jägering was considered "missing since August 14, 1944 in Warsaw." What Anna had changed—no doubt, unconsciously—was the context. Perhaps she protected herself from a truth that would be too painful to live with otherwise. Perhaps, by adjusting the context of his death, she could salvage the memory of the father she had known and loved before war made him a soldier: a man who worked with his hands, who smelled of freshly planed wood, who made things that were beautiful and useful. Perhaps Anna's misremembering was not a mistake at all, but a daughter's memorial to her father.

Discussing the relative epistemological weight of memory and imagination, Aristotle assigned them to different temporal spheres. Memory, he declared, belonged to the realm of the past, imagination to the realm of the future. We can summon the past; it can literally be re-called. But we can't re-call the future; it is yet to come.[9] We can just evoke it, call it forth, through imagination.

Yet, as the psychology and neuroscience of memory have amply shown, the boundaries between memory and imagination are permeable. We can cross them without even knowing it. We can even inhabit both realms at once. Moreover, our capacity for memory contains a paradox: we can remember something that we didn't experience physically, but only know from our imagination. Sometimes, psychoanalysts Françoise Davoine and Jean-Max

Gaudillière explain, this "human ability to produce living paradoxes" can be a way of coping with a painful dilemma: there are things we can't bear to remember even as they are impossible to forget.[10]

I am awed by the power of memory to protect us from what we know. Memory is not accountable to factual evidence. It adjusts facts to emotional truths. We know that terrors lurk in the shadows of the past, so we learn to tread lightly. We shroud ourselves in forgetting. We erect walls and map safe passage through the danger zones. And when our fear is so great that we can't go on, we sometimes close our eyes and let the guardians of our unconscious guide us.

The last time I saw Anna was a year before her death. It was 2013 and I had come to Münster to see her. She was weak and suffering from debilitating joint and muscle pain. To get around, she had to use a wheelchair.

It was the first time she didn't come to greet me when I rang the bell. A much younger, dark-haired woman opened the door for me. She smiled and introduced herself as Anna. "Anna from Poland," she explained with a laugh, acknowledging the curious coincidence of the doubled Annas. My Anna, "German Anna," as we jokingly renamed her for now, could no longer live without assistance. A woman from Poland had been hired to take care of her. At first, my Anna later confessed to me, she had resisted the idea. She had always thought of Polish people as the enemy—they had killed her father. But she needed help and this Polish woman offered it. A relationship of convenience started and soon a friendship had taken shape.

When my Anna heard me at the door, she called her greeting from the living room and I went to hug her. She was sitting on the couch, two fat pillows propping up her back, and a blanket keeping her legs warm. I sat next to her, while Polish Anna made coffee in the kitchen.

I had brought pictures of my children to show her and we got out pictures of Anna's family, present and past. Soon the three of us—the two Annas and I—were sitting on the couch together, going through photographs. There is Anna in 1938, thick, curly hair barely tamed into two fat braids, sitting for her official first-day-of-school photograph. There she is again with her pet lamb. She smiles at the camera, while the lamb butts its head against her thigh. And there she is at her First Communion, her head crowned with a white rose garland and a small gold crucifix around her neck. "Easter 1940," the caption reads. The following year Anna's father was drafted into the Wehrmacht and sent to war.

"What happened to him?" Polish Anna asked.

"He died in Warsaw."

I get the framed photograph of Bernhard Jägering from Anna's room upstairs: a simple private in a Wehrmacht uniform, his wool field cap at a rakish tilt aslant his forehead. His daughter is twice as old now as he was then.

Anna Bancken with a 1941 photograph of her father, Bernhard Jägering, in his Wehrmacht uniform. (Photograph by author, 2005)

A man from Velen goes to war and is killed in Warsaw. Now his daughter sits next to a woman from Lublin. Our different histories drift through the room as memories.

Suddenly, Anna from Lublin gets up and puts on dance music. "Frau Anna," she announces, "let's dance."

My Anna looks fearful. "I'll fall," she objects, nervously.

"I will hold you, Frau Anna. Trust me. I won't let you fall."

Then Anna from Lublin reaches out both arms and gently pulls Anna from Velen to her feet. She holds her close in a tight embrace and waits for her to find her balance. Finally, my Anna nods and laughs, "I'm ready."

The sounds of Strauss' "Blue Danube" fill the living room, while Polish Anna and German Anna dance.[11]

Memories of Betrayal

As a child, I thought that Heaven was reserved for Catholics. All others would have to stay in limbo, unredeemed until the end of time. Their only chance to escape this fate was to be baptized Catholic. They didn't even have to ask; I could do it for them.

I longed for such an opportunity. Preparing for my First Communion as a fervent seven-year-old, I dreamed of saving some poor, doomed soul. In the car with my parents, I kept watch for a possible accident. If someone were injured and at risk of dying, I knew what to do. I had prepared myself. I was ready. I would overcome my terror of blood and wounds, set aside my shame of touching strangers, and baptize them in the name of Jesus Christ, our Lord. *In nomine patris ... et filii ... et spiritu sanctu*, I would say and make the sign of the cross on their forehead. *In the name of the Father ... and the Son ... and the Holy Spirit.* So may it be done. *Amen.*

I assumed that everyone in Velen was Catholic. The rhythms of Catholic rituals mapped people's lives. Births were hallowed by christenings, marriages sanctified by the priest, and the dead remembered in special masses. The year was organized around the liturgical calendar: Advent and Christmas, Lent and Easter, Ascension and Pentecost. On their name days people prayed to their special saints.

There were a few Protestants, but they were a tiny minority, and they didn't even have a church. No stained glass windows, no pews, no organ—just wooden chairs in a big, bare room. What did they do in there, I sometimes wondered. And Jews ... Were there any Jews in Velen? As a child, I didn't even think to ask.

At the time I was baptized, St. Andreas' was the only church in Velen. A Protestant church wouldn't be built until the early 1950s, when refugees from eastern Europe brought their Lutheran beliefs and practices with them. And there was no longer a Jewish place of worship. The room above the butcher shop where the Franks once celebrated Shabbat still existed. But it was now just a regular room.

One of the reasons for my visit to Anna in the summer of 2005 was to have her tell me what she knew about the Jews of Velen.

The day after our excursion to Velen, Anna invited me to accompany her to the Münster cemetery, where she was tending her husband's grave. It had been a hot, dry summer, the earth was parched, and the plants needed regular watering. It was an easy walk from her house to the cemetery and, she suggested, "we can talk on the way." We took some garden tools and a small begonia and set out.

"Tell me about the Jews in Velen," I asked. She began with the Franks.

"There was one Jewish family in Velen: the Franks. Avram and Frieda (a Cohen from Coesfeld) and their children, Edith and Siegfried. Avram was the butcher in Velen. They lived above the butcher shop. Avram's three unmarried sisters—Lina, Dora, and Bertha ('the three aunts,' Veleners used to call them) lived next door."

I was struck by the names. Avram was emphatically Jewish. Frieda, Bertha, and Siegfried were just as emphatically not. Siegfried was the Nibelungen hero. Frieda had the Germanic root for peace.[1] As I thought of the Johns, Josephs, Marias, and Annas so prevalent in Velen, I saw how the dilemma of German-Jewish assimilation marked the very names that Jewish families gave their children. Siegfried and Sigmund, Bertha and Frieda were definitely not Jewish names. They were also not Christian names. But they were decidedly German.

"Was Siegfried a common name back then in Velen?" I asked Anna. "Were there any other Veleners with names like that?"

"No." Anna was positive. "There was only Siegfried Frank."

"Were the Franks the only Jews in Velen?" I resumed my inquiry.

"There were also the Landaus," Anna continued. "Avram's oldest sister, Amalie—Male, as she was known in Velen—married a Jewish man, Meyer Landau. He was from Coesfeld, like her sister-in-law, Frieda. They settled in Velen and had two daughters, Ida and Lene."

"And the daughters?" I pressed on. "What became of them?"

"They married Germans. Ida married Franz Sandmann, the Velen electrician ... You remember their store? And Lene married another Coesfeld man, a Herr Tiwisina."

Anna went on, adding details, but my mind was wandering. I tried to pull it back (*pay attention*, I scolded myself, *this is the history you came to learn*), but all these names of people I didn't know were getting jumbled. They had such a similar ring: *Landau, Sandmann, Avram, Male, Ida, Frieda, Frank*. Who were they again? Who was Frank and who was Landau? Who was related to whom and how?

I was mixing up names and getting more and more confused. Anna was still talking, but I had lost the thread. I was only picking up random fragments: *Ida and Franz ... married in Velen ... St. Andreas' ... Catholic. Their son, Günther, Catholic, too ... Ida and Lene ... in school with my mother ... excused from religion class ... other kids envied ... Ida and Lene free to ... outside in the schoolyard.*

What was wrong with me? Why couldn't I follow what she was saying? My attention was distracted by something she had said earlier that hadn't felt right. I tried to think back to where I got stuck.

They married Germans. That's what it was.

Anna had been talking about Ida and Lene Landau. She told me that Ida married Franz Sandmann, the Velen electrician, and Lene married a Coesfeld man named Tiwisina. But just before that, she had said, they "married Germans." That's where I lost the thread of her story. I wanted to object that Ida and Lene were German too. So was their Jewish mother, Amalia Landau. And their Jewish father, Meyer Landau.

I didn't say any of this to Anna. It didn't seem my place to correct her. Despite their Jewish parents, and their Jewish grandparents on both their father's and mother's sides, even going back as far as their Jewish great-grandparents, Ida and Lene were as German as the Catholic men they married. I knew that Anna knew that too. Yet to say that "they married Germans" obscured that fact. It effectively accepted the Nazi separation of German from Jew.

"So what happened during the war?" I asked Anna, wondering, even as I asked it, why I reverted to this phrase, when what I meant wasn't "during the war" but "during the Nazi years." Turns of phrases, like ways of thinking, came ready-made, carrying unreflected histories with them.

Anna's initial response, "They had to wear the Jewish star," took me aback at first. Her way of answering, like my way of asking, seemed somehow ready-made, less something she remembered than a generic association with Nazi history. Her answer seemed impersonal, detached.

It wasn't until later, upon re-reading Victor Klemperer's postwar reflections on the Third Reich and its mobilization of cultural symbols in its race war, that I considered her response in a different light. Klemperer recalls that whenever he asked himself and others, "which was the worst day for the Jews during those twelve years of hell, I always, without exception, received the same answer ... September 19, 1941."[2] That was the day, he explains, when German Jews were publicly marked as Jews. "From that day it was compulsory to wear the Jewish star, the yellow piece of cloth that today still stands for plague and quarantine, and which in the Middle Ages was the color used to identify the Jews." It didn't just identify them; it branded them. From that point on, Klemperer continues, "I was recognizable to everyone all the time, and being recognizable isolated and outlawed me." "Now, for the first time," he concludes bitterly, "ghettoization was complete." Perhaps, I thought, this was the shock Anna too had registered: the shock of realizing that the social body had just been rent. "We," unmarked as Germans, were on one side. "They," marked as Jews, were on the other.

I wondered what else Anna recalled, but I didn't press her. Memory has its own rhythm, so I waited. She eventually returned to the Franks. "People were told they could no longer buy meat from the Franks," she said. "Some ordinance was passed. Most people just ignored it and continued to buy from them ... out of sympathy ... to show their support ... and because it was the only place to get good meat in Velen. But they'd go secretly, to the back, not the front door."

I tried to picture the scene. Women with cloth shopping bags go around the back of the shop, as if they aren't customers, just neighbors visiting. They stop at the garden gate, perhaps to see if they are being watched.[3] They hesitate at the back door. Should they knock? Or just go in? Once inside the store, do they act like customers or do they feel awkward? Do they stay and chit-chat, exchange village gossip, or get their business over with and leave? Perhaps some of them solve the problem by having their children go in their stead; they can just hand Frau Frank a written list of their order. I imagine Frau Frank putting on her apron, as she did every day for work, getting ready to wait on her customers. In her shop, behind the counter, she is Frau Frank, the butcher's wife. Everyone in Velen knows her. Indoors, she isn't marked as Jewish.

By now Anna and I had reached the cemetery and our conversation flagged as we busied ourselves at her husband's gravesite. We watered, picked wilted blooms off the flowering shrubs, and planted the begonia. I looked around at the park-like landscape and inhaled the fragrant scent of summer roses. It felt peaceful. Memories of the dead drew us inward. Yet the aesthetic attention to detail—the graves well tended, the walkways raked—didn't feel entirely innocent. I couldn't help wondering if this attention to detail helped Germans organize their genocide with such efficiency.

Our work at the cemetery was finished. We put the watering can away, tossed the clippings into the compost, and headed home. For a while, we didn't talk. It was hot and we were tired. When Anna finally broke the silence, her words were startling. "All gone," she suddenly noted, into the stillness of this summer day. "They were all taken away."

"The Franks were deported," she went on. "At least the grown-ups were: the parents, Avram and Frieda … and the three aunts, Lina, Dora, and Bertha. Soon after the Franks left, another family came to take their place. They moved into the Franks' apartment and took over their butcher shop." That family, the Laumanns, Anna explained, had moved to Velen from a city in the Ruhr after their butcher shop and home were destroyed in the aerial bombings.[4] "They were a big family, the Laumanns," Anna added.

"After the Franks left, everything was different," she continued. "The butcher shop was never the same."

"And the Frank children?" I asked. "What happened to Edith and Siegfried?"

Anna hesitated and shook her head. She looked uncertain. "I heard the children were sent away. To England, I think. Maybe Siegfried? … Or was it Edith? … A children's transport?" Her answers were inflected like questions. Maybe both Frank children went to England? Maybe neither of them did? Maybe they died or were killed? Or maybe they were still alive somewhere? She shook her head again.

"There were rumors that they both survived," she went on. "But no one seems to know exactly. All we know is that none of the Franks returned to

Velen." We walked on for a while without speaking. We were almost at Anna's house.

"Sometimes their names came up in conversation," Anna finished, as we turned into her street. "But no one knew anything definite."

While Anna rested, I went over what she had told me: how many Jews had lived in Velen under Nazi rule, who they were, and what became of them. The names muddled in my mind. To sort them out, I decided to list them. I drew two columns on a sheet of paper, one for each family. In one column, I listed the Frank family: the parents (Avram and Frieda), their two children (Edith and Siegfried), and the three aunts (Lina, Dora, and Bertha). In the other column, I listed the Landaus: the widowed mother (Amalia, known as Male) and her two daughters (Ida and Lene). I initially included Male's husband, Meyer Landau, in the Landau column, but then erased his name. He died long before the war, and it was the war years that I was after.

I had a total of ten names. My history of Velen Jews in the Hitler years would be a short one. It looked pretty straightforward and clear.

Yet as I reviewed the list, my confusion resurfaced. Did Ida and Lene Landau even belong here? If they were already married at the time, they were no longer Jewish but Catholic, like the men they married. Should I still count them as Jews anyway? I bracketed their names, then erased the brackets, then bracketed them again. I added their married names, crossed them out, and penciled them in again. Which laws should define their identity? The eraser smudge around their names betrayed my uncertainty. I drew lines linking the ten people on my lists. I erased the lines, corrected, and redrew them. Who was related to whom and how? I stared at the mess of names and smudge of lines. What did I know now other than ten names I hadn't known before? And what did knowing them tell me? Or, more precisely, how did knowing them matter to me?

These were questions I couldn't yet answer. But a few weeks after my visit to Münster, I realized that the names mattered to me in ways I hadn't yet registered. I was visiting a childhood friend of my mother's from Velen. She was in her eighties and hadn't been to Velen in many years. Her memories of "back then" had faded. But she remembered the butcher.

"He was a Jewish man."

My reaction shocked me. A flash of anger I hadn't known was there shot through me. I wanted to shout, "He had a name! His name was Avram Frank! The name of the butcher in Velen was Frank!" But my throat was tight and closed like a fist and I said nothing. My anger collapsed as abruptly as it had surfaced. It left a sense of unacknowledged shame in its wake.

That evening after supper, Anna made tea and we sat in the living room. The books of Velen history we had looked through earlier, when we were talking about the war, still lay on the table. We looked at them again, but found nothing useful. There was no mention in these books of the history of Velen Jews or what happened to them in the 1930s and '40s. All we had were pieces of story and fragments of memory.

While we sat there in the dusk, watching the garden fade into twilight, Anna summoned such a memory fragment. It was a scene from long ago, from a past that she seldom entered anymore. It was sometime during the war, she said. Her father had already gone to Russia, so it must have been after 1941. She was around ten. She remembered being in the front room of their house in Velen, standing by the window, when she saw a group of women walking down the road outside their house. It was the road that led from the center of town to the train station.

I knew the route well. I had walked it many times myself. During the months that we lived in Velen after leaving Canada, I had taken the train to Coesfeld almost every day and walked from my grandparents' house to the station. My mother had done much the same during her school years, taking the train back and forth between Velen and Münster. For most of the twentieth century, it was trains that connected villages like Velen to the larger world, from towns and cities nearby to places far beyond regional borders. Not until the 1970s, as more and people acquired private cars, was the local train line finally discontinued.

As she watched the women walking down the road come closer, Anna recalled, she saw that it was actually two groups. "I have forgotten many of the details," she said, "but I see their faces. I knew them … I knew them well." In the telling, it's as if she still sees them. First, the three Frank aunts: Lina, Dora, and Bertha. They walk slowly, slightly bent forward, in a shuffling, old-woman gait. They are dressed warmly—more warmly than usual for a summer day—but it's early morning and the air is chilly. The second group follows close behind. It's the fourth Frank sister, Male Landau, and her two grown daughters, Ida and Lene. Their arms are linked. Male is in the middle, Ida and Lene are on either side. They are walking to the Velen train station on a summer morning. And while Anna was just a child at the time, she recalled knowing that once they left on the train they would not be returning to Velen.

"Did they walk alone?" I asked Anna. "Just these six women? Did anyone go along with them?"

Anna couldn't recall. In her memory, all she sees is the women walking. I tried to picture the scene as Anna described it.

Six women are walking down Bahnhof Street.[5] From their house to the station, it will take about fifteen minutes. They walk slowly; the three aunts are old. On their right, they pass the village cemetery and the red-bricked elementary school on the left. Over the rooftops they see the steeple of St. Andreas'. At the corner of Bahnhof and Schürkamp Streets, where the houses thin and give way to the first plots of farm land, they pass the wayside statue of St. Andreas, Velen's patron saint. From there, it is just a five-minute walk to the station.

It's a weekday morning, so even though it's early people are out, heading for work, going to the fields, feeding their animals.[6] Children are on their way to school. The dairy plant by the train station has begun its deliveries; the breakfast rolls at the bakery are still warm. Some people are just returning from early morning mass. Some will be on the train to Münster with the six women.

If you were in Velen that morning, you might have seen them. You might have passed them on the street and said good morning. But even if you weren't out yet, you might have seen what ten-year-old Anna saw from her living room window: six women wearing the Jewish star walking to the station.

If you were a Velener, you would have known the women. As members of their families. As neighbors or classmates. As friends. Perhaps you wondered where they were going that day. Did you ask? And when they didn't return, did you ask what happened?

As I imagined that long-ago morning in Velen, I recalled the chilling way an old friend of my mother's once described the fate of Velen's Jews. "One day, they simply disappeared."

No, they didn't, I now wanted to tell her. They did not "disappear." And they certainly didn't disappear "simply." They walked in broad daylight for all to see from the center of town along the main village road to the station. Everyone who saw them walk by would have known what was happening. And when they didn't return, everyone would have known that too.

Forever after, Anna told me, her mother cried when the Franks were mentioned or when something happened that reminded her of them. "They were good people," she always told her daughter, who, now remembering her mother's tears, started crying too. "They were good people. They had done nothing wrong."

Lying in bed that night, unable to sleep, unable to think, unable to distract myself, as usual, with reading, I kept revisiting the scene Anna had described. I wasn't sleeping, yet the images my mind conjured had the surreal vividness of dreams.

From a window in my grandparents' house I saw three women walking in the direction of the Velen train station. The older woman was flanked by the two younger ones; their arms were linked. One of the younger women carried a travel bag. The older woman in the middle looked like my grandmother. She wore the same beige gabardine coat that my grandmother liked to wear and the same sturdy shoes that my mother called "sensible"—shoes for walking that didn't give you blisters. But it was not my grandmother. I could see a Jewish star on her coat. Had they known each other, I wondered? They might have bowled together at the women's bowling league that met every other Thursday. Perhaps they had met at Buddenkotte's hair salon, where my grandmother had her hair set every Friday and every six weeks went for color and a perm.

I wondered what the three women might be saying to one another as they walked to the station that morning. If I were in the mother's shoes, my children beside me, like Male Landau's daughters, what would I say to them? What would I want them to say to me? Sometimes the big words—of love and longing or regret—remain unspoken because they weigh too heavily. Sometimes the everyday words—"Are you cold? Do you want your sweater?"—seem unduly light. Most likely, I would say nothing. I would just cherish the physical closeness of beloved bodies, the comfort of their arms encircling mine. I would put one foot in front of the other and let my mind go blank.

When I fell asleep that night, my sleep was dreamless.

The next morning at breakfast, I told Anna that thoughts of Male Landau had evoked such vivid memories of my grandmother that I could have touched her. Anna retrieved the memory fragment she had summoned the previous evening but, to my astonishment, it had changed. Instead of six women—two groups of three—Anna now described three women walking together: Male Landau and her daughters, Ida and Lene. The three aunts—Lina, Bertha and Dora—weren't in the picture.

What happened? Had I heard it wrong? Had I misremembered or confused things? The names had a similar ring and rhythm; I could have mixed them up: Lina, Lene … Bertha, Dora, Amalia. We couldn't explain the discrepant versions. But this was the correct one, Anna insisted: Male, Ida, and Lene. Only one person left on the train that day: Male Landau. Her daughters, Ida and Lene, returned home. The three aunts were taken away some other day. That was Anna's revised and corrected story.

These shifting memories were unsettling. Which of them was true? "Where exactly were you when you saw them walking?" I asked Anna, hoping to reconstruct what she might have seen. That's when she explained that she hadn't actually seen them. It had been her mother. What Anna "saw" was a reconstructed version of her mother's memory.

I was dismayed to realize that she didn't know for sure which—if any—of her remembered accounts were accurate. Maybe each was a partial version of a bigger story. However, what dismayed me even more was to realize that I preferred Anna's first account to the corrected one: six women was more weighty, more dramatic, than three. I was ashamed of my reaction. It felt unseemly. The smaller number should be cause for rejoicing, not dismay. I was trapped in the dilemma of numbers.

The story of Jews under Nazi rule is commonly told on an epic scale. We map the Holocaust in terms of millions. I didn't know how to fit the story of Velen's Jews—ten people, two families, one woman deported on a given day— into a history of this scale. In a count of 6 million, how do we measure one?

The power of the numbers argument is based on a simple logic: higher numbers make the case more grave. The greater the losses, the more serious the crime. The more harm you can show, the more damning the indictment. six million count more than 600. Six Jews deported in Velen count more than one. The problem is that by building a case on numbers, we turn people into instruments of our argument. We make them numbers. And in doing so, we lose sight of them as persons. We risk dehumanizing them all over again.

This dilemma of numbers made me feel dizzy. I couldn't think past the number one. One woman—Amalia Landau, known in Velen as Male—was taken from the place that had been her home. Her daughters walked to the station with her. They carried her bags, put her on the train, and went home without her. Their mother never came back. That is the Holocaust story from

"What should they have done? Was hätten sie tun sollen?" Light projection—a slowly rotating circle that projected its question, in German and English, directly onto the museum floor, on display in the Jewish Museum, Berlin, 2001– 2002. Exhibition curated by the design firm Würth & Winderoll. (Photograph by author, 2001)

Velen as I heard it from Anna. It's a story that shifts attention from the horror of millions dead to remind me of this particular one.

The abstraction of genocide overwhelms my imagination. Numbers blur. Didn't everyone, in the end—whether they were deported, fled, or went into exile, whether they were killed or left to die—suffer as an individual? Even when they were herded by the thousands into cattle cars, killed by starvation, massacred at the edge of mass pits, or gassed, people didn't suffer and die as a collective. They lived, suffered, and died as individuals. Each in his or her way. Death, like birth, happens individually. This is how a genocide unfolds: one ... then another ... and then another one after that. Each in turn is the one that matters.

Yet sometimes the weight of each one in turn feels unbearable. Sometimes the abstraction of numbers is all we are able to bear.

Later that day, Anna and I revisited the story of Male Landau. "What happened to her daughters, Ida and Lene?" I asked. "Did they stay in Velen? Did they leave? Were they taken away too?"

Anna's answer seemed to evade my questions, as she told me something about Ida's husband, Franz. Franz Sandmann, she said, never served in the army. Even when all eligible men were mobilized, he stayed in Velen. "People said they probably didn't want him, because his wife was a Jew." Yet even as she said this, Anna looked skeptical. "It could also have been that he was needed in Velen," she continued. "Franz was a master electrician and we relied on him for all things electrical. Even the street lights depended on Franz Sandmann."

"But what about Ida and Lene?" I persisted.

They might have gone to Holland, Anna thought, but she wasn't sure. "It may have been somewhere else." She hesitated. "They were gone for a while ... toward the end of the war," she finally offered. She spoke slowly, as if her memory was foggy. Her answer, or lack of it, surprised me. Anna wasn't usually vague. More than her vagueness, though, I found her words disturbing. *They were gone*, she said. Not *they left* or *they were deported*. It was abstract, impersonal. As if one day something simply happened.

"Gone where?" I asked. "And what do you mean, *gone*?" Our conversation was beginning to feel eerie.

"Theresienstadt," Anna proposed, her rising inflection betraying her uncertainty. "They went to Theresienstadt, I think. Toward the end of the war. People said they were put to work in the laundry." As far as she knew, they were only gone briefly. When the war was over, they returned. Anna's voice was regaining its ring of certainty. For events after the war her memory fog seemed to dissipate. "After the war," Anna said, "Ida and Lene returned to Velen." They lived there for the rest of their lives, and when they died, they were buried in the Velen cemetery with their Catholic husbands. "The Sandmanns were a Catholic family," Anna reminded me. "Lene and her husband, Herr Tiwisina, were Catholic too."

I was struck by the shifts from uncertainty to certainty in Anna's account: what she knew, what she didn't know, what she wasn't sure of. In a village where everyone knew everyone else's business—particularly who came and went, when and where—the very vagueness of her answers was telling. It suggested that when Ida and Lene returned after the war, the question of what happened to them while they were gone wasn't clearly answered. Perhaps because it had never been clearly asked.

"What did people say when they came back?" I asked Anna. "And what did Ida and Lene have to say?"

"It wasn't talked about," she said, simply.

This "it" that wasn't talked about was probably the fog that obscured Anna's memory, the elided time between no-longer-innocent and not-yet-guilty. The time when women like Ida and Lene—along with the other members of their family lost to Nazi violence—disappeared from public awareness because Germans didn't know through what lens to see them. If those who "were gone," as Anna had put it, were victims of a crime, then those who remained were either participants in the crime or complicit. People didn't talk about "it," because they didn't know how.

The rest of that day I kept thinking about Ida and Lene. After their mother's death in Theresienstadt and after they had been sent to Nazi camps themselves, how did they bear the public silence about the Holocaust? How did it affect them in their private lives? After all, the separation of German from Jew cut right through their families. Ida Sandmann was sent to Theresienstadt because she was deemed a Jew, while her husband, Franz, and son, Günther, stayed in Velen because they were registered Aryans.[7] How did their different traumas affect the relationships among them: Ida's sense of abandonment and betrayal; her husband's powerlessness to protect his wife; their son's confusion when his mother suddenly left and just as suddenly returned, with no explanation that could possibly make sense to a boy of ten. Were they able to restore trust and talk about these things? Or did they learn to live with memories they couldn't share?

Just before I left Münster, Anna added a coda to this story in the form of an incident involving her mother and Ida Sandmann, when both women (they were the same age, Anna explained) were in their seventies. Ida and Franz Sandmann were living with their son, Günther, at the time, and Frau Sandmann often worked in the small electrical goods store that Günther had opened on the ground floor of his house in Velen.

Like the Sandmanns, Anna and her mother had also been living in the same house, sharing companionship and domestic responsibilities. But recently Anna had married and moved to Münster, leaving her mother alone in the Velen home she had always shared with her daughter. The incident Anna remembered occurred at around that time. Not long after Anna's move to Münster, her mother fell seriously ill. The doctors didn't know what ailed her or how to help. She was suffering from a condition they had no name for.

"One day," Anna recounted, "I was back in Velen to see my mother, when I saw Frau Sandmann at a distance down the street. I smiled and waved and continued walking, but she rushed over and wanted to talk. She was visibly distressed. She seemed to know what was wrong with my mother and wanted to tell me. *Your mother is homesick*, Frau Sandmann told me. *She is homesick for you. She is sick for the child she misses.*"

Anna was silent for a moment and looked at me. "I think she was telling me about herself years earlier. My mother's illness revived memories of that time. I think it was as close as Frau Sandmann could get to talking about what she had felt when she was taken from her home and family, away from her child. I think she was telling me, this is the grief I suffered ... this was the heartache for which there was no cure."

That fall, I returned to Velen for a brief follow-up. There was something I wanted to see. Anna had mentioned a memorial that I hadn't known about. Hidden in plain sight, in the heart of Velen on Bahnhof Street, was a small memorial to Velen's Jews, so modest and unassuming that I had walked past it numerous times without noticing it.

Anna had given clear directions. It was across the street from the Franks' former home and butcher shop. "Right across from the *Judenstegge*," she had added. The moment she said *Judenstegge*, Jews' steps, she looked dismayed, as if she had said something inappropriate. *Judenstegge* was a word from the past that Veleners no longer used. It carried memories of betrayal and danger. She blushed, visibly flustered. "That's what we called it then," she stumbled through an explanation. "To get to the Frank house, from the street to their front door, there were several steps ... we called them the Jews' steps."

The memorial was a plain stone slab about 2 feet high, in size and shape not unlike a gravestone. The top of the stone had three small peaks, like the steep roofs of traditional houses in this area. When I later asked Anna what the peaks represented, she wasn't sure. "Perhaps," she guessed, "they represent the three houses where Velen's Jews once lived: the Franks, the three old Frank aunts, and Male Landau."

I took a photograph of the memorial and another of the old Frank house. It looked like all the other sturdy brick houses along Bahnhof Street with their high-pitched roofs, heavy wood doors, and flower-filled gardens. An ordinary Velen house. The only difference was that it looked neglected. The front steps were in disrepair and it needed painting. Before I left, I copied the inscription on the memorial marker into my notebook:

It happened here as well. Until 1942, the Jewish families of Velen lived on this street, popularly called the JUDENSTEGGE. After 1933 they fell victim to the National Socialist regime of terror and suffered discrimination and humiliation, the deprivation of rights and expulsion, deportation and murder. May their suffering be our mandate for tolerance toward all minorities and all those who think differently than ourselves.

Velen, 9–1–1989

Back in Atlanta, sorting through my notes from Germany that summer, I was struck by the discrepancies, uncertainties, and outright errors in Anna's account of what had happened to Velen's Jews. She hadn't just muddled a few details, like whether she had seen six—or just three—Jewish women walking to the train station one summer morning. Much of what she had told me was incorrect. It began with the Franks. She had described them as "Avram and Frieda and their children, Edith and Siegfried," adding that "Frieda was a Cohen from Coesfeld." Yet Avram (whom all official records, including documents that he himself had produced and signed, identified as Abraham, not Avram), was not married to Frieda, "a Cohen from Coesfeld," but to Helene, a Humberg from Dingden. When I found a Frieda in the records, it wasn't Abraham's wife, but his wife's younger sister, who didn't even live in Velen.[8] Perhaps the "Cohen from Coesfeld" Anna was thinking of was Ida, Abraham Frank's younger sister. For while Ida Frank wasn't born "a Cohen from Coesfeld," she became one when she married Albert Cohen, a Coesfeld merchant.[9] And since Frieda and Ida, in German, sound almost alike, Anna could have conflated Frieda (Abraham's sister-in-law) with Ida (Abraham's sister) and falsely remembered them as Abraham's wife—a composite of three related Jewish women.

I found other errors. Abraham's three unmarried sisters—Lina, Dora, and Bertha, "the three old aunts"—were not deported, as Anna had suggested. They died of natural causes unrelated to the Holocaust: Dora in 1929, Lina in 1939, and Bertha in February 1941, ten months before the first Münsterland Jews were deported.

Anna's claim that Amalia (Male) Frank had married "a Jewish man from Coesfeld" was also incorrect. Male Frank *had* married "a Jewish man," but he wasn't from Coesfeld. Her husband, Meyer Landau, was a Velen native. Born in Velen in 1826, the second son of Hermann Landau, a Jewish cattle trader, and his wife, Helena (born Helena Levi), he had lived in Velen all his life. He grew up there, married and had five children there, and died there in 1911.

Apart from these factual errors, there were many things Anna just didn't know, like what became of Siegfried and Edith Frank after they left Velen; what happened to Ida and Lene, Male Landau's daughters, when they were deported; and how Veleners responded when they returned after the war.

I thought Anna's eyewitness perspective would give me the most authentic and accurate account of what happened to Velen's Jews in the Nazi years. That assumption had been misguided. My error reminded me of something I had read in the sociologist Maurice Halbwachs' work on group memory. Eyewitness testimony, he had argued, was inherently unreliable. At first his claim had seemed counter-intuitive. Yet Anna's struggle to align her memory with the facts caused me to reassess his argument.

Proper witnessing, Halbwachs proposed, requires emotional distance. Too much closeness risks distorting what we think we see, and that distortion shapes what and how we remember. In short, he concluded, the emotional impact of an event, particularly one that we experience as traumatic, undermines our ability to provide reliable witness testimony. Halbwachs argues:

> [W]hen an event occurs that is worth remembering and reporting, it is precisely the presence of direct witnesses which increases the chances that some of its features will be changed ... This is especially the case when the event is of a nature that arouses deep emotions in groups of people, giving rise to passionate discussions ... Having been stunned and moved by these events, how could they have maintained the necessary detachment to see everything completely and clearly?[10]

Halbwachs' claim that we can't be relied upon to give an accurate account when we witness an event that "arouses deep emotions" and gives rise to "passionate discussions" afterwards offers an explanation for Anna's muddled and partial recollection. Even if what she witnessed may not in itself at the time have seemed traumatic (three or six women that she, or her mother, saw walking to the train station), the catastrophic outcome of that event became visible in the retrospective light of history. In the limited and partial ways that any one person registers what we call "history," Anna was a witness as a child to a genocide in the process of unfolding. In that light, Halbwachs' question, "how could [she] have maintained the necessary detachment to see everything completely and clearly?" resonates with the truth of her experience.

Witnessing a traumatic event often happens in delayed phases. The event itself comes first. You feel the shock of its initial impact. But the full effect of what happened doesn't hit you until later, perhaps on more than one occasion, as the extent of the damage becomes evident and you realize that it wasn't just the one tree you saw felled by lightning but that an entire forest was destroyed. Under the weight of this repeated impact, memory often warps or buckles. Sometimes it shatters. It rarely survives intact. Postwar memory of the Nazi years bears the marks of these successive shocks.

The story that Anna told was based on memory. To know what actually happened, I consulted history.

There Was a Butcher Here, Once

History bases its claims to truth on facts. I asked it, as I had Anna, a simple question. "Tell me about the Jews in Velen." Anna had said there was one Jewish family: the Franks.

"Well," history answered. "It was like this."

In the beginning, there were two Jewish families in Velen: the Franks and the Landaus. Around 1816 a Jewish cattle trader, Hermann Landau, moved to Velen with his wife, Julie, after the birth of their first child, Liefmann. Another young Jewish family had settled in Velen at around the same time. Levy Frank, a butcher by trade, had moved to Velen from his native Bavaria with his wife Friederika.[1] Their first child, Helena, was born the same year as Liefmann Landau. And so, as the Landaus and the Franks established their businesses and started raising families, Jewish life in Velen began. By the mid-1830s, a small Jewish community had formed. The Franks had eight children, the Landaus six,[2] and both families were active participants in the local economy.

For a variety of reasons, few of their children stayed in Velen through adulthood. Some died young, others left to get married or establish their own business elsewhere. However, one Landau son (Meyer) and two Frank children (Helena and Samuel) stayed.[3] Meyer Landau started a small business and Samuel Frank followed in his father's footsteps and became a butcher. Both Meyer Landau and Samuel Frank married and started their own families. The Franks, in particular, thrived. Samuel and his wife, Julie, like Samuel's parents before him, had eight children. The Landau line was less fortunate. Meyer Landau's first wife and all of their children died,[4] leaving him a widowed man in his sixties. But the Franks, with four eligible daughters, lived next door, so a year after his first wife's death, Meyer Landau married the eldest Frank daughter, Amalia. If Meyer Landau didn't want to spend the rest of his life alone, and if Amalia Frank wanted to marry within her Jewish faith and stay close to her aging parents and younger siblings,[5] their union was the perfect solution. When they married in 1895, Amalia Frank was thirty-five and Meyer Landau was sixty-nine.[6] Their first daughter, Helene (known as Lene), was born that same year. A second daughter, Ida, followed five years later.

In 1907, Samuel Frank's second son, Abraham (his first son, Louis, had moved away), decided to start his own butcher business.[7] Both his parents were dead and Abraham, still unmarried, was in his thirties. It was time to establish his independence. He purchased property in the heart of town on Bahnhof Street, next to the Landau home, where his sister, Amalia, lived with her family, and made plans to build his own house. Four years later, when Meyer Landau died, leaving Amalia a widow and single parent of two daughters (Lene was fifteen and Ida nine), Abraham Frank assumed the role of family patriarch, shouldering responsibility for his four older sisters (Lina, Bertha, and Dora—the three unmarried "old aunts," and the recently widowed Amalia) and two young nieces.[8]

Abraham Frank's new house was built in the traditional style of rural Westphalia. A two-story red brick house with a high-pitched tile roof, it had family quarters upstairs, commercial space on the ground floor, and a small garden plot in back. The large room downstairs, with a street front entrance, became the butcher shop; the four rooms upstairs provided space for a growing family. When the house was finished, Abraham took the next step. In 1912, he married Helene Humberg, a young Jewish woman from a neighboring town. Helene had roots in Velen herself. Her grandfather was Liefmann Landau, the son of Herman and Julie Landau, the first Jewish family to settle in this town. A year after they married, Abraham and Helene Frank had their first child and they named him Siegfried. Five years later, they had a daughter, Edith. With these names—the Germanic Siegfried and the Anglo-Saxon Edith—they broke with tradition in two ways. They broke with the Jewish tradition of repeating family names across generations. And they broke with the tradition of giving their children Jewish names. "Siegfried" and "Edith" would not mark their children as Jews.

A generation earlier, both the Franks and the Landaus had lived in large, multigenerational families. At times, there were up to nine people in the Landau household (parents, grandparents, and four to five children),[9] and for a while the Frank household numbered up to twelve: the parents (Samuel and Julie) and their eight children; Samuel's younger brother, Moyses, who lived with them until he married; and Helena, Samuel's eldest, unmarried sister.

By 1913, when Abraham and Helene Frank started their own family, Velen's Jewish population had shrunk to ten.[10] It shrank even more when

Abraham Frank's older sister, Dora, died and Amalia Landau's eldest daughter married and left.[11] By 1930, only eight members of Velen's original two Jewish families remained in Velen. And since Amalia Landau's second daughter, Ida, married Franz Sandman the same year that her sister Lene married Johannes Tiwisina, Amalia was officially the only Landau left. Anna's recollection that in her childhood "there was one Jewish family in Velen: the Franks" was thus technically correct.

By consulting history and cross-checking records, I had added details to Anna's account and corrected errors. But I hadn't simplified the matter. On the contrary, it had become more intricate. As I explored the histories of the Frank and Landau families, following the roots and branches of their family trees across generations, I was still left with a tangle of names I struggled to keep straight. I kept mixing people up. Not only did the Frank and Landau families intermarry, but in over three generations of Franks and Landaus in Velen alone, I found four Helenas, three Idas, and multiple Berthas, Rosas, Amalias, and Abrahams. To make things simpler, I considered leaving people out or not including their names, just referring to them as "wife," say, or "children."

But in the end, I couldn't do it. I couldn't leave a person out or erase their name. Too many people had been left out already, their names erased from history. In this brief history of one small place, I wanted to account for them. I wanted to know who they were, how they lived, and what their place was in my natal village. At the very least, I wanted to name them.

By the time the Nazi regime came to power in the early 1930s, Velen's Jewish families had been part of the community for almost five generations. To see and treat them as different people and not as fellow Veleners was a complex process. It had to be orchestrated step by step, over time. Separating "Germans" from "Jews" in a small and close-knit village community was not only personal. It disrupted social habits. It threatened emotional bonds. It rent the very fabric of village life, where everyone shopped at the same stores, saw the same doctor, and drank at the same pubs, and where all the children sat on the same benches in the village school.

Apart from their faith and particular religious observations—they kept kosher and observed Shabbat—the Franks were no different from other Velen families. They celebrated with them, grieved losses with them, conducted neighborhood business with them. On Christian holidays, they even joined in the traditional festivities.[12] Edith Frank invited girlfriends to her house for sleepovers, and her brother, Siegfried, played soccer in the Velen league. He even joined his Catholic classmates for religion class. Abraham Frank was a founding member of Velen's Volunteer Fire Brigade, and in 1929 he represented the Butcher Guild in the twenty-fifth anniversary celebration of the Catholic Journeyman's Association.

In early 1933, right after the election of Adolf Hitler as Reich Chancellor, a Nazi party office opened in Velen. But it took more than an office to inculcate a Nazi mindset. To effect the change of perspective that would segregate Jewish members of the community into a separate group marked as "Jews" would take a steady stream of laws, decrees, and ordinances issued over many years.

In rural areas a particular point of attack was the traditional involvement of Jews in both the cattle trade and the slaughter and butchering of livestock, the very work that the Frank and Landau families had traditionally done. Abraham Frank, like his father, Samuel Frank, his grandfather, Levy Frank, and his uncle, Moyses Frank, had learned to practice his butcher trade in observance of kosher law; his kosher slaughter knives were among his most prized possessions. In one way or another, almost his entire extended family was involved in the cattle business, from the trade and slaughter of livestock to the butchering and sale of meat. His sisters, Ida and Amalia, had married into Jewish families in the cattle trade business. Ida's husband, Albert Cohen, Amalia's father-in-law, Hermann Landau, and two of her brothers-in-law, Carl and Levy Landau, were all cattle traders. The same applied to Abraham's wife, Helene, with one brother a butcher, another a cattle trader, and another cattle trader as brother-in-law.

From the early 1930s on, a steady drumbeat of anti-Semitic regulations targeting the cattle and butcher trades systematically undercut the ability of rural Jews to make a living. Some of the initial attempts to curtail the involvement of Jews trading in cattle could still appear innocuous, an example being the April 19, 1933 ordinance passed in the southern German state of Baden prohibiting "the use of the Jewish language (Yiddish) on cattle markets," followed by an almost identical ordinance in Bavaria the following year.[13] But this prohibition was just a sideswipe. The real blow came two days later. On April 21, 1933, a law passed simultaneously by the Reich Ministry of the Interior, the Reich Ministry of Justice, and the Reich Ministry of Food and Agriculture—effective immediately across all of Germany—required all livestock to be stunned or anesthetized before it was slaughtered. This new Reich law effectively outlawed kosher slaughter, putting Jews who held to kosher law out of work. Insult was added to this injury a few months later when the Reich Association of National Cattle Traders announced that, while current membership was not yet affected, henceforth "German cattle traders of Jewish origin" were barred from the Association.

These acts of outright exclusion were accompanied by harassment and intimidation, sometimes in the form of petty rules and arbitrary measures designed to humiliate and demoralize. In the German state of Württemberg, for example, Jewish cattle traders who addressed German farmers or their adult children with the informal "Du" could be arrested for public nuisance.[14] A bizarre Bavarian directive about cattle breeding took the illogic of anti-Semitic prejudice to an absurd extreme. Jewish cows, it decreed, were not allowed to mate with German bulls. Even proximity produced contamination. German cows that had shared a stable with Jewish livestock were barred from mating with a German bull for a year, allowing time to purge the racial contamination.[15] Even cattle in the German Reich were subject to Aryan bloodline thinking.

For a while, the Franks could bend to the pressures and manage. But the web of restrictions imposed on their work took their toll. By March 1935, Abraham Frank was no longer able to pay his municipal taxes. He asked them to be forgiven or at least reprieved. "I am not currently in a position to pay taxes," began his formal appeal to the Velen mayor. "As you well know," he continued, "my business is under severe attack. And I have to support my two older sisters." Yet after this opening plea for help, his sense of outrage erupted and his letter ended with a fierce expression of unbowed pride.

> I trust that justice will continue to prevail, even now, in the Third Reich. My parents, grandparents, and great-grandparents were all born in Germany and have always lived here. There is evidence of this for 200 years. If things continue like this in Velen, I must demand support.
>
> With respectful greetings,
> A. Frank

When Abraham Frank wrote this letter in March 1935, proudly declaring a German heritage going back for centuries, his Germanness was not yet in question. German Jews were still legally German. A few months later, the so-called Nuremberg Laws ended this status. Jews were officially no longer Germans; they were just Jews. And Jews, to the Nazi mindset, had no place in Germany. They had to be removed. Two months after Abraham Frank wrote to the Velen mayor pointing out his German roots, this process of removal was set in motion.

On May 17, 1935, the regional Gestapo in Münster ordered local authorities across Westphalia to account for all resident Jews within their jurisdiction. The matter, they were told, should "be handled with as much discretion as possible." By June 15, local Jews were to submit ("in duplicate copies") the following information: given name, family name, profession, date of birth, and precise address. The order was signed, notarized, and marked "confidential!"

Authorities in Velen reported seven Jews: Abraham, Helene, Siegfried, and Edith Frank (Bahnhof Street 17a), Amalia Landau (Bahnhof Street 17b), and Lina and Bertha Frank (Bahnhof Street 21a). With this information the path toward deportation was cleared.

By 1936 Abraham Frank was financially ruined. But when he tried to lease his shop to a man he had trained and trusted as a former apprentice,[16] Velen's mayor, a Nazi loyalist, intervened, urging the immediate "removal of the non-Aryan butcher" from his current premises and recommending the "Aryan" butcher and Nazi party member Bernhard Laumann as his successor.[17] The maneuver succeeded. Veleners' meat production was henceforth securely in Aryan hands.

Not long after losing their butcher shop, the Franks also lost their house. It, too, was sold to the Laumanns. By 1939, everything the Franks had worked for was gone. As their resources dwindled, they depended on others to get by. Sympathetic neighbors, the Föckers, gave them a place to live by converting the attic rooms in their house to a small apartment, and when Nazi hoodlums came to threaten the Franks, Ferdinand Föcker protected his tenants. A local farmer, Wilhelm Tepferd, supplied them with food from his farm and supported them even after he was warned of penalties for "inappropriate" contact between an Aryan and Jews. Luise Schmähing, who ran a small grocery store on Bahnhof Street across from where Abraham had lived as a child, helped with groceries and daily necessities.

Yet, as many others shrank from contact with them, Abraham and Helene Frank found themselves more and more alone. Abraham's sister Lina died in 1939 and four of Helene's siblings, along with their families, left Germany.[18] Most crushingly, both the Frank children left too. Edith left for England that spring and Siegfried went into hiding. After his arrest the previous November during the Kristallnacht pogrom, he was released to the Netherlands instead of being deported. Edith was twenty-one and Siegfried was twenty-five. It was the last time the Franks saw either of their children.

No one can know how they survived this rending of their family, whether their hearts hardened in self-protection or broke like glass when it freezes. Perhaps the need to survive carried them through.

After Edith's departure, the Franks' isolation deepened. At the same time, their sphere of activity shrank. They were not allowed to leave their quarters after four in the afternoon, and leaving town required special permission. They could only buy food from two merchants, one of whom was the new Aryan butcher who now owned their shop. The final humiliation was the September 1941 edict requiring all Jews to wear the "Jewish star," thus branding them publicly as pariahs. A few weeks later, the Reich Security Main Office made "friendly relations" between "persons of German blood" and Jews illegal. Offending Germans could be sent to a concentration camp for several months, but for Jews the punishment was life-threatening. "[I]n all cases," the decree stated, "[t]he Jewish part shall ... be committed to a concentration camp for protective custody until further notice."[19]

With even such minimal shelter as "friendly relations" removed, the Franks had nothing and no one to protect them from deportation. The order was imminent. The Münster Gestapo informed local authorities that on December 11, 1941, Jews in this part of Westphalia would be "evacuated." Lists were finalized, names and addresses checked. The "evacuation" list for Velen had three names: Abraham Frank, Helene Frank, and Leopold Humberg, Helene's unmarried older brother, who had moved to Velen to be with his sister after all his other siblings had emigrated or fled.

At the last minute, Leopold's status as a disabled World War I veteran earned him a reprieve. Meanwhile Abraham and Helene Frank got ready. Helene saw her eye doctor to get new glasses. Abraham, who was about to turn seventy, got a note from his doctor that he had arthritis and needed an eiderdown. They distributed their belongings among acquaintances and friends. Abraham left his precious kosher butcher knives with a trusted neighbor. They had a painter print their names and address on a set of suitcases. Helene's last errand was to the Schmähing's grocery store to get the ground coffee that she had ordered, but the order was late and she had a curfew and couldn't wait. When the delivery came, Frau Schmähing sent her daughter to bring Frau Frank her coffee. But the Velen policeman sent to surveil their residence took it and sent the girl home.

This was their last night in the town that had been their home. Abraham was born there. Helene made it her home when she married Abraham. Now they were alone. No one could visit them and they were confined to their quarters. How did they spend their last hours? Perhaps they reviewed their final list of things to pack. Had they forgotten anything? Was there anything else they should add? The directive issued by the Gestapo headquarters in Münster specified what they could take and Helene carefully checked off each item. Bedding with blanket. Adequate clothing: outer and undergarments. Decent shoes. Three weeks' worth of non-perishable food stuffs (bread, flour, barley, legumes). Eating utensils (a plate or pot) with spoon; knives and forks are strictly forbidden! No valuables. No jewelry except wedding rings. A limit of one suitcase per person.[20] The other suitcases that Abraham ordered would have to stay behind.

It was still dark the next morning when they walked to the corner of Bahnhof and Coesfeld Streets, where they had been told to expect the bus that would come to get them. The designated stop was just across the street from their house. The policeman assigned to watch them stood guard as they waited.

When the bus arrived, the driver left the engine running. The schedule was tight. Departure time from Velen was 7.10 a.m., and people at the next stop were already waiting. Boarding was quick. The bus was already half-full with Jews from other towns in the area. Abraham's younger sister, Ida Cohen, had boarded the bus in Coesfeld. Five of his cousins and two nieces and nephews were on the bus too. Abraham and Helene took a seat and the bus departed.

That same day—December 11, 1941—the Franks' residency in Velen was officially terminated. Their utility services were cut off, the doors to their house were padlocked, and Abraham and Helene Frank were struck from the Velen town registry. The last entry on the Franks in the registry identifies them as "Jews." They were allowed no other social identity. Abraham was no longer identified as a butcher; Helene was no longer identified as his wife. Next to their name, it simply says "no profession."[21] And under "next place of residence" it says "unknown."

Yet it was not unknown. They were sent to Riga. Not, however, to take up residence. They were sent to Riga to die. From Velen, they were taken to Münster, where hundreds of local Jews were assembled for deportation. Two days later, a train with some four hundred deportees, among them the Franks and members of their extended families, headed east for what was officially billed as a "work assignment." Hundreds more Jews were added along the way. When they arrived in Riga shortly before midnight on December 15, 1941, they had been on the train for over sixty hours and were 1,700 kilometers from home. They had traveled across the European continent, through northern Germany and German-occupied Poland, across Lithuania and half of Latvia, until they reached Riga on the Baltic Sea. It was the largest ghetto for Reich Jews in eastern Europe, Nazi authorities boasted. Surrounded by a 10 foot high double-barbed wire fence, and patrolled by guards with German shepherds, it was not a place of residence but a prison.[22]

When the transport from Münster arrived, Riga was blanketed in snow. The barracks were icy. Food, when it didn't rot, froze. Icicles formed stalactites on the ceiling and people kept their winter coats on indoors. Every piece of clothing the Franks had packed and been able to salvage became critical.[23]

Beyond a rumor that Abraham Frank was seen in 1943 in Warsaw, where the SS put German prisoners to work repairing railroad tracks, the only information on the fate of the Franks is the manifest showing that they boarded the train for Riga in Münster. There is no recorded date of death. Official records simply list them as "missing."

On March 2, 1942, three months after they boarded the bus in Velen, their material possessions—furniture, household items, and personal effects—were displayed in a Velen pub and auctioned. Many Veleners, it is said, came to bid. The Frank family home, where Abraham had lived as a child, was declared Reich property and rented to Velen's chief of police in recognition of his service to the Nazi Party.

After the Franks were gone, Velen's Mayor Becker, as ardent a Nazi as his eager chief of police, reported to the regional authorities that only three Jews were left in his jurisdiction: eighty-one-year-old Amalia Landau; her daughter, Ida Sandmann; and Leopold Humberg, the brother of Helene Frank. Two of them, he noted, merited special dispensation: Leopold Humberg as a decorated World War I veteran, and Ida Sandmann as the wife of "an Aryan electrician."[24]

But special dispensations no longer curbed the Nazi zeal to purge the German Reich of all things Jewish. Amalia Landau and Leopold Humberg were ordered to report to the police to register for "evacuation." The same Velen policeman who had put Abraham and Helene Frank on the bus for Riga took Amalia and Leopold to their designated registration site for deportation. He picked them up at their house, walked them to the station, sat with them on the train, and delivered them to the police as ordered. It was early morning on July 26, 1942 when the three set out.

On their walk down Bahnhof Street, they would have passed the Jägering home, where a little girl named Anna, who later recalled seeing three Jews walking to the station on a summer morning, was looking out of her front window. The three people walking by were not, as she misremembered, Amalia Landau and her two daughters, but Amalia Landau, Leopold Humberg, and the Velen policeman. The scene her memory conjured up was not what she saw, but a composite of the stories she heard from others.

When Amalia and Leopold arrived in Münster, they were crowded into makeshift quarters where they waited until the last deportees had arrived. Five days later, hungry, thirsty, and suffering from the heat and lack of sleep, they were finally loaded onto a special deportation train composed of seven empty freight cars. Four of the seven cars were filled with the very elderly, many of them patients taken out of nursing homes, hospitals, and even hospice care. Frail and ill, wrapped in blankets, they were laid out side by side, like planks on the floor of the freight cars. At around midnight on July 31, the doors were locked and the train departed. Destination: Theresienstadt. Leopold Humberg died there four months later. Amalia Landau survived two more years.[25] At midnight on July 31, 1942, Nazi party headquarters was informed that "Gau Westfalen-Nord ist judenfrei"—Northern Westphalia is Jew-free.[26]

But Velen was not yet "Jew-free," as the Party prematurely crowed. There was still Ida Sandmann. In 1935, when Velen authorities submitted to the Gestapo their requested list of Velen Jews, they had left her out. It was a puzzling omission. As the daughter of two Jewish parents, Meyer Landau and Amalia Frank, Ida Sandmann was clearly Jewish by Nazi standards. Why she was not listed is unclear. Perhaps in May 1935 the new meaning of the word "Jew" had not sunk in yet. Before the Nuremberg Laws were passed that fall, Ida Sandmann could still have been considered Catholic. She had converted to Catholicism, consecrated her marriage in a Catholic church, and was raising her children as Catholics. To Velen eyes, the Sandmanns were a Catholic family.[27] Or perhaps leaving her off the list was a small but bold act of resistance by an unnamed clerk in the Velen town registry, appalled by the politics of exclusion she was asked to support.

Ten years later, the net had tightened and Ida could no longer escape. On February 1, 1945, just weeks before Germany conceded defeat in the disastrous war it had started, Ida Sandmann, like her mother before her, was sent to Theresienstadt. Her Catholic faith and Aryan husband no longer shielded her from the fate to which Nazi authorities had condemned her as a Jew.

Unlike her mother, however, Ida Sandmann survived the camp. Less than half a year after she was deported, she returned to Velen. But she didn't return unchanged. "Discouraged" (*mutlos*) is how her husband later described her. She had used all her resources of courage to survive the camp. What she needed to survive in Velen after the camp was not courage but forbearance.

Her very presence made people uncomfortable. Most Germans didn't know how to deal with survivors of the camps, especially those who returned to their own communities. What should they say? Should they apologize for what had happened, acknowledge what they had—or had not—done? Should they ask the survivors what they experienced? And if they asked, were they ready for the answers? They didn't even know what to call these survivors. Contorted terms like "former concentrationers" (*ehemalige Konzentrationäre*) betrayed their discomfort.

Returning home after surviving Auschwitz and Buchenwald, the protagonist of Imre Kertész's autobiographical fiction *Fateless* registers the awkwardness and even hostility born of this discomfort. When people ask what he experienced ("Did you have to go through many horrors?"), he deflects: "That depends on what you call a horror."[28] But when they counsel him, "'you must forget the terrors,'" he firmly rejects their proposed solution as impossible. He can't just "start a new life." All he can do is continue his old one.

For Ida Sandmann, continuing her old life meant restoring her sense of self in a community that had abandoned if not betrayed her. And it meant returning to a place of traumatic loss. Her mother was gone, killed in Theresienstadt. Her eighteen-year-old daughter had died the same year as her mother of complications following tonsillitis amidst rumors that "there were other causes ... not natural ones" for her death.[29]

Since the early nineteenth century, when Hermann Landau and Levy Frank moved to Velen to develop their businesses and raise their families, Jewish life had been part of village life. That life was over. The Franks and Landaus were gone. Ida's relatives had either been killed or forced into exile. The family she returned to was just two people: her husband and eleven-year-old son.

In the privacy of the Sandmann family, did they talk about what had happened—what they experienced, what they remembered, what they felt? Did Ida tell her husband and son of the camp where she spent four months less than a year after her mother died there? Did Franz confess to his fear that, after losing his daughter, he had lost his wife, and that their son, Günther, would grow up without a mother? Did he tell of the times when his grief was so overwhelming that he wept when he talked of her with his neighbor? "Sometimes the old man would sit at our kitchen table and just cry," the neighbor's son recounted when I asked him what he remembered of that time.[30] Did Günther tell his mother about his eleventh birthday, two weeks after she had left, and his fear that, like his sister and grandmother, she was gone forever? Or did they let the routines of daily life cover up the wounds?

Ida and Franz Sandmann both died in Velen, the village where they were born: Ida in 1987 aged eighty-two, Franz seven years later aged ninety-two. They were buried side by side in the Velen cemetery.

On one of my visits to Velen, an acquaintance commented that their son, Günther, was "the only one left."[31] What she meant was "the only" Jew, "the only" survivor of Velen's Jewish community. Yet Günther Sandmann didn't think of himself as Jewish. He was born and had lived his life as a Catholic. By all accounts, therefore, there were no Jews left in Velen. The Nazi genocide had been effective. Jewish life in towns and rural communities across Westphalia had been destroyed.

After the war, Veleners were asked to account for the Jews in their community. How many had lived there before what a February 1946 survey referred to, bizarrely, as "Hitlerism" (*Hitlerismus*)? And how many were living there now? Nine was the answer to how many there had been. And two were living there now: Ida Sandmann and her sister, Lene.[32]

The survey didn't ask what became of their property. It didn't have to. The evidence was clear. The house where Abraham and Helene Frank lived and had their butcher shop had been sold to an "Aryan" with Nazi credentials. Abraham's parental home, where Samuel and Julie Frank had raised eight children, had been expropriated as "Jewish property" and rented to the Nazi chief of police, just as the former Landau house had been rented to another of Velen's most ardent Nazi officials.

In the early 1950s, Abraham and Helene Frank's daughter, Edith, who had moved to England and survived the war, submitted a formal request for restitution of Frank family property: the financial assets confiscated by the state when it annulled their citizenship and the material possessions claimed as state property when her parents were deported. The list included furniture and personal effects, bedding, table linens, and clothing.[33]

But it didn't take surveys of how many Jews were missing or itemized lists of property that had been stolen from them to remind Veleners of what had happened during the Nazi years. They knew.

In cities, where people were deported in large numbers, often in mass actions, you might be able to claim that you didn't exactly know what was happening. Perhaps no one you knew personally had been arrested or deported … and, after all, it was war, and in war, as the saying goes, stuff happens.

In a rural community, such distancing is impossible. You can't feign ignorance. Even if you don't know everyone directly, you know *of* them. Word spreads. When Velen's Jews were deported, Veleners could not pretend to be ignorant. They would have known who helped them, who betrayed them, and who profited from their persecution. Even if they didn't know why exactly they left or what became of them, they knew that they were gone and did not return.

Everyone knew when the Franks left their house and butcher shop and a new family, the Laumanns, moved in, just as they knew when Edith and Siegfried Frank left Velen. The Föckers knew the violence of anti-Semitism first hand, from when the Franks lived in their house and Nazi hoodlums attacked them. Luise Schmähing and farmer Tepferd knew the shame and despair of a family whose livelihood had been destroyed when they tried to help the Franks by supplying them with groceries. Frau Wellermann knew the anguish of a husband who could not protect his wife from deportation when Franz Sandmann sat at her kitchen table and cried. The village policeman who assisted in deporting Velen's Jews knew the rush of power when he strutted about in his uniform. Even those who were only involved indirectly—who filled out the paperwork, signed the orders, delivered the deportation notices, cut off the utilities to the empty homes of deported Jews, put their houses up for sale, and auctioned off their possessions—they too knew, at least partially, what was happening.

How people know things—how they learn of them and pass them on—affects what and how they remember. Only shared knowledge, knowledge that circulates within a group or community, Maurice Halbwachs declared, can be retained over time in memory. What isn't shared dissipates and eventually can no longer be retrieved. It is by sharing things within "social frameworks of memory," Halbwachs insisted, that the shape of what we know as our past evolves. Indeed, he maintained, outside the social frameworks that shape our sense of identity—familial, national, religious, ethnic, or political formations—we have no memory. Memories are formed and sustained within social contexts. Outside these contexts, like plants without oxygen, they die.[34]

This link between forms of knowledge and the shape of memory is reflected in the different ways that war and the Holocaust figure in the past that Veleners recall. During the Nazi years, the war was a constant focus of public attention on the radio, in the local paper, and by word of mouth. The priest announced the names of the dead from the Sunday pulpit, each name recalling someone the congregants knew. These deaths were mourned publicly and openly. After mass, people gathered outside the church or in the pub to exchange information on the state of the war and its impact on the local community. And every evening, the night watchman who doubled as the town crier through the war years, patrolled the streets on his bicycle. Ringing a large cowbell, he stopped at key sites with the latest updates.[35]

The deportation of Velen's Jews was not communicated in this public way. The priest didn't announce them from the pulpit and the town crier didn't call them out with his bell. When people shared what they knew, they did so confidentially, in private conversations or behind closed doors.

The relative presence of these different histories in the communal memory of the town is inseparable from the ways they have—or have not—been acknowledged publicly. War is readily acknowledged in Velen's cultural landscape, from the large memorial sculpture on the town hall grounds and the book of the war dead in St. Andreas' church to the rows of headstones for fallen soldiers at the entrance to the cemetery. Remembrance of the Holocaust has, until recently, been much less visible. Not entirely absent, but off to the side.

In 2012, the landscape of Velen memory changed. It started with a simple school project. Ulrich Wollheim, a social science teacher in Velen's middle school, wanted his students to learn about history through primary research instead of from books, and his tenth grade class accepted the challenge: they would explore the fate of the Jews in Velen during the Third Reich.

Four girls formed a small research task force. "No boys?" I asked Herr Wollheim. "They showed no interest," he shrugged. "The girls were eager to get involved." They consulted archives. They collected stories. They interviewed surviving witnesses, including Günther Sandmann, the lone descendant of Velen's Jewish community still in Velen.

In the process, they not only moved parts of local history from the shadows into the light, but found new details that changed the contours of Velen's memory. Among other things, they added a missing chapter to the story of the Franks. Buried in the history of persecution and death, they found a love story.

Updated records from Yad Vashem reveal that, after his flight to the Netherlands, Siegfried Frank was arrested again and sent to Westerbork (the camp where Dutch authorities detained Jews who had entered the country illegally). Stays at Westerbork were usually brief. Most inmates were moved to Nazi concentration camps within weeks. Siegfried Frank, however, stayed at Westerbork for almost five years, during which time he fell in love with a fellow Westphalian from a town less than 30 miles from Velen. Twenty-one-year-old Margot Cohen had been sent to Westerbork with her two-year-old daughter, Sophia Juliana Lindemann. In July 1942 Margot Cohen and Siegfried Frank were married.

Their happiness was short lived. In September 1944, Siegfried was moved to Theresienstadt, then to Auschwitz, and finally, in January 1945, to Buchenwald. During this final transfer, he was shot and killed. Margot and her daughter Sophia were murdered in Auschwitz on October 6, 1944.

I take note of their deaths. I record their names. Three people in the mass of 6 million. But the horror of their death is not all I choose to remember. I want to recall their moments of happiness too.

Teacher Wollheim's students wanted to do more than write a paper and get a grade. They wanted to leave a trace of their research in Velen's public memory. In June 2012, at their initiative, a *Stolperstein* memorial was installed to remember the Jews from Velen who had been deported and killed. Four small commemorative stones, each a little under 4 square inches, were set into the sidewalk in front of two houses on Bahnhof Street. The first three, in front of Bahnhof Street 13, where the Franks' butcher shop and house had been, remembered Abraham, Siegfried, and Helene Frank.[36] The fourth, in front of what was now a savings and loan bank but had once been the site of the Frank's first home in Velen, remembered Leopold Humberg, who was deported from there in 1942 together with his sister-in-law, Amalia Landau.[37]

That fall, I went to Velen to see these memorials. I sat on the front steps of the Franks' former butcher shop and watched people go by. No one stopped to look at the stones. Everyone seemed busy. They had things to do. The past wasn't on their mind. They didn't even seem to be aware of the memorials.

The building behind me felt and looked abandoned. The front room, where the store used to be, was empty, the window shuttered. Nobody seemed to have used the entrance in some time. I had heard that three of the Laumanns still lived there, but they were very old, I was told, and kept to themselves in the back rooms of the house. No signs of human habitation were visible.

Workers were setting up to start repairs on the house next door. They stopped, curious to know what I was doing there. I pointed to the Franks' former house and asked if anyone still lived there.

"In back," one of them said, "the Laumanns."

"And in front?"

"Nothing. Nothing's in front."

"Nothing?"

"There was a butcher shop here," he answered. "Once."

So, what remains of the time when Velen still had Jewish families, a small Jewish community connected to other small Jewish communities in neighboring towns? A shuttered building that once housed a thriving butcher shop, where Abraham and Helene Frank ran a business and raised their children. A modern, glass-fronted savings and loan bank that had replaced the house where Samuel and Julie Frank had raised their eight children. And four small memorial stones to remind passersby of what had been lost.

A passerby stops to read the inscription on the Stolperstein memorial to Abraham Frank, Siegfried Frank, and Helene Frank (née Humberg) in front of their former house and butcher shop on Bahnhof Street, Velen. (Photograph by author, 2012).

As I watched Veleners going about their business, oblivious to the small memorial stones underfoot, I wondered whether things in the material world—a stone, a landscape, a table—hold memories of the past even when we don't perceive its traces. Somewhere in Velen, I imagined, was the table where the Franks once sat, breaking bread and reciting the Shabbat blessings. Another family, in another household, sat at the table now, again breaking bread and asking for God's blessing. They probably knew nothing of the table's history. It was just a table to them. What stories it could tell them if they asked it. No one, I suspected, asked.

My Nazi Family

"It was wonderful," he said, leaning closer. I was talking with Johannes Liesner, an old colleague of my grandfather's in Velen. They had worked together in the Landsberg administration for years. Herr Liesner's eyes peered over his bifocals. They were a startling, electric blue. "It was wonderful," he said again, focusing his gaze on me. "I have to be honest ... it was a wonderful time for me."

I had asked him how he remembered the Nazi years in Velen (*What was it like for you?*) and this was his answer. I was startled, but also pleased. Finally someone who didn't say the predictable, *how terrible it all was* or imply that *it had been some huge mistake.* On the contrary, he admitted he had fond memories of those years. *A wonderful time*, he said.

I hadn't met him before, but my grandfather had often spoken of him warmly. Before my visit to Velen in 2012, I had contacted him and asked if we could meet. He invited me to his home for afternoon coffee with his wife, Cäcilia. When he greeted me at the door, he remarked that I reminded him of my grandmother, Maria. "The same eyes," he said, "as Frau Bushoff. You have your grandmother's smile."

We sat and talked over coffee and cake until afternoon shaded to evening. The Liesners were curious about my interest in Velen history and open to sharing their memories and thoughts. They had been very fond of both my grandparents, they told me. "But especially your grandfather," Herr Liesner offered. "Herr Bushoff was the finest man." They began working together in 1947, when Johannes Liesner got a job in the bookkeeping department of the Landsberg estate, eventually advancing to the position of head bookkeeper. My grandfather was his boss.

Johannes Liesner was born in 1932, the same year as my Velen friend Anna. In elementary school, he reminisced, they were classmates. But his most vivid memories were of his boyhood years in the Hitler Youth. The excitement of the marches. The fellowship of the gatherings. The camaraderie of their activities. The songs. The flags. He loved it all. More than anything else, he loved the uniform. Johannes still remembered his pride when he wore it. Brown shirt. Black pants. Black neck scarf, with the leather tie. "But the best part was the belt! Black leather, with a metal buckle, just like soldiers in the army. I never had clothes like that before. For me, as a boy, it was thrilling." He paused and took a sip of coffee. I saw the old man's tremor in his hand. "All that other stuff," he added, "we didn't know about at the time." At the end of the war, he was fourteen.

I had finally found someone willing to admit Nazi sympathies, even if it was just nostalgia for a spiffy uniform. The discrepancy between the magnitude of Nazi crimes and the tiny number of identified criminals had always troubled me. Where had all the Nazi-tolerant Germans gone? Outside Germany, many people routinely associated Germans with Nazis, while inside Germany, everyone seemed to disavow them. My childhood fantasy that my parents had been Nazis was a perverse attempt to reconcile the difference.

Stereotypical German traits—being punctual, orderly, dutiful, *korrekt*— were equated with Nazi behavior. My father sometimes elicited that reaction. People would note "how German" he was with a note of censure, as if he might suddenly snap to attention, click his heels, and shout *jawohl*. We ourselves were guilty of this slippage.

"If you had to represent our father in a single, one-man scene, how would you play him?" I once asked my brother. Thomas grinned. For a seasoned actor, this didn't need rehearsal.

"*François*," he barked in a French accent, his face and gestures also turning French, "*François, où sont les pommes de terre?*" Where are the potatoes? He clicked his heels, jerked his head up, and shot his arm out in a Nazi salute.

I laughed, remembering the incident my brother replayed. It was in Gabon, when our father was ambassador. François, the cook, had forgotten our father's rule that fish was always served with potatoes, whereupon our father had angrily and arrogantly dressed him down. My brother's representation was on target. I might have picked the same incident.

"But the Hitler parody," I objected, "that's unfair and untrue. *Heil Hitler* ... that was not our father."

"You're right," Thomas conceded. "That wasn't him. I got carried away by the scene."

Yet there was truth in it all the same. Not the Nazi part. It was his attitude that conjured up the image. My father wasn't mindlessly obedient—he didn't run with the herd—but he respected prevailing forms, or at least accommodated them as much as possible. Conformity was a matter of cultural style for him. There was a right and proper way to do things. Any other way was dismissed as wrong. It was a stance he had been taught from childhood. Already as a child he called his parents by the formal *Mutter* and *Vater*, instead of *Mutti* or *Vati*, or some other more affectionate terms. Even his beloved grandmother was always formally addressed as *Grossmutter*, never *Oma*.

My father believed in good form. He valued it. It was integral to his sense of identity. And he was willing to pay the price. He observed the rules. "To rebel," the historian Tony Judt remarked, "one must dispense with good form," and my father was unable to do that.[1] In my father's household, you came to dinner dressed properly. You sat up straight, kept your elbows at your side, and used your napkin. You never slurped your soup. And when fish was served, it came with potatoes. When my son was young, he referred to his grandfather as "the ambassador."

This adherence to proper form was evident again in my father's response to the postwar denazification process. When he filled out the required six-page questionnaire in which every German over eighteen had to account for the manner and degree of their involvement with Nazi activities, he followed the instructions to a tee, printing all of his answers to the 131 questions neatly and "clearly in block letters." And when his answer to a given question, such as the details of his military service ("Give a chronological history of your employment and military service beginning with 1st of January 1931"), exceeded the allotted twelve lines, he added another sheet that he glued to the questionnaire as a supplement, carefully penciling in twelve additional lines with a ruler. Then, when he had filled out all six pages, he started over, copying each of his answers—word for word—on a duplicate form to keep as a record.[2]

The principle of denazification was noble, inspired by the idealist assumption that good abounds once you extirpate evil. But the practice quickly became a logistical nightmare. In May 1945, when the US Office of Military Government (OMGUS) drew up its questions and printed the questionnaires, it hadn't considered the practical implications that soon became evident. In the American zone alone, over 13 million German men and women were filling out questionnaires and submitting them for clearance certification. The Military Government was overwhelmed. It didn't have the personnel to read millions of documents written by hand and in German. Nor did it have the legal and administrative means to follow up on the information that the questionnaires disclosed. The solution was obvious: hand it over to Germans and let them sort things out themselves.

To accomplish that, "Law No. 104 for Liberation from National Socialism and Militarism" (effective March 5, 1946 in the parts of Germany under

American military control—Bavaria, Greater Hesse, and Württemberg-Baden), relegated the denazification process to German authorities. One of the signatories of this new German law was the man who, three years later, would become the first President of the German Federal Republic, Theodor Heuss.[3] Law No. 104 aimed to secure a lasting foundation for a democratic Germany by calling all persons to account who had actively supported the National Socialist reign of terror or violated basic principles of justice and human rights in its name.[4] The questionnaire was designed to identify those culpable.

It began with standard biographical details (name, address, place of birth, profession, etc.), dwelling on religion for five full questions (including which religious affiliation you currently claimed and which you claimed in the 1939 census). Education came next, with the note, "If a special Nazi school or military academy, so specify," followed by employment and military service to include "paramilitary organizations" from January 1931 on.

However, the main concern was "Membership in Organizations." Over half of the questions—76 out of 131—focused on this issue, beginning with membership in the Nazi Party itself and continuing through a list of fifty-three subsidiary or affiliated organizations. My father's record in this regard was clean. His only Nazi-affiliated membership—with the German Worker's Front (Deutsche Arbeitsfront, DAF)—effectively preceded the Nazi state. When independent trade unions were abolished in 1933 and replaced by the Nazi-controlled DAF, his trade union membership was just transferred to the new structure.

His questionnaire completed, my father submitted it to the local Denazification Committee on November 16, 1946.

Two days later, the first of three letters in support of his clearance application was put in the mail. It was from Manfred Förster. Typed on official Förster Company letterhead, it emphasized "Dr. Walter Bammer's internationalist sensibilities" and vouched for his anti-fascist credentials ("*ein einwandfreier Antifaschist*"). As a loyal citizen of Czechoslovakia, Manfred's letter stated, Dr. Bammer had always opposed Sudeten German nationalist politics. He earned distinction as the only German candidate at the Czech military academy and was promoted early. The concluding lines of Manfred's letter address the issue at the heart of the postwar reckoning with Nazi Germany: Nazi anti-Semitism and its impact on relationships between Jews and non-Jews. "Despite the rule of National Socialism in Germany," Manfred wrote, "and the hardships that I myself suffered because of this regime, my relations (*herzliche Beziehungen*) with Herr Bammer and his family always stayed close."

A second letter of support came from a Jewish friend of Walter's father, who had emigrated to the United States in 1938. With his German name, Hans

Bacher, Americanized to John H. Backer, he had returned to Europe after the war as a civilian member of OMGUS and was stationed in Frankfurt.[5] John Backer addressed his letter to Walter directly. "Dear Herr Doctor," he wrote, "having known you in the context of your family and its members' political beliefs, I have no doubt that you never adopted National Socialist ideas, but always held to democratic principles." By way of conclusion, he addressed the question of whether Walter's service in the Wehrmacht was a culpable offense. He determined it wasn't. "As a German and a soldier," he declared, "you only did your duty when you were drafted into the Wehrmacht." From the perspective of the American military authorities, John Backer's letter concluded, Walter Bammer presented "no political concern."

The third and last letter followed that April. It addressed head on the question that Manfred Förster had merely raised obliquely: Walter's relationship to Jews. Written in the stiff, formal language of a man versed less in the art of writing than the statements of facts, and typed on the brittle brown paper that spoke of postwar penury, it was headed "Declaration." Noting that he had known "Herr Dr. Walter Bammer" since childhood and attended elementary school with him, the author affirms that throughout his youth Walter had close Jewish friends and that, when he began his legal career in 1937, he started with a Jewish firm in Prague. The letter ends with the observation that he had always known Walter Bammer as someone who "associated freely with everyone, without regard to their race, status, or nationality." It is signed (illegible first name) Gekar, "member of the K.P.Č. since 1925, now S.E.D. and police officer at the Löbau train station."[6]

As I read these testimonials I was struck by how quickly political tides turn. Just a few years earlier, my father had compiled information for his Ancestry Passport proving that his family tree was Aryan-pure. Now the contaminating factor was Nazi affiliation. And the best way to dispel it was by documenting close relations to Jews.

In early June, half a year after my father submitted his questionnaire to local authorities, he received a postcard from the German Minister for Political Liberation in Frankfurt, the administrative headquarters for the denazification process. The card informed him that within the categories established by the Law for Liberation from National Socialism and Militarism he was cleared of guilt. Neither an *offender* (an activist, a militarist, or a profiteer), nor a *follower*, nor an *exonerated person* (someone whose guilt had been established and forgiven), he was free to proceed with life in the new Germany.

Six weeks later, on July 23, 1947, his official Clearance Certificate arrived. Printed on the same plain brown stock as the other documents from that time, it was a simple postcard-size piece of paper. Signed by the chair of the local Denazification Committee, it confirmed that Dr. Bammer, Walter, born January 11, 1913, resident of Velen, Westphalia, "has been cleared under the provisions of Military Government Ordinance No. 79."[7]

A month earlier, on June 20, 1947, my mother too had been officially cleared of guilt under the denazification provisions. Already in April, her German Identity Card, issued in four languages (German, English, French, and Russian) by the Allied Control Council, had been given the requisite seal of political approval. As the official document that all Germans had to carry at all times and "present to any public official or member of the police force upon request without delay," it confirmed that Ursula Bammer, née Bushoff, born December 2, 1922 in Velen, Westphalia; nationality: German; height: 168 cm; and figure: slender, had been "Reviewed politically" and found acceptable. The only error on Ursula's Identity Card was her eye color. A clerk had entered "blue." Perhaps "gray-green" didn't seem sufficiently German. Or perhaps small adjustments to the facts helped smooth rough regime transitions.

As I look at my parents' postwar documents, another such adjustment strikes me: the stamp from the Frankfurt police department on Ursula's German Identity Card still carries the same German eagle as in Nazi times, but it no longer holds a swastika in its grip. The place where the swastika had been is voided.

Walter's parents were cleared at around the same time. His father's case was straightforward and easy. He had navigated the transitions between regimes successfully. He had accommodated the Nazi regime by suspending his affiliation with the Social Democrats, even as he eschewed affiliation with the Nazi Party. After the war his non-Nazi credentials were an asset that he reinforced by renewing his Social Democratic Party membership.

Walter's mother wasn't so savvy. While she never joined the Nazi Party, she became a member of the Nazi-affiliated NS-Frauenschaft through her work as a volunteer Red Cross nurse. As an umbrella organization for various groups and associations devoted to so-called women's concerns, the Frauenschaft functioned as the women's wing of the Nazi Party and as such was accountable within the party structure.[8] For this involvement with Nazi activities, Hildegard Bammer was held responsible after the war. A brief entry in my mother's diary on June 17, 1945 records the outcome: "Walter's mother is punished for her membership in the Nazi party by being made to clean the quarters where the troops are housed."

Absent further details, I conjure a scenario. Armed with a bucket of soapy water and a brush, Hildegard Bammer scrubs the walls and floors of the soldiers' barracks. On her hands and knees, she cleans the bathroom—the grimy tiles, the shit-streaked toilets, the splattered urinals. I try to square this scene with the image of the grandmother Bammer I grew up with: her delicate health, her quiet elegance, her grace. She carried herself like a dancer, people said of her. One of the only pictures of her from that time is a formal portrait in her nurse's uniform. Her striped blouse with the starched, white collar is clean and pressed and her hair is concealed under her white nurse's cap. The small Red Cross pin at her throat draws my gaze.

My grandmother Bushoff was another story. I had known for some time that she had been a member of the NS-Frauenschaft. It had come up once in conversation, but was dismissed as no big deal, just a small adjustment to what she was doing anyway. As my mother explained it, when an NS-Frauenschaft chapter was created in Velen, activities previously organized within the context of the church were simply integrated into its new framework. The Catholic Women's Group of St. Andreas' parish was incorporated into the local NS-Frauenschaft. It was called *Gleichschaltung*, realignment. The Party simply took the place of the Church. Nothing really changed, my mother shrugged. The basic activities continued: gossipy gatherings over cake and coffee, community service to the needy and poor, and the annual spring pilgrimage to the Marian shrine in Kevelaer that had always been as much a social as a religious event.[9] The Nazi party framework just expanded the range of their engagements.

The first big event marking this expanded context was May Day 1934. It coincided with the first anniversary of the Velen Frauenschaft chapter. For the occasion, the Nazi Party had ordered Velen to be adorned with swastika flags and banners and the women of St. Andreas', now recast as Frauenschaft women, mobilized to meet the charge. Directed by a cadre of professional seamstresses and tailors, they worked around the clock for days and produced a rush of flags that covered the village with billowing swastikas.

When I first learned of my grandmother's Frauenschaft involvement, I found the *Gleichschaltung* argument compelling. I reasoned that this Party affiliation didn't change who she was, much less who she was to me. She wasn't a fascist or an anti-Semite. She was warm and generous and kind.

Certainly my grandmother Bushoff didn't look like the Nazi women in popular images. Those women coarse and ugly, dressed in work clothes, and had rough manners. They looked (and probably were, I thought) hard and mean. My Oma was different. She was soft. She was silky blouses, the smell of talcum, and the taste of bonbons. Her smell embodied all that was feminine in my childhood world. When she bent to kiss me, the cloud of perfumed powder made my nose itch, but I loved to bury my face in her silk jabot and inhale the fragrance. In the evening, when I said goodnight, I sometimes caught her in her bedtime ritual. On the stool by her dresser mirror, her hair in a hairnet and her face covered with Nivea cream, she looked like a clown in a whiteface. "To smooth the wrinkles," she explained, while I hugged her gingerly, trying to avoid getting cream on my clothes. To this day, the smell of Nivea evokes my Oma.

Maria Bushoff was used to being spoiled. In her youth, she was known as one of the five beautiful Thoma sisters and her husband couldn't say no when she had a wish. He indulged her with little treats—chocolates, a glass of egg liquor, a pastry. Even in lean times, when potatoes and lentils were the daily fare, she could nuzzle his shoulder and plead for "maybe, a little roast on Sunday?" and he would instruct the maid to prepare a little roast "for the lady."

Yet I loved her, this spoiled and self-indulgent woman. I loved her extravagance, her embrace of sensual pleasures without shame. I loved her outrageousness, her breach of decorum, her wild laughter. Swabbing at her eyes with a cotton diaper, she would gasp for help. "Help," she almost choked from laughing. "Help, I'm going to pee my pants." I wanted to be bold like her, unafraid to want things.

But her Nazi involvement was a different matter. On reflection, she no longer seemed so innocent. *No big deal* was an insufficient response. My unease deepened when I learned that she wasn't just a member of the local Frauenschaft; she was its head!

At first I almost missed the mention. I was reading a description of the Velen Frauenschaft and its founding on May 21, 1933, a few months after

My grandmother, Maria Bushoff, and me on my second birthday, September 1948.

Hitler's appointment as Reich Chancellor. A Party representative had been sent to recruit local women as members. Women, she said, held the future of the fatherland in their hands. They were responsible for shaping the new Germany alongside their men. The Frauenschaft needed their involvement.

Her appeal worked. That same day, some thirty Velen women joined and within a week, the local chapter had over eighty members. Two prominent women from Velen's most-respected families took on the leadership and the wife of the Landsberg estate director was elected head. It took me a moment to realize that I was reading about my grandmother Bushoff.

Did her appointment matter? What difference, if any, did it make? One could object that beyond sponsoring occasional swastika-decorated events in the local community, the Velen Frauenschaft head wasn't authorized to make—or execute—decisions of import. Yet for the Nazi Party, locally and regionally, the appointment of Maria Bushoff was a coup. As the wife of one of the most respected men in the village hierarchy, a man whose position as director of the Landsberg estate signified authority, Frau Bushoff lent social prestige to the Nazi-affiliated Frauenschaft and helped legitimate local Nazi Party activities.

The real shock, however, was not discovering that my grandmother was head of the Velen Frauenschaft chapter. It's what I learned about my grandfather along the way.

I had just received a copy of Norbert Fasse's meticulously researched regional history with a focus on the Nazi years and wondered if my grandparents were mentioned. I checked the index and there, under "B," was my grandfather: "Bushoff, Hans." He wasn't just mentioned. There were a total of eighteen entries to his name. One of them was a photograph: a formal three-quarter profile shot.[10] High forehead, prominent nose and ears, wispy hair and receding hairline, a perfect egg-shaped head. This same photo of my grandfather Bushoff was in my family album. *Pg. Hans Bushoff,* the caption read. I was momentarily puzzled. What did "Pg." mean? Then I remembered: it meant *Parteigenosse,* the term that Nazis used for "Party member."[11] I stared at the small black and white photograph in the history book. My Opa Bushoff, a Nazi party member? And judging from the number of entries to his name, not a minor one. This was a revelation. Unlike my grandmother Bushoff's involvement in the Velen Frauenschaft, my grandfather's membership in the Nazi Party had never come up.

It wasn't mentioned in family conversations or in any of the official eulogies after his death. When he died in 1969, Hans Bushoff was remembered as a devoted public citizen who had served his community over the years. He had assisted the hospital as legal advisor, played a key role in town planning matters, and been the driving force in the preservation of local culture.

He was born in the neighboring town of Borken in 1884 and christened Johann Christoph Adolf Bushoff. Records show the Bushoff family residing in the area for many generations. His father was a doctor, and his mother, a dark-haired, melancholic beauty always remembered by her maiden name, Antonia Süss, died when he was a baby. Ten years later, when he was eleven, his father died, leaving Hans and his half-sister, Toni, to be raised by his stepmother, his father's second wife.

Perhaps it was his early experience of profound loss, perhaps a mark of Westphalian peasant culture, that shaped his lifelong impulse to preserve things. He salvaged what he could from the past: endangered parts of the native landscape, old stamps and coins, the ways and traditions of local culture and Westphalian history. His greatest passion and most enduring commitment was the *Heimatverein*, the local heritage association. Not only was he one of its founding members, he chaired it for its first thirteen years.

He kept careful records of the things he saved. Each stamp and coin in his collection was itemized. Each had its place in a prescribed, well-ordered system. His collections were little worlds he could preserve. He never seemed happier than when he worked on his stamp collection. When he let me help him, I felt like a ministrant in a sacred ritual. Gently grasping each stamp at its serrated edge with special tweezers, we slipped it into its paper sleeve and recorded its date of release and place of origin on a tiny label. He taught me to work with care and attend to details. You can't allow yourself to get distracted, he admonished me when I started chattering. He sat, I stood, his woolen jacket sleeve against my cheek, as we silently bent over the stamps together. The lamplight glanced off his glasses and the world felt calm.

My grandfather Bushoff was a quiet man. He always preferred listening to talking. He never played with his grandchildren as grandparents sometimes do when they want to entertain or amuse them. The rare occasions when he did were all the more special. When he asked, out of the blue, "Would you like to see a trick?" he immediately had our attention. A coin would appear from behind his left ear and disappear without a trace behind the right one. He would reverse the process and slip the coin in his pocket.

His ears were an endless source of fascination to us as children. When he removed his glasses and knit cap and asked, with a grin, *Can you do this?*, we knew what was coming and were rapt. We watched him narrow his eyes, pinch his lips, and frown in concentration. Then we saw his ears move, first imperceptibly, until they slowly flapped back and forth, like a butterfly opening and closing its wings.

But these performances were rare. Hans Bushoff didn't like to be in the spotlight or attract attention. He was a background man. He didn't eschew authority, but preferred service to leadership positions. After his Abitur, he studied law in Münster and Freiburg, but instead of practicing law he took an administrative position as manager of the Landsberg estate. Like his physician father, who had chosen public service over private practice,[12] he became a public servant in private employ, a so-called "private public servant" or *Privatbeamter*.

At once public servants and private employees, men in such positions (and most indeed were men) often worked in quasi-feudal conditions. They responded accordingly, showing unwavering loyalty to their employers whom they saw as masters, and obediently submitting to the hierarchies of their time and place. Politically and culturally, they were usually deeply conservative.

In Westphalia, particularly in the majority-Catholic rural areas, the political party of choice for people in such positions was the Center party (Deutsche Zentrumspartei, or Zentrum, for short), and Velen was no exception to this rule. In the 1932 election of Reichstag delegates, over 70 percent of Velen voters chose the Zentrum party; only 10 percent voted National Socialist. A year later, the gap had decreased slightly, yet Zentrum votes (60 percent) still vastly outnumbered votes for the NSDAP (20 percent).

But in March 1933, my grandfather, who up to then had always voted Zentrum, joined the Nazi party. He not only joined, he asked that his membership be dated retroactively to January 5 of that year. The politics of this request were clear. By pre-dating his membership to several weeks before Hitler's January 20 appointment as Reich chancellor, he signaled his desire to be seen as a supporter of the Nazi party from the beginning and from the ground up. This gesture of loyalty soon received its due. Hans Bushoff was put in charge of cultural activities and film for the Velen chapter (*Ortsgruppenkultur- und filmwart*), and within a few years he had become one of the most respected men in the local party.

His early affiliation with and visible support of the Nazi party can be understood in several different ways: a *Realpolitik* assessment that the Zentrum party wouldn't survive Nazi propaganda challenges; a basic sympathy for the kind of Blood and Soil ideology that National Socialism espoused; a directly personal, job-related calculation. Most likely, all three were in play, but the latter was almost certainly the most urgent.

In the early 1930s, the Landsberg estate was in serious trouble. In the financial crisis of 1929/30 that devastated global and local economies the estate had lost four-fifths of its holdings and investments. The devastation was complete a year later when fire destroyed much of the Velen castle. To avoid bankruptcy, much less restore the largely ruined castle, a government subvention was needed. But public funding was contingent on public use of the facilities in question, so Landsberg management proposed using the restored castle as an academy for customs officials. This plan meant working closely with government officials, and after 1933, it meant working with Nazi party representatives. The party emblem on the estate manager's lapel was useful, if not compulsory. It provided access. It opened doors.

Opening doors for the Landsberg estate was critical in many ways, some of which they preferred to keep hidden. Among the latter were negotiations with Nazi authorities for use of Landsberg land. Since much of the family's assets were vested in property, notably extensive land holdings across Westphalia, sale or lease of land was a primary source of their income. When Nazi authorities moved to set up labor camps—some as work camps administered by the Reich Labor Service, some as forced labor camps for political prisoners—the Landsberg estate was open for business.[13] As a faithful servant to his Landsberg master and an efficient manager of the estate, my grandfather might well have handled the negotiations. Even if he didn't, he would have played a role in—or been informed of—the resulting deals.

When I met with Günther Sandmann on my visit to Velen in 2012, I mentioned my grandfather's Nazi party membership. His response was immediate and unequivocal. "He had no choice," he exclaimed. "He was the general manager of the Landsberg estate. Resign or join the party. Those were your grandfather's only choices."

Perhaps realizing that he had raised his voice, Günther Sandmann paused, leaned back in his chair, and removed his glasses. He looked at me and held my gaze. "There were all kinds of people in the party," he went on. "There was this kind and there was that kind. And Johannes Bushoff …" His voice trailed off. When it returned, it was strong and steady. "Your grandfather," he said, "he was never *that* kind. For a man in his position, he had no choice."

In the review of my grandfather's Nazi activities that the British Military Government conducted after the war, his defense echoed the sentiments of Günther Sandmann. Yes, he confirmed, he was a Party member, but not an ideologue. Unlike Velen's mayor Becker or Velen's equally fanatical chief of police, he had never been "*that* kind" of a Nazi. On the contrary, as he declared in his statement to the Denazification Committee, he had "only become a member [of the Nazi party] in order to steer the local movement toward a more moderate path."[14] His explanation persuaded the authorities and Hans Bushoff was granted clearance.[15]

A new postwar order was emerging in fits and starts. Some people, like my grandfather Bushoff, were absolved of crimes during the Nazi regime. Others were found guilty and punished. The Velen castle that had been used to treat wounded soldiers during the war became a regional internment center for Nazi criminals. The moat was strung with barbed wire to prevent escapes and the corpses of men who preferred drowning to facing trial were sometimes found tangled in the reeds in the morning. As punishment for assisting the Nazis in establishing forced labor camps, the Landsberg family had to give large tracts of land to the Netherlands for war reparations.

Four years after the end of the war, when my grandfather's denazification review was conducted, the Potsdam Agreement that "all members of the Nazi party who have been more than nominal participants ... are to be removed from public or semi-public office and from positions of responsibility in important private undertakings" had ceded to the postwar interests of recovery and reconstruction. Hans Bushoff retained his job as manager of the Landsberg estate and remained an influential voice in Velen's civic life for the next two decades.

It's impossible to know whether my grandfather's claim that he intended his position inside the party as a way to check its more radical impulses was sincere, disingenuous, or nakedly tactical. Yet, even if it was sincere, his choice didn't absolve him of responsibility. He knew what was happening. As a "well-respected citizen of the local community" (to quote his obituary in the paper) and a leading member of the Velen branch of the ruling party, he would have known when someone in the community died or disappeared, when people left or were deported, when a new family moved in and where they moved to, and when a local business changed hands. He would have known what happened to the Franks and Landaus and what the reasons were.

Could he have said or done something to make a difference, "to steer the local movement toward a more moderate path," as his appeal claimed? When I put this question to the historian, Norbert Fasse, his answer was, "Not really. There is nothing different that your grandfather could have done."

"But as one of the men in power," I persisted, "couldn't he have intervened ... at least to protect people like the Franks and Landaus?"

Again, Norbert Fasse demurred. The structural hierarchy of Nazi authority, he explained, impeded intervention. Deportations were organized and administered top-down. Decisions were made in Münster, in the Gestapo headquarters, and were sent to local authorities in the form of orders. The orders were executed in Velen by town officials and the police, and when they were done they reported the results back to Münster. Local officials had no say in the decisions they were tasked to implement. "What could your grandfather have done for the Franks and Landaus?" he took up my question. "Tell them things were bad and getting worse? Warn them? Tell them they should save themselves and flee?"

He stopped and looked at me. "How were they supposed to do that? Where were they supposed to go?"

I had no answers. My questions seemed naïve. But before he ended, Herr Fasse offered a concession.

"People like your grandfather couldn't stop the deportations," he repeated. "But they could do something. They could treat people targeted as Jews with kindness and respect as fellow human beings. The way Frau Schmähing did when she brought Frau Frank her coffee the evening before the Franks were sent to Riga. Small human gestures like these couldn't stop the genocide ... but they made a difference."

Be careful what you wish for, the adage goes. I had wished for a Nazi family and now I had one. While their degrees of involvement differed, three of my four grandparents had been Nazis: both grandmothers and one of my grandfathers. My first reaction was disbelief and shame. I felt exposed, discovered. If they found out, what would people think? It was too late to admit that my Nazi-family wish had never been serious. It was too late for me to say, just kidding.

However, once the shock settled, I started wondering what had actually changed. I already knew that not every Nazi was a murderer, a monster, an evil person. Among the millions of Nazis in Germany (who, by definition, included all those who had joined the Party) were scores of ordinary people like my Oma Bammer in her nurse's uniform, my Oma Bushoff with her silk jabot, and my Opa Bushoff with his stamp collection. What my grandparents meant to me—how I remembered them—also remained more or less the same.

In the end, perhaps the biggest shock was not discovering Nazis in my family, but realizing how little that fact mattered in itself. What mattered was how that discovery changed my focus. The important question, I realized, was not what would people think if they learned of my Nazi family. The important question was, what did I think from where I now stood? What did it mean to be a human with a history? What did "innocent" and "guilty" mean? What distinguished a perpetrator from a victim or a follower? Reckoning with the past wasn't resolved by applying labels.

There were many reasons why people joined the Nazi party. They inclined that way. They were lured. They were pressured. Some did it for the camaraderie or the uniform. Some because it promised them a voice. Some because a herd had formed and they were sheep.[16] Velen's baker Kremer joined because he had a small business to run and he wanted a chance to provide the party-run labor camps in the area with bread. Velen's bailiff, Ludwig Oenning, nicknamed "Stewel Amtmann" (Boots Bailiff) for the jackboots he liked to wear with his uniform, was drawn by the allure.

Even genocides start small, fueled by myriad mundane and trivial motives. The Nazi Holocaust started that way too. Before the gas chambers and the crematoria, before the deportations and night-and-fog raids, there

My grandmother Hildegard Bammer, as a volunteer Red Cross nurse, *c.* 1941.

My grandparents Maria and Hans Bushoff, 1943.

were the fancy uniforms, the shiny belt buckles, the leather boots. There were the parades, the songs and slogans, the group belonging. Genocide was the outcome, not the reason, most people joined. Yet, as one of the witnesses in Peter Weiss' play, *The Investigation*, insists, no matter why they joined, professing shock at the genocidal outcome was disingenuous:

> We must get rid of our exalted attitude
> that this camp world
> is beyond our comprehension
> We all knew the society
> which had produced the regime
> that could bring about such a camp
> we were familiar with this order
> from its very beginnings.[17]

By joining, didn't they assume partial responsibility for the politics enacted in their name?

I don't know why my grandfather joined the Nazi party or what he thought about his decision, looking back. Was it mostly a matter of practical expediency? Did he have "no choice"? Did his conservative principles and his commitment to German heritage preservation make the Nazi Blood and Soil ideology seem just? Or was he, like Stewel Amtmann, compelled by the allure of power, even if it only meant being the Cultural Affairs chair of a small Party chapter in a small Westphalian town?

Whatever his reasons and however insignificant his role in the larger scheme of things (a history in which he hardly merited a footnote), in his time and place he was Pg. Hans Bushoff. He lent his authority and energies to the work the party did, which included, from the very outset, the work of killing. He supported a system that put a lien on part of his soul. "He was one of the most kind-hearted persons I ever knew," my father once said of my grandfather. Could he be a good and decent man and also be a Nazi? I believe so. Yet the calculus that allows such conclusions is a painful one.

When I confided to a friend my shock at discovering my grandfather's Nazi past, her reaction surprised me. She almost seemed bemused. "What made you think that in your family there would be no Nazis?" I couldn't answer her. She was asking me to look at my own blind spot.

I always thought that I wanted to know the truth about Nazi history—what happened, where and when, who was guilty—and over the years I assembled a trove of facts: the chronology of the genocide, the names of key criminals and killing places, the dates and outcome of trials, accounts by victims. January 20, 1942, the date of the Wannsee Conference, was more present to me than the birthdays of friends. This data was the dark background to growing up German after the Holocaust. I prided myself on my willingness to face that truth.

But looking back, I am not so sure about facing truth. I had read many books—on Nazi Germany, the Holocaust, the history of European Jews, the psychology and politics of memory, trauma, genocide—that probed the truth of history. But the personal and private truth, the family truth, that was different. I approached it, but with one eye shut. What had people in my family known and done, what sediments of guilt and shame, grief and pain, had they lived with? These weren't questions that I pursued with much conviction. I went toward them, but veered off when I got too close.

We call it truth when it is based on evidence and confirmed as fact. But our truths contain elements of choice. They are informed by need, driven by desire, and shaped by a maelstrom of competing feelings. Even faced with evidence that disproves what is fact, we often—stubbornly, bravely, foolishly, desperately—hold to positions to which we have become attached.

It was easy for me to blame my parents for their silences. For my postwar German generation, blame was the stance of choice. But I seldom asked them questions in ways that allowed for listening. I was too angry or afraid to grant what might have been their truth. Judging was easy. Empathy was harder. Understanding was almost out of reach.

While my mother was alive, I was unwilling to hear what she might have told me. My eagerness to blame her silenced us both, and by the time I was ready to listen it was too late.

In my father's case, time was more forgiving. He was old and his memory was waning, but when he was in his early nineties we started talking about our German past. I came with questions and he returned with answers. We kept talking through the remainder of his years. When he died in 2009 aged ninety-six, we hadn't finished. But we had started the critical process that Freud called memory work: of working through a difficult past together.

This process of working through, for me, is not over as long as the present continues to redraw the shape of the past. For that reason, I have no conclusion and no real ending. Reckoning aims for justice and hopes for forgiveness. And like justice and forgiveness, its measure is time.[18]

Epilogue
Forgetting Anne Frank

In 1991, when my twins were five, I took them to Germany for a month-long visit. My parents were getting older (my father was seventy-eight and my mother in her late sixties) and I wanted my children to know their grandparents while we still had time. In the past, I had flown to Frankfurt and gone directly to Bonn from the airport, but this time we flew to Amsterdam first. We would spend a day there, getting over jet lag, and take the train to Bonn the next day.

I had booked a room in a historic inn on one of the canals in the heart of the city. It was May, spring was in the air, and we went walking. Nicolas and Bettina were thrilled. They loved the tall, skinny, colored buildings, the canals where they expected streets, and the houseboats with cats and geranium flower pots. They loved the prostitutes in lacy underwear sitting in window seats on view for customers. "They're so pretty," they both agreed, and the red lamps on the tables next to them were pretty too. Back in our hotel room, the children bounced on the beds while I put my feet up. Then we wrapped ourselves in eiderdowns and watched television until late at night. We were free and easy, travelers on jet time, just passing through.

But we were not just passing through. I had a plan.

The next morning, before our train left, we headed for the Anne Frank House. There, in the back of the house on 263 Prinsengracht, in what Anne called the Secret Annex (*Achterhuis*), she and her family hid from the Gestapo for over two years until August 1944 when they were arrested. A few months later, Anne died of typhus in the Nazi concentration camp of Bergen-Belsen. I had chosen our hotel for its location near the Prinsengracht.

But not near enough, I soon discovered. Soon after we set out, I realized that I must have misread the map. Or just forgotten how long everything takes with two five-year-olds in a place with so many distractions. I was getting anxious and increasingly impatient. "Hurry up," I urged them, "we don't have much time. You're going to have to walk faster."

I tried to cajole them. "This will be fun," I promised. "We're going to see where a little girl called Anne lived."

When they didn't mind me, I snapped, "What's the matter with you? I want you to pay attention." I finally grabbed their hands and pulled them along with me.

When we arrived, there was a line. My anxiety spiked and I checked my watch. We got in line and waited. Finally, it was our turn and we went in. We climbed up and down stairs, filed through a maze of corridors, and saw the attic where the Franks had lived. Nicolas and Bettina looked at the furniture. They didn't know the purpose of our visit. What could they see from the narrow windows, they wondered.

"Nothing," they concluded, when I held them up. "Just sky ... and the tops of buildings."

I checked my watch again. It was time to go.

But I wasn't done yet. I hadn't finished what I came to do. Before we left, I pulled them over to a bench by the canal. The breeze was chilly and I squatted to button their coats up.

"You must remember this, Bettina and Nicolas," I said, as I grasped their hands. "You must remember Anne Frank. Her story is part of your history." The weight of the lesson I wanted to teach them made my voice sound harsh. I tried to soften it by adding, "She was just a child." But instead of softening, my voice cracked.

My children looked at me. They were silent.

I held their gaze. "She was just a child," I repeated, at a loss for words. My throat tightened and I tried to swallow.

"Like my two precious ones, right here," I rallied and folded them into a hug. They squirmed to free themselves, their giggles telling me that they weren't worried. Whatever was troubling me was not their problem. Then, holding hands, we ran to the hotel, grabbed our luggage, and took a cab to the central station.

Years later, when my children were in middle school, *The Diary of Anne Frank* was required reading. I reminded them of their visit to the Anne Frank House when they were five.

They looked at me blankly.

They couldn't possibly have forgotten. I tried to jog their memory. "Remember how we ran along the canals ... how I lifted you up to look out of the attic windows ... how I told you not to forget Anne Frank!" But they didn't remember and my evident dismay didn't faze them. They laughed.

"Don't look so worried, Mami. It's no big deal. We've just forgotten." Bettina patted my arm, as if I were the child and she the reassuring grown-up. "It was long ago ... and we were just children."

I was frustrated and confused and angry, as if they had cheated me somehow. I felt defeated. What was important to me hadn't registered with them. The lesson I had wanted to teach them had failed. I had wanted to take the swastika raincoat that I had been carrying all these years and hand it to the next generation. But they didn't want it. It wasn't made for them. It was mine to either wear or get rid of.

And so the problem of the past that my parents and I faced had become a problem for me and my children. The dilemma had come full circle. What do we do with the legacy of the past when we have the history of our own time to deal with?

Carrying the past forward is easier to say than do. We can't always find the words or the right words. And sometimes, even if and when we have the words, those we are speaking to aren't able to hear them.

It's not the facts that are the problem. Facts can be resolved. They are matters of record. It's the feelings those facts evoke that cause problems. One generation's guilt can be the next generation's shame, and that shame can become another generation's resentment. Like water, the past is fluid, mutable. It can evaporate or be absorbed into other matter. It provides sustenance for things to grow. Under pressure, it boils. And occasionally it forms into storm clouds.

When I was a German girl in Canada, the past was a living present that I could feel. We embodied it as a German family to the world around us. People saw it in the way we looked. They heard it in the way we talked. Yet what they saw and heard was inaccessible to me. I couldn't identify the response we triggered. I didn't know its cause. *Hate*, this word a child my age threw at me on the playground, gave a name to it. But at the time I didn't grasp its meaning. I asked my mother, but she didn't tell me. I knew we must have done something wrong—so wrong that it couldn't ever be corrected—but throughout my childhood the nature of that wrong remained a mystery. It didn't just confuse, it frightened me. If I didn't know what we had done, I couldn't know what we should do differently. An explanation, I thought, would make me feel safer.

Taking my children to Amsterdam to have them learn about Anne Frank was an attempt to fill the silence that had scared me at their age. I wanted to give them the explanation I had looked for when I was five, an answer to the question, "Why do people hate me before they even know who I am?" But that was my question. It was not my children's. I had given them an answer to a question they didn't have.

We say the past is the past, but it rarely is. Our questions continue, while the answers change. What had disturbed me when I was young hardly fazed my children, while for my parents it was a daily source of shame. But it is only in retrospect that these differences between us became clear to me. One incident in particular drove it home.

It was 1987. Winter in Bonn had been cold and rainy and my mother's arthritis was acting up. "Come to Atlanta," I wrote my parents. "Spend some time with us. And come in April. A Southern spring is an experience that you won't forget."

They wrote back, "We'll be there for Easter."

At the time of their visit, an exhibition on Auschwitz was on display in the Emory University library. I had seen it when it first went up, but I wanted to go again when my parents came. I suggested that we go together and they agreed. Friends took their parents to the botanical gardens or the art museum, but for us this seemed the obvious place to go.

Yet if you were to ask me why it was obvious, why I had to take my parents to an Auschwitz exhibition, I would be at a loss. I had no plan, no particular expectations. Just a deep sense of obligation: we had to go. Whenever an event that addressed the Holocaust was scheduled, I felt obliged to participate. Like Saturday confession and Sunday mass in my Catholic childhood, it was a commitment that I assumed as a duty. It was my German responsibility, I thought.

But going with my parents changed things. What had been habitual— perhaps an unconscious act of contrition on my part—became deliberate in our shared decision. It implied the willingness to face ourselves and each other, as Germans, in the wake of Auschwitz. What were we responsible for? Who were we accountable to? How did the Holocaust affect our relationship to one another?

I don't know what I thought would happen, what I hoped or feared. Did I want my parents to acknowledge the burden of a history that had shadowed me throughout my life, or the veil of silence that had hung between us? Was I angry at them? Resentful? Curious? Was I staging a confrontation? Envisioning a redemptive moment? Was this to be a reckoning in the name of Auschwitz? Whom and what was this for?

At the library my parents signed in as visitors. We walked up to the main floor, past the desk where you check out books, to the gallery where the exhibition filled the atrium. I had always loved the expansive openness of this space, but now—crammed with documents, maps, and photographs—it felt overwhelming. We stopped at the threshold. Where to start? I fought the impulse to say, "Let's go for a walk instead," and escape into the springtime sunshine. We stood there, undecided, hesitant. Then a woman came over and smiled a welcome.

"Good morning," she said, explaining that she was a volunteer docent from the Atlanta Jewish community. I glanced at her nametag.

"Would you like me to take you around the exhibition?" She smiled again.

I was about to say, "Yes, thank you, we would like that," when my father answered first, although for a moment I wasn't sure it was his voice. It didn't sound like him. I glanced over at my father. He looked flushed and seemed distraught. The docent turned to him, but he looked away. We waited.

"But … we are German," he finally said, in a voice so low I could barely hear him. I saw the vein on his temple pulsing. It was quiet around us. I felt hot.

"Oh," our docent answered. She was quiet too. The word "German" hovered. My mind stumbled over my father's *But* …

Then our docent rallied. "That's all right," she said. She spoke calmly, the way you reassure a frightened child. "Where are you from?" she went on. Her tone was warm and conversational. Her words were light, her Southern accent a melody.

My father fumbled with a button on his overcoat. The veins and age spots on his hands stood out. He suddenly looked like an old and tired man to me, not the vigorous seventy-four-year-old I knew. He didn't answer the docent's question. Silence was a darkness and he couldn't see. He seemed lost in history and couldn't find his way. We continued waiting. Finally our docent stepped into the silence to find him. She would walk with him part of the way.

"Well," she asked, "how do you like Atlanta?" She smiled in his direction.

My father looked up and returned her smile. "We are from Bonn," he said. "We came to Atlanta to see our daughter." He touched my arm. "She told us, come in April when the azaleas are in bloom … a Southern spring …"

Their words stretched a lifeline from the shame of a German past into the generosity of a Southern welcome. His voice trailed off. When it returned, it was strong and steady. "Our daughter was right," my father continued. "It is beautiful here. It's like seeing what Mozart sounds like."

Then we walked into the exhibition with our docent.

To say I will "never forget" is an idle promise. It is not a promise I can keep. I can make an effort to remember, but not forgetting and remembering are different. Memory is fickle and unreliable. It doesn't hew to a particular position or moral stance. It has no loyalties. It ignores commitments. It doesn't hold itself accountable to truth. Memory can lie. Memory can invent. Memory can dissimulate. It can even include forgetting.

So how do we find our way through the past if we can't trust memory? What orients us? Who will be our guide?

Aristotle's claim that we remember the past and imagine the future seems self-evident.[1] Yet it is only partly true. When we enter the past, we don't leave the present. Like explorers of caves or deep-sea divers, we attach our lifelines where we set out: the boat, the dock, the mouth of the cave, the companions waiting. "Wait here," we say, "I'll be back." Thus secured, as we move forward we are stretched between two poles: the place to which we are going and the place to which we'll return. Similarly, remembering extends us in two directions: the past that we are recalling and the present from which our recall sounds.

The past is the place where the dead live. We call them forth—in memories, in dreams, in imagination. We endow them with faces and bodies. We see them. We hear them. We feel their presence. I sometimes can't tell whether what I know is something I experienced, something I imagined, or something someone somewhere told me. Did it happen to me or did I read it in a book or see it in an exhibition like the one on Auschwitz?

In a dream, I hear a child. It's my daughter crying. She is in danger and I run to help. But when I get there, it is not my daughter, but a child I only know from a photograph. There was a war. She was hurt ... or maybe just frightened. I don't remember which war it was. Perhaps one that we're currently engaged in or one that involved me in the past. It could be Iraq, or Vietnam, or Bosnia, or Germany before I was born. I can't place her or my relationship to her. She is a stranger whom I don't know.

Yet I know her deeply.
I hear my own child and the child I once was in her cry.
This is how I experience the past.
It is in the present as I live it now.

Sometimes I summon it.
Sometimes it summons me.

I listen.
I try to respond.
I await the reckoning.

Sources and Acknowledgments

This book began as a work of theory. The initial title was "The Work of Memory." But midway along that journey I lost my way. Like Dante's ill-fated traveler in *The Inferno*, I found myself on a tangled path. There were fearsome challenges. There was the psychology and neuroscience of memory that I had to tackle. There was the historiography of Nazi Germany and the Holocaust, and all of World War II. There was the rich body of creative work—from literature through visual art to public installations—on the unresolved traumas of the past. I labored mightily to chart a path through these materials, filling folders, boxes, and filing cabinet drawers with notes and drafts. The bigger the job got, the more I faltered, until I reached a word-choked silence and finally stopped.

The direction was right, but the path was wrong. I needed to find a different one. That's when my Virgil appeared in the unlikely form of a short text by T.W. Adorno. I didn't know about it then, but Adorno had written "Education after Auschwitz" in April 1966, around the time I got my Abitur and went to university. When I rediscovered it in my struggle to think through issues of history, memory, and German identity "after Auschwitz," this essay proposed an answer. You can't think your way out with theory, Adorno declared. You have to work your way out through practice. For those who carry the burden of guilt for the Nazi genocide, whether perpetrators or those born after like me, reckoning with the past in a meaningful way must take the form of "critical self-reflection" (*kritische Selbstreflexion*). Adorno's injunction compelled me away from the high road of theory to blaze a trail through subjective experience.[1]

Freud provided a roadmap. Three key essays—"Remembering, Repeating, and Working Through," "Mourning and Melancholia," and "The Uncanny"—offered suggestions as to how I might proceed.[2] At the very outset, Freud reminded me that remembering difficult pasts takes work. It takes the courage to admit there is a problem; it takes the willingness to "work through" our entanglement in that past. Moreover, Freud insists, we can't do this work alone: we need others to help us.

Many of those who assisted me along the way are recognized and named in my endnotes. But some proved particularly helpful. Ian Kershaw's deep engagement with what he called "Hitler's Germany" and Saul Friedlander's magisterial history of Nazi Germany and the Jews modeled an approach to scholarship that always keeps the human cost of events in focus.[3] Historians like Nicholas Stargardt, Marion Kaplan, R.M. Douglas, Sönke Neitzel, and Ulrich Völklein focused attention on particular dimensions of the German experience.[4] Scholars of regional and local history, like Norbert Fasse or Gisela Möllenhoff and Rita Schlautmann-Overmeyer, rarely get the attention accorded those who write the "big" histories, yet their work was invaluable to me in its precision and granular attention to detail. So-called "popular" (as opposed, one assumes, to "academic") historians like Rick Atkinson and Erik Larson showed me ways to carve out dramatic plot, while Jonathan Spence, the eminent scholar of Chinese history, transformed the way I saw how history could be written.[5] Finally, Tony Judt, always a philosopher as much as a historian, reminded me not to lose sight of the big questions.[6]

But not at the cost of the details. Details are critical and the tedious work of providing them often goes unrecognized. Yet without that work, much of history would be lost or remain inaccessible. In the dusty attic of the Velen Stadtarchiv the archivist Natalia Linke retrieved documents on Velen's Jewish history for me that made the past come alive. In Hamburg, Gerhard Koerth and Erika Schüler, volunteers in the Sütterlinstube-Hamburg, took my mother's 1945 diary that I found indecipherable, because she had written it in the old German Sütterlin script, and returned it to me in the form of a printable Word file.[7] Joseph Walk's compendium of over 20,000 anti-Semitic laws, ordinances, and decrees drew a chilling picture of the systematic progression toward genocide in Nazi Germany and was an indispensable resource.

My most heartfelt thanks goes to those who shared their memories and stories with me. Some of them, notably my parents and Anna Bancken, died before I finished my book. I hope my work honors the trust they placed in me. If empathy, as Rebecca Solnit describes it, "is first of all an act of imagination ... and then a way of traveling from here to there,"[8] the physical journeys that my work involved entailed a corresponding willingness to bridge interpersonal distances. Those who spoke with me about the German past displayed that willingness with singular generosity. They included people in Velen—Günther Sandmann, Johannes and Cäcilia Liesner, Alfons Wellermann, Ulrich Wollheim, and the mayor at the time, Thomas Brüggemann. My time with Anna Bancken was its own chapter in my life. Her emotional honesty was rare and infectious. But no matter what we did or talked about, we always ended up in her kitchen, cooking or washing up, while I dried the dishes. Over time, my conversations with Anna extended to her stepson Martin Bancken and his wife Anna (the "Polish Anna" I describe in "Memories of War"), as well as her niece and nephew-in-law, Annette Woestmann and Thomas Graessner. Arnold Hermans, the director of the Annette School in Münster, gave generously of his time. I spent a memorable evening with Gisela Brüggemann, the daughter of my mother's friend, Gisela Wolters, talking about our mothers and their lifelong friendship. For years, going to Berlin meant the pleasure of time with Heide and Peter Vogel. Heide was the daughter of my father's childhood friend Heinz Vatter, and Peter was her German-Jewish husband. Over wine and often long into the night, we talked about German history and our different German pasts. The day we spent together at the former Nazi concentration camp of Ravensbrück will always remain with me. In Warsaw, I spent several memorable days as the guest of Wacława Grudzinska, the mother of my friend and then-colleague at Emory Irena Grudzinska Gross. During the Nazi years, Pani Grudzinska was imprisoned at Ravensbrück. We didn't directly address the history that hung between us, but it was the backdrop of our conversations about her city and its German past. Since I didn't speak Polish, we used a mixture of German and French to talk. My former Liebfrauen School teacher, Marianne Gester, and her husband, Freder, welcomed me so generously over the years that their home became my second home in Bonn. In conversations that began at breakfast and continued over dinner in the evening, we talked about the German past and its present traces. Much of what I was able to work through I owe to them.

When I began writing this book, I worried about my flawed memory. I couldn't recall the most memorable things—the year my mother died, my children's first words, starting school in Canada. I thought my spotty recollection revealed a deeper deficit, both moral and intellectual. The work of experimental and cognitive psychologists like Daniel Schacter and Elizabeth Loftus reassured me that my memory "problems" were just part and parcel of how people process experience.[9] I was neither bad nor stupid, just your average person who remembers, misremembers, and forgets. Critical studies in the field of psychoanalysis, beginning with Freud, and continuing through recent work on trauma, postmemory, and what Christopher Bollas calls "the unthought known," deepened my understanding of the complex pathways of human memory. Emotionally and intellectually, we live in more than one time at once. As the philosopher Ernst Bloch reminded us, we often find ourselves to be "non-synchronous" with our own time.[10] For their research and reflections on this non-synchronicity, I am indebted to the work of scholars like Nicolas Abraham and Maria Torok, Nadine Fresco, Esther Rashkin, Marianne Hirsch, Cathy Caruth, Ruth Leys, Gabriele Schwab, and Eva Hoffman.[11]

Thoughts and ideas are not a work until we give them shape, such as through writing a book. That shaping is a daunting process. As an act of creation, it feels transcendent. As an act of fixing, it inspires dread. How could I account for the ways the German past shaped my life and how could I give that account form? I turned to writers who had preceded me for guidance. To name them all is impossible. There were too many. However, some were particularly inspiring. Their honesty, the courage with which they faced their truth, and the aesthetic power of their creation offered models. Among those writing about the Nazi past from the perspective of non-Jewish Germans, the work of Christa Wolf has always moved me. From her early autobiographical fiction, *The Quest for Christa T.*, to her memoir of girlhood in Nazi Germany, *Patterns of Childhood*, she has tried to reckon with the past, even when struggling against the limits of her own blind spots.[12] The work of Uwe Timm and Roger Frie reveals the same measure of commitment to truth.[13] Confronting the trauma of the Nazi past from the Jewish perspective, three very different works—Sarah Kofman's *Rue Ordener, Rue Labat*, Ruth Kluger's *Still Alive: A Holocaust Girlhood Remembered*, and most recently Susan Faludi's *In the Darkroom*—inspire me with the power of their moral courage and aesthetic brilliance.[14] Primo Levi and W.G. Sebald have accompanied me from the start.[15] Two women have profoundly influenced both my work and approach to writing by the ways they have modeled truth-telling. Deborah Lipstadt showed me and the world that speaking truth to power is a force for change.[16] Evelyn Torton Beck taught me that you can only be really whole if you can acknowledge all the parts of yourself, past and present.[17]

As I tried my hand at putting my story into words, readers came along to help me. My Atlanta writing group—Elizabeth Gallu, Laurie Patton, and Rosemary Magee—encouraged my first halting steps beyond the conventions of academic writing into new terrain, where the writerly and the scholarly found common purpose. I owe them my enduring thanks. Others read parts along the way: Sue Lanser, Natasha Trethewey, Irene Kacandes, Deborah Lipstadt, Jan Gross. When I told him about my two grandfathers (the kind and gentle one who joined the Nazi party and the demanding, selfish one who remained politically "pure"), Jan didn't seem surprised. He laughed, "It could take fortitude to not become a Nazi."

A variety of people read (or heard) drafts of the work at different stages— colleagues, friends, and students. I thank all of them for their responses: those who answered my questions, those who questioned my answers, and those whose questions and answers generated new ones of my own. Occasionally, a colleague seemed unnerved by my deviation from the norms of scholarly form and tried to rescue me. My work was "unprofessional and self-indulgent," as one of them warned me. I also thank the skeptics. Their concerns strengthened my resolve and forced me to make clear what I was doing. Toward the end, when I had completed a whole draft, two readers were particularly helpful. Natalie Catasus brought an artist's eye and poet's sensibility to my work. Esther Rashkin was the editor whom writers dream of and seldom find. She read with care and empathy. She read with a rare and deeply generous ability to listen. I am profoundly grateful.

And to those who were there from the beginning and for the long haul, I couldn't have done it without you. Richard Street, red pen in hand, read every chapter (and many more than once), with a writer's sensibility and a historian's questions. Ever sensitive to the pathos of lives under pressure, he helped me bring their stories to life in my work. My son, Nicolas Bammer-Whitaker, was my constant companion on the journey of this book. He helped me get through the valley of doubt and shared the moments of triumph. Most importantly, he kept me honest. "Is that what you really believe?" he would ask. His question became my inner compass. My daughter, Bettina Jendrek, believed in me and this project from the outset. Her faith was infectious. And when my energies flagged, she restored them with flowers, chocolates, and the simple human gestures of love.

A word on images. Some of the images included in the book function as illustrations (this is what x, y, or z looked like). As a whole, however, I wanted them to work in more expansive ways: to comment on or interrupt the narrative, to create space within the flow of text for reflection. Images invite us to stop, focus, breathe, and consider what is there before us. Visual artists create worlds and tell stories in the form of images. I learn from their approach and am grateful to such guides as Anna Grimshaw, whose work continues to expand and deepen the ways I look at the world and see. The collaboration between John Berger and Jean Mohr, who treat words and images as complementary, not subordinate, to one another, is a constant inspiration.

Making a book entails infinitely more than just writing it. For their role in the production process, there are countless people to thank. The few I mention here must stand for the many I cannot name. The editors of the "Psychoanalytic Horizons" series—Peter Rudnytsky, Mari Ruti, and Esther Rashkin—have been affirming and supportive from the outset, as has Haaris Naqvi, the Editorial Director of Bloomsbury Academic US. Various people provided invaluable technical help along the way. Molly Slavin turned messy references into tidy endnotes; Nathan Lomas at Image Flow turned my images into beautiful, high-resolution files. Jim Johnstone restored my laptop to life when it gave up the ghost close to the finish line.

In the fall semester 2010, I taught an undergraduate seminar on "Holocaust Memoirs" at Emory University with my friend and colleague in Jewish Studies, Deborah Lipstadt. We had decided to include some of our own work in the syllabus. Deborah's contribution was her recently published book *History on Trial*. Mine was a draft of "Walking to Buchenwald," an earlier version of a chapter from this book. At the end of the class, when we discussed my work, one of the students came up to me and clasped my hand. "I grew up with stories of Germans," she said. "They were Nazis who killed Jews, including members of my extended family." She paused. "I never thought of Germans as people," she resumed. "Until now." She paused again. "Thank you."

Now it is my turn to thank her back. What she found in that early chapter draft is what I wanted my book to show: that Germans, for better or worse, were (and are) people. Even those, like my grandparents, who were Nazis. They were (and are) people with all that personhood entails: selfish, generous, timid, impetuous, kind, mean, vulnerable, resilient. They act nobly, they do terrible things, they err. But no matter what they do, they are responsible for their acts and choices. My story of growing up German after the Holocaust examines how we engage the present in light of the past. I wanted to use a particular case to explore the universal question of what it means to be a human with a history.

Notes

Epigraph

*   Written in 1939 in Danish exile from Nazi Germany. Bertolt Brecht, "An die Nachgeborenen." In *Gesammelte Werke*, vol. 9. *Gedichte* 2. Frankfurt/Main: Suhrkamp, 1967, pp. 722–725. My translation.

Prologue
Swastika Raincoat

1   Gitta Sereny, "Children of the Reich." In *The Healing Wound: Experiences and Reflections. Germany, 1938–2001.* New York: W.W. Norton, 2001, p. 286.

Part One

1   Eelco Runia, *Moved by the Past: Discontinuity and Historical Mutation.* New York: Columbia University Press, 2014, p. 5.

In the Aftermath

1   The Allied control period lasted from July 5, 1945 to May 23, 1949.
2   "Editorial: Moods of Victory," *Life*, vol. 18, no. 20 (May 14, 1945), p. 40D.
3   Victor Klemperer, *The Language of the Third Reich: LTI. The Philologist's Notebook*, translated by Martin Brady. London and New York: Continuum, 2006, p. 104.
4   One of the outcomes of the Second Quebec Conference held in September 1944 and attended by the heads of state and combined Chiefs of Staff of the American and British governments, the Morgenthau Plan proposed to convert Germany to "a country primarily agricultural and pastoral in character."
5   Sidney Olson, "Defeated Land," *Life*, vol. 18, no. 20 (May 14, 1945), p. 39.
6   W.G. Sebald, *On the Natural History of Destruction*, translated by Anthea Bell. New York: Modern Library, 2003, p. 4.

7   By late 1946, daily food rations in the British zone were an estimated 700–1,000 calories.

8   Victor Gollancz, *In Darkest Germany: The Record of a Visit*. Hinsdale, IL: Henry Regnery Company, 1947, p. 25. Gollancz's dispatches from Germany between October 2 and November 15, 1945 were featured in newspapers across Britain.

9   Walter Bammer, *Tagebuch 1945–46* (September 12, 1946). Unpublished, unpaginated manuscript. My translation. Subsequent references to this diary will be included in the body of the text.

10 "Editorial."

11 "Suicides," *Life*, vol. 18, no. 20 (May 14, 1945), p. 32.

12 Otto Hagel and Hansel Mieth, "We Return to Fellbach," *Life*, vol. 28, no. 26 (June 26, 1950), p. 108.

13 Ursula Bammer, *Tagebuch 1945–46* (April 21, 1945). Unpublished, unpaginated manuscript. My translation. Subsequent references to this diary will be included in the body of the text.

14 Françoise Davoine and Jean-Max Gaudillière, *History Beyond Trauma: Whereof One Cannot Speak, Thereof One Cannot Stay Silent*, translated by Susan Fairfield. New York: Other Press, 2004, p. xxx.

15 "The War Ends in Europe," *Life*, vol. 18, no. 20 (May 14, 1945), p. 27.

16 In *Revisiting Zero Hour 1945: The Emergence of Postwar German Culture* (Washington: American Institute for Contemporary German Studies, 1996), the editors Stephen Brockmann and Frank Trommler provide an outline of the genesis and use of the term "Zero Hour" in postwar Germany.

17 Discussing the valuation popularly attached to the concept of a "point zero" derived from the realms of scientific and mathematical computation, the German Wikipedia entry notes that "[t]he zero point … is the starting point for the measurement or computation of values … [it] divides actual values into two domains: *positive* and *negative*." http://www.de.wikipedia. org/wiki/Nullpunkt. My translation.

18 The term is Eva Hoffman's. She explains it thus: "The second generation after every calamity is the hinge generation, in which the meanings of awful events can remain arrested and fixed at the point of trauma; or in which they can be transformed into new sets of relations with the world, and new understanding." Eva Hoffman, *After Such Knowledge: Memory, History, and the Legacy of the Holocaust*. New York: Public Affairs, 2004, p. 103.

19 Primo Levi, "The Truce," translated by Ann Goldstein. In *The Complete Works of Primo Levi*, vol. 1. New York: Liveright Publishing Corporation, 2015, p. 321.

20 Hans-Werner Richter, "Warum schweigt die junge Generation?" *Der Ruf*, vol. 1, no. 2 (September 1, 1946). Quoted in Brockmann and Trommler, p. 38, fn. 30.

21 Levi, "Truce," 394–395.

22 Klemperer, *The Language of the Third Reich*, p. 11.

23 Klemperer, *The Language of the Third Reich*, p. 14.

24 Davoine and Gaudillière, *History Beyond Trauma*, p. 16.

25 "It is unbearable to think the tiny word 'I' in connection with the word 'Auschwitz.'" Christa Wolf, *Patterns of Childhood*, translated by Ursula Molinaro and Hedwig Rappolt. New York: Farrar, Straus and Giroux, 1980, p. 230. The German original puts it slightly differently, observing that "es … unerträglich ist, bei dem Wort 'Auschwitz' das kleine Wort 'ich' mitdenken zu müssen." Christa Wolf, *Kindheitsmuster*. Berlin/Weimar: Aufbau Verlag, 1976, p. 303.

26 The so-called Nuremberg Laws, issued September 15, 1935, outlined a two-step process. Step one, the Law for the Protection of German Blood and German Honour, made a legal distinction between persons of "German blood" (thenceforth designated "Aryan") and others. Step two, the Reich Citizenship Law, spelled out the consequences of this blood criterion: only those "of German blood" ("Aryans") were full Reich citizens (*Reichsbürger*) with all attendant rights. Those "not of German blood" were assigned the inferior status of mere "state subjects," ineligible to vote, hold public office, or be employed as civil servants in any capacity.

27 Reference to Lan Duong, *Treacherous Subjects: Gender, Culture, and Trans-Vietnamese Feminism*. Philadelphia: Temple University, 2012 found in Viet Thanh Nguyen, *Nothing Ever Dies: Vietnam and the Memory of War*. Cambridge, MA: Harvard University Press, 2016, p. 61.

28 Olson, "Defeated Land," p. 39.

29 The first German postwar census was conducted in October 1946 by the Allied Control Council across the four Allied Zones. Among a total of 65 million Germans 23 million lived in the British Zone, where Velen was situated. The count for Velen was 1,724 (771 males and 953 females).

30 The official New King James Version of this passage from Psalm 91 is: "He shall give his angels charge over you, to keep you in all your ways." My translation hews more closely to the German text that my parents used: "Denn er hat seinen Engeln befohlen über dir, dass sie dich behüten auf allen deinen Wegen."

31 This poem opened Celan's poetry collection, *Der Sand in den Urnen* (*The Sand in the Urns*). Vienna: A. Sexl, 1948. The full passage reads, "The angels are dead and the Lord has gone blind … and no one will guard for me those who have gone to their sleep and are resting." ("Denn tod sind die Engel und blind ward der Herr … und keiner ist, der mir betreue im Schlaf die zur Ruhe hier gingen."). Paul Celan, "A Song in the Wilderness"/"Ein Lied in der Wüste," translated by John Felstiner. In *Selected Poems and Prose of Paul Celan*. New York: W.W. Norton, 2001, pp. 18–19.

32 Found in Michael R. Marrus, "The Nuremberg Trial: Fifty Years After," *The American Scholar*, vol. 66, no. 4 (Autumn 1997), pp. 563–570.

33 What became known as the Nuremberg Trial was just the first, albeit the most famous, of a series of related trials. Following the October 1, 1946 verdicts, twelve additional trials, known collectively as the Subsequent

Nuremberg Trials, tried German industrialists, as well as members of the
Gestapo and Schutzstaffel (SS), for war crimes.

34 One of the twenty-three original defendants (Hermann Göring) committed
suicide before the verdict was issued.

35 The so-called long drop method of hanging deployed in this case resulted
in a slow (up to 28 minutes) death by strangulation instead of the intended
quick death from a broken neck in the standard drop method.

36 Twelve death sentences were pronounced, but only eleven executed, as
Martin Bormann was tried *in absentia*.

37 W.H. Auden, "Musée des Beaux Arts" (1939). http://www.poetrybyheart.
org.uk/poems/musee-des-beaux-arts/.

Lost in the Past

1 Riefenstahl produced, directed, and starred in *The Blue Light*; Carl Mayer
and Bela Balazs cowrote the script. The success of this film and Hitler's
admiration for Riefenstahl's genius landed her the commission to film the
1934 rally of the National Socialist Party in Nuremberg that resulted in
Triumph of the Will, a landmark in the history of documentary film.

2 Riefenstahl's pioneering film and editing techniques included the ground-
breaking use of moving cameras, telephoto and close-up lenses, combined
with radically unconventional camera angles.

3 Gollancz (November 8, 1946), p. 31.

4 His point of reference is a report by the British House of Commons to the
effect that "a diet of 1,200 calories may be characterized as slow starvation"
Gollancz (December 4, 1946), p. 37.

5 Gollancz (November 30, 1946), p. 75.

6 See Victor Gollancz, "Shoes and Other Things." In *In Darkest Germany*,
pp. 73–88.

7 The Federal Republic of Germany (West Germany) was founded in May
1949, followed by the German Democratic Republic (East Germany) that
October. Since my story is shaped largely by the West German context, my
references to "Germany" are to the Federal Republic, unless mentioned
otherwise.

8 After the megalomania of the Third Reich, the opening lines of the German
national anthem—"Germany, Germany above all others/Above all others
in the world"—hit the wrong note. The second stanza, which began with a
paean to "German women and German loyalty" was similarly out of step
with postwar perspectives. That left the innocuous third and final verse,
whose opening line struck the right democratic note with its invocation of
"unity, justice, and freedom." In 1952, the first postwar chancellor Konrad
Adenauer and the first postwar president Theodor Heuss decreed that the

first two stanzas of the anthem were henceforth banned, leaving only the
third to be sung.

9 The so-called Basic Law (*Grundgesetz*) has served as Germany's constitution
since it was passed by the West German parliament in May 1949. Article 1,
section 1 begins by affirming the fundamental principle of human rights:
"The dignity of every person is inviolable."

10 Ursula Bammer, *Tagebuch 1945–46*, September 21, 1945.

11 Ian Kershaw, *Hitler: Biography*. New York: W.W. Norton, 1998, p. 430.

12 In the realm of psychoanalysis, see, among others, Nicholas Abraham and
Maria Torok, *The Shell and the Kernel*. Chicago: University of Chicago
Press, 1994; Christopher Bollas, *The Shadow of the Object: Psychoanalysis
of the Unthought Known*. New York: Columbia University Press, 1989; and
Nadine Fresco, "Remembering the Unknown," translated by Alan Sheridan.
In *International Review of Psycho-Analysis*, vol. 11 (1984), pp. 417–427.
Blaise Pascal's "*le coeur a ses raisons que la raison ne connaît pas*" offers an
earlier, pre-scientific formulation of this insight.

13 Bollas, *The Shadow of the Object*, p. 282.

14 Bollas, *The Shadow of the Object*, p. 281.

Following the Clues

1 David Grossman, *See Under: Love*, translated by Betsy Rosenberg (New
York: Washington Square Press, 1989) and Carl Friedman, *Nightfather*,
translated by Arnold and Erica Pomerans (New York: Persea Books,
1994), both use a child's perspective to portray the gradual discovery
that the "secret" their elders are keeping from them is their Holocaust
experience.

2 Both the wartime destruction and the postwar reconstruction were of
such massive a scope that the national anthem of the newly founded
German Democratic Republic began by marking this point of departure
in its opening lines, "Risen from the ruins and facing the future"
("*Auferstanden aus den Ruinen, und der Zukunft zugewandt*"). The lyrics
by Johannes Becher were set to music by Brecht's long-time collaborator
Hanns Eisler.

3 The so-called Marshall Plan, officially the European Recovery Program,
went into effect in April 1948 and ended in 1952.

4 Olson, "Defeated Land," p. 110.

5 The website of the West German Foreign Ministry (*Auswärtiges Amt*)
notes that it was "re-established" under the postwar regime. In fact,
it was never "disestablished." Created in 1871 under the first German
Chancellor, Bismarck, it continued through the Weimar Republic and the
Third Reich.

6   Walter and Ursula Bammer, *Angelika I: 1946–1951*. Unpublished photo
    album and journal. The SS *Ryndam* was 15,000 tons. By comparison, the SS
    Rotterdam, Holland America Line's flagship, was almost 39,000 tons, and its
    SS *Nieuw Amsterdam* 36,000 tons.

7   Lisa Appignanesi, *Losing the Dead: A Family Memoir*. Toronto: McArthur &
    Company, 1999, p. 12.

8   The Convention on Relations between the Three Powers and the Federal
    Republic of Germany (*Vertrag über die Beziehungen der Bundesrepublik und
    den Drei Mächten*) was signed on May 26, 1952, but not implemented until
    May 1955.

9   The Treaty on the Final Settlement with Respect to Germany (*Vertrag
    über die abschließende Regelung in bezug auf Deutschland*)—popularly
    known as the Two Plus Four Agreement (the "Two" referring to the two
    former Germanies, East and West, and the "Four" to the four erstwhile
    Allies)—was signed on September 12, 1990, before the reunification of
    Germany, to prevent unresolved issues from World War II (such as the
    question of Germany's borders) from compromising the status of this "Final
    Settlement." Although legally binding, this Treaty is not a formal peace
    treaty. Text references are taken from the Preamble.

10 The Preamble notes that the Treaty is not only based on "principles [that]
    have laid firm foundations for the establishment of a just and lasting
    peaceful order in Europe," but that this "peaceful order" has been the
    foundation on which the signatories "have been living together" for the
    past forty-five years.

11 Klemperer, *The Language of the Third Reich*, p. 13. "Pg" (*Parteigenosse*) was
    the common abbreviation for a member (*Genosse*) of the Nazi Party.

12 The total initially agreed to was around 3.5 billion Deutschmark.

13 Norbert Frei and Peter Hayes, "The German Foreign Office and the Past,"
    Bulletin of the German Historical Institute, vol. 49 (Fall 2011), p. 65.

14 Holger Nehring, "Skeletons in the Filing Cabinet," *Bulletin of the German
    Historical Institute*, vol. 49 (Fall 2011), p. 97.

15 Ralf Beste, Georg Bönisch, Thomas Darnstadt, Jan Friedmann, Michael
    Fröhlingsdorf, and Klaus Wiegrefe, "Welle der Wahrheiten," *Der Spiegel*,
    January 2, 2012. http:www.spiegel.de/spiegel/print/d-83422497.html.

16 Christopher Browning, "German Foreign Office Revisited," *Bulletin of the
    German Historical Institute*, vol. 49 (Fall 2011), p. 72.

17 Ralf Best and Christoph Schult, "Ende der Vertuschung," *Der Spiegel*,
    April 11, 2005. http:www.spiegel.de/spiegel/print/d-39997520.html.

18 Volker Ullrich, "Hitler's Brown Diplomats," *Bulletin of the German
    Historical Institute*, vol. 49 (Fall 2011), p. 108. Among the more notorious
    cases detailed by Ullrich is that of Franz Krapf, a former member both of
    the Nationalsozialistische Deutsche Arbeiterpartei (the National Socialist
    German Workers' Party, NSDAP) and the SS, who in 1966 was appointed
    German ambassador to Japan and in 1971 head of Germany's Permanent

NATO Delegation. Another is the case of Herbert Müller, a former member of the Hitler administration's Jewish Department (*Judenreferat*), who, under the revised name of Herbert Müller-Roschach, served as German ambassador to Portugal in the 1960s. For details, see Browning, "German Foreign Office Revisited," p. 75.

19 Best and Schult, "Ende der Vertuschung."

20 Michael Wildt, Ulrike Jureit, and Birgit Otte, *Crimes of the German Wehrmacht: Dimensions of a War of Annihilation*, translated by Paula Bradish. Hamburg: Hamburger Edition, 2004. Quoted in Beste et al., "Welle der Wahrheiten."

21 The 2017 website of the German Foreign Ministry identifies cultural, along with political and economic, relations as one of the three cornerstones of German foreign policy. In line with this commitment, cultural institutions and programs like the Goethe Institutes, the German Academic Exchange Service (DAAD), the Alexander-von-Humboldt Foundation, the international radio broadcast, Deutsche Welle, and the Central Agency for Schools Abroad, are funded and administered by the Foreign Ministry.

22 The irony is that other countries, notably the United States, were actively working to acquire German technological, rather than cultural, expertise. Wernher von Braun, the German aerospace engineer responsible for developing the V-2 rocket deployed by Germany against England during World War II, was recruited for American military counterintelligence as early as June 1945. By 1961, when a young Werner Herzog was making his first short film, Wernher von Braun had become the first director of NASA's Marshall Space Flight Center.

23 As the Foreign Ministry's website puts it, "Culture and communication are key elements of a credible, sustainable German foreign policy and go straight to people's hearts and minds." www.auswaertiges-amt.de/EN/AAmt/Abteilungen/KulturUndKommunikation-node.htm/.

Family Ties

1 The essential details of this Protocol had been worked out three years earlier, when the so-called German Treaty (or, as it was officially called, the Convention on Relations between the Three Powers and the Federal Republic of Germany) was signed, but it was not ratified until May 1955.

2 The incorporation of Germany and Italy into what had begun as the European Defense Community (founded in 1948 by the UK, France, Belgium, Luxemburg, and the Netherlands) marked the formation of the WEU, and in May 1955 Germany was admitted to NATO.

Between the Word-Gaps

1 Etymologically, nostalgia (from Gk. *nostos* = return home + *-algia* = longing), is a form of suffering caused by the loss of (or inability to return to) home. Before its meaning shifted in the early twentieth century to signify a wistful longing for a lost past, nostalgia was regarded—and treated—as a medical condition. First identified in 1668 by a Swiss doctor, Johannes Hofer, as an illness caused by physical displacement from one's homeland, nostalgia was included in the German handbook of medical terms (*Deutsches Krankheitsnamen-Buch*) as late as 1899.

2 Georg Lukács explores the concept of transcendental homelessness, as "the urge to be at home everywhere," in his 1920 *Theory of the Novel*. At the time, the concept held great appeal to the young Teddie Wiesengrund (T.W. Adorno) and his friend Siegfried Kracauer, who fancied themselves "Agents of the Transcendentally Homeless" and sometimes signed letters or notes to each other as "transcendentally homeless."

3 Founded in 1876, from 1917 onwards the Liebfrauen School was run by the School Sisters of Notre Dame. Since 1975, it has been under the authority of the Roman Catholic Archdiocese of Cologne.

4 The opening lines of Kluger's memoir are: "Their secret was death, not sex. That's what the grown-ups were talking about, sitting up late around the table." Ruth Kluger, *Still Alive: A Holocaust Girlhood Remembered*. New York: Feminist Press at CUNY, 2001, p. 15.

5 This question comes in the middle of Celan's breathless opening sentence that in the first published version extended over thirteen print lines. Paul Celan, "Gespräch im Gebirg," *Die Neue Rundschau*, vol. 71, no. 2 (1960), pp. 199–202.

6 First published in 1960, "Gespräch" is Celan's only literary prose text.

7 By 1960, Celan had published four volumes of poetry. His first collection, *Der Sand aus den Urnen* (1948) received little critical attention, but his second, *Mohn und Gedächtnis* (Munich: Deutsche Verlags-Anstalt, 1952), which included his famous "Todesfuge" ("Death Fugue"), won him international critical acclaim. They were followed by *Von Schwelle zu Schwelle*. Munich: Deutsche Verlags-Anstalt, 1955, and *Sprachgitter*. Berlin: S. Fischer, 1959.

8 "Death Fugue/Todesfuge" was one of Celan's earliest poems. In *Selected Poems and Prose of Paul Celan*, translated by John Felstiner. New York: W.W. Norton, 2001, pp. 30–33. Although, like all of Celan's works, it was written in German, it was first published in 1947 in Romanian translation in Celan's native Romania. Over fifty years later, the German literary critic, Wolfgang Emmerich, declared it the "poem of the century"(*Paul Celan*. Reinbek: Rowohl, 1999) and Celan's American translator and biographer, John Felstiner, compared it to Picasso's *Guernica* (*Paul Celan: Poet, Survivor, Jew*. New Haven: Yale University Press, 2001, p. 26).

9   Born Paul Antschel, Celan (who adopted the anagram of Ancel, the
     Romanian spelling of his family name, as his pen name) was born in
     Czernowitz, Romania, the only child of German-speaking Jewish parents.
     When German forces occupied Romania in 1941, his parents were deported
     and murdered and Celan spent several years in forced labor camps.
     After the war, he left Communist-controlled Romania for a brief stint in
     Vienna before settling in Paris in 1948, where he lived until his suicide in
     1970. While Celan never returned to live in a German-speaking country,
     he inhabited a German cultural world, teaching German language and
     literature at the École Normale Supérieure and composing all of his literary
     work in German.

10   Unlike Celan, Adorno, the son of a Jewish father and a Catholic mother, did
     not suffer the traumatic impact of the Holocaust directly, having already left
     Germany for England in 1934. In 1938, he left Europe altogether for exile
     in the United States, moving first to New York, then Princeton, and finally
     California, where he lived until 1948 and was naturalized as an American
     citizen. In 1949, Adorno returned to Germany, where he lived until his
     death, teaching sociology at the University of Frankfurt and rebuilding the
     Institute for Social Research in collaboration with his friend and colleague
     Max Horkheimer.

11   This phrase, "*nach Auschwitz ein Gedicht zu schreiben, ist barbarisch,*"
     stands as one of the most contentious statements about the possibility of
     meaning after the Holocaust. It is the concluding passage of Adorno's 1949
     essay "Cultural Criticism and Society," reprinted as the opening piece in his
     1955 collection *Prismen*. The longer passage, in English translation, reads:
     "Cultural criticism finds itself today faced with the final state of the dialectic
     of culture and barbarism. To write poetry after Auschwitz is barbaric. And
     this corrodes even the knowledge of why it has become impossible to write
     poetry today. Absolute reification, which presupposed intellectual progress
     as one of its elements, is now preparing to absorb the mind entirely. Critical
     intelligence cannot be equal to this challenge as long as it confines itself
     to self-satisfied contemplation." (Theodor W. Adorno, "Cultural Criticism
     and Society," translated by Samuel Weber and Shierry Nicholson Weber. In
     Prisms. Cambridge, MA: The MIT Press, 1981, p. 34). Adorno revisited this
     claim and its implications several times in his later work, most explicitly in
     Notes on Literature and *Negative Dialectics*.

12   Celan and Adorno had planned to meet in July 1959 in the Engadin
     valley in the Swiss Alps, in the same town where Nietzsche had spent his
     summers. Celan wrote "Gespräch im Gebirg" immediately afterwards,
     dating it August 1959.

13   Germans initially continued to use Nazi terminology, such as "Final
     Solution" (*Endlösung*) or the symbolic term "Auschwitz" (as in "after
     Auschwitz"), to refer to the Nazi genocide of European Jewry. Although
     "Holocaust" was used as early as 1942 in the British press and occasionally

in Israel in the 1950s, it entered public circulation through the international reporting of the 1961 Eichmann Trial. By 1968, "Holocaust" had become so commonly used that the US Library of Congress began classifying all work on the Nazi genocide of Jews under "Holocaust-Jewish, 1939–1945." In Germany, the term "Holocaust" didn't enter public discourse until 1979, when the American television mini-series *Holocaust* aired in Germany. That event galvanized public discourse, leading the Society for German Language (*Gesellschaft für deutsche Sprache*) to proclaim "Holocaust" the "Word of the Year." Despite the currency of "Holocaust," however, many people, notably Jews both in and outside Israel, prefer the term "Shoah."

14 As the following is a dialogue with, not a discussion of, the text, I have put passages from Celan's text in italics, rather than the standard quotation marks, in order to allow for a more fluid reading. References are to Paul Celan, "Conversation in the Mountains" (translated by John Felstiner. In *Selected Poems and Prose of Paul Celan*. New York: W.W. Norton, 2001, pp. 397–400). Quoted passages proceed progressively through the text (397–400), before returning to the beginning (397) and the middle (398).

15 German uneasiness with the status of German Jews in postwar Germany was evident in the strange designation, "*jüdische Mitbürger*" (Jewish fellow-citizens), as if their actual citizenship status had to be qualified, or emphasized, through the prefix "*Mit*" ("fellow").

16 Adorno's father, Oscar Alexander Wiesengrund was born Jewish, but had already converted to Protestantism by the time of his son's birth in 1903. Adorno's mother, the opera singer Maria Calvelli-Adorno della Piana, was a descendant of an aristocratic family from Corsica.

17 The full passage with which Auerbach concludes his afterword reads, "*Möge meine Untersuchung ihre Leser erreichen; sowohl meine überlebenden Freunde von einst wie auch alle anderen, für die sie bestimmt ist; und dazu beitragen, diejenigen wieder zusammenzuführen, die die Liebe zu unserer abendländischen Geschichte ohne Trübung bewahrt haben.*" Erich Auerbach, *Mimesis: Dargestellte Wirklichkeit in der abendländischen Literatur*. Bern and Munich: Francke Verlag, 1946, p. 518.

18 Lyrics by Bertolt Brecht and music by Kurt Weill.

19 The "Seeräuberjenny" song begins: "*Meine Herren, heute sehen Sie mich Gläser abwaschen/Und ich mache das Bett für jeden./Und Sie geben mir einen Penny und ich bedanke mich schnell/Und Sie sehen meine Lumpen und dies lumpige Hotel/Und Sie wissen nicht, mit wem Sie reden.*" My translation.

20 "*Und wenn dann der Kopf fällt, sage ich 'Hoppla!'*" are the concluding lines of the final stanza.

21 Comparable to American states, *Länder* (singular, *Land*) are the semi-autonomous political units of the German federal state. Before unification, (West) Germany had ten *Länder*; the current unified Germany has sixteen. Educational policy in Germany is established and administered at the *Land* level.

Ambushed by History

1   Arendt's reports on the Eichmann trial, initially published serially in *The New Yorker*, appeared in book form in 1963. The German version followed in 1964. *Origins of Totalitarianism* was initially published in English in 1951. A reworked German version appeared in 1955.

2   West German complaints that it depicted Germans unfairly led the French secretary in charge of the competition selection to withdraw it as France's official entry at Cannes. After French protests against its withdrawal, the film was shown "*hors compétition*" at Cannes and subsequently presented at an official screening at the Berlin Film Festival.

3   The Austrian composer Hanns Eisler (1898–1962) worked closely with Brecht from the late 1920s onward. Their joint projects, with Eisler setting Brecht's texts to music, included the 1930 agitprop play "Die Maßnahme" ("The Measures Taken") and the 1932 film, *Kuhle Wampe oder: Wem gehort die Welt?* (*Kuhle Wampe or Who Owns the World?*), which featured the "Solidarity Song" as a leitmotif. Exiled from Nazi Germany because of his Jewish parentage and communist affiliation, Eisler spent the years 1938–48 in the United States, where, in 1947, he co-authored *Composing for the Films* (reissued in 2007 by Continuum) with T.W. Adorno. In 1949, Eisler settled in East Berlin, capital of the newly established German Democratic Republic, for which he composed a new national anthem.

4   The Auschwitz Trials began with three initial trials—the first 1963–1965, the second 1965–1966, and the third 1967–1968—and concluded with three follow-up trials in the 1970s.

5   One defendant, Hans Stark, was indicted under the juvenile criminal code because he was only nineteen when he started work at Auschwitz. Two defendants were dropped from the case for reasons of illness. The camp commander, Rudolf Höss, had already been tried, sentenced to death, and executed in 1947 in Poland.

6   The accuracy and even authenticity of this quote, attributed to Hitler in his address to military commanders in Obersalzberg on August 22, 1939, are disputed, but the underlying sentiment has become a truism.

7   For an elaboration of this principle of the reciprocal relationship between history and memory see Maurice Halbwachs, *The Collective Memory*, translated by Francis J. Ditter and Vida Yazdi Ditter. New York: Harper & Row, 1980 and *On Collective Memory*, translated by Lewis A. Coser. Chicago: University of Chicago Press, 1992. Positing that "it is in society that people normally acquire their memories" and that "[i]t is also in society that they recall, recognize, and localize their memories," Halbwachs concludes that "it is to the degree that our individual thought places itself in these [social frameworks for memory]… that it is capable of the act of recollection." Without grounding itself in the collective understanding of a given history at a given time, memories cannot be sustained: "We can remember only on condition of retrieving the position of past events that

interest us from the frameworks of collective memory" (Halbwachs, *On Collective Memory*, pp. 38 and 172).

8   Quotes taken from the prefatory Judgment preceding the verdict in the Eichmann trial: www.asser.nl/upload/documents/… /Eichmann_Appeals_ Judgement_29-5-1962.pdf.

9   The public phase of the trial extended from April 11 to August 14, 1961.

10 The first Frankfurt Auschwitz trial took almost two years (December 20, 1963–August 19, 1965).

11 Founded in 1950, the ARD (Arbeitsgemeinschaft der öffentlich-rechtlichen Rundfunkanstalten der Bundesrepublik Deutschland) was the first nationwide television network in postwar West Germany. A second network, the ZDF (Zweites Deutsches Fernsehen), was added in 1963. Both were public. Private commercial television did not exist in Germany until 1984.

12 In 1960 only 17.6 percent of German households had televisions sets. By mid-decade this number had almost doubled (to 47.3 percent), but was still less than half (Siegfried, 77). Still, consumer surveys show that as early as 1963 television had become the preferred medium for news and entertainment in German households.

13 The German term, *Zeitzeugen*, literally means witnesses (*Zeugen*) to their time (*Zeit*).

14 The wide-ranging figures are based on estimates by different sources, www.yadvashem.org/odot/Microsoft Word - 6622.pdf.

Passing Through Bitburg

1   "Leaving on a Jet Plane," words and music by John Denver. Copyright © 1967, 1969; Renewed 1995 BMB Ruby Songs and Reservoir Media Music. All Rights for BMG Ruby Songs Administered by BMG Rights Management (US) LLC. All Rights for Reservoir Media Music Administered in the World excluding UK, Eire, South Africa, New Zealand and Australia by Reservoir Media Management, Inc. All Rights Reserved. Used by Permission. *Reprinted by Permission of Hal Leonard LLC.*

2   The Nuremberg Trial condemned the Waffen-SS as a criminal organization guilty of war crimes.

Resident Alien

1   This is the subtitle of Grass's *Headbirths*, a hybrid of fiction, travelogue, satire, and political commentary from 1979–1980 (Günter Grass, *Headbirths, or, The Germans Are Dying Out*, translated by Ralph Mannheim. London: Seeker,

1982). *Headbirths* builds on Grass's political essays of the 1970s that reflect on the meaning of Germanness and the legitimacy of the German state in the wake of Auschwitz. A selection of these essays appeared in English translation as *Two States – One Nation? Against the Unthinking Clamor for German Reunification*, translated by Krishna Wilson with A.S. Wensinger. San Diego: Harcourt Brace Jovanovich, 1990.

2   Reference to Duong Thu Huong, *Novel Without a Name*, translated by Phan Huy Duong and Nina McPherson. New York: William Morrow & Company, 1991, p. 225, found in Nguyen, *Nothing Ever Dies*, p. 61.

3   Defined as a "journal of politics and culture," *konkret* was founded in 1957 by Klaus Rainer Röhl, Ulrike Meinhof's husband from 1961 to 1968. Meinhof worked for the journal as an editor and journalist and was editor-in-chief from 1960 to 1964. She resigned in 1969, accusing the journal of becoming "an instrument of the counter-revolution." Her essay "Jürgen Bartsch und die Gesellschaft" originally appeared in *konkret*, No. 1 (1968) and was reprinted in Ulrike Meinhof, *Die Würde des Menschen ist antastbar: Aufsätze und Polemiken*. Berlin: Klaus Wagenbach, 1980, pp. 112–116.

4   The title of Meinhof's collected essays, *Die Würde des Menschen ist antastbar* (The Dignity of Human Beings is Violable) rhetorically inverts this constitutional principle.

5   During RAF attacks on government, industry, and right-wing media facilities, three American soldiers and two German policeman were killed.

6   Baader, Ensslin, and Raspe did not outlive the year they were sentenced. All three died in prison in October 1977.

7   The image of Vietnamese peasants confronting modern militaries with primitive tools is mostly a romanticized myth. Both the South Vietnamese Viet Cong and the North Vietnamese Army were well equipped with modern weaponry—assault rifles, machine guns, rocket-propelled grenades, anti-aircraft missiles, and even tanks—supplied by China and Soviet bloc countries.

8   Written as "Dona, Dona" in 1941 by Sholom Secunda (music) and Aaron Zeitlin (lyrics in Yiddish), the English version, "Donna, Donna," with lyrics by Arthur Kevess and Teddi Schwartz, was recorded by Joan Baez in 1960.

9   The work of the Brazilian educator, Paolo Freire, particularly his 1968 *Pedagogy of the Oppressed*, was formative in the development of a critical pedagogy at that time.

Proof of Ancestry

1   While the provenance of the designation Sudeten German is disputed, its historical significance is not. It dates back to the nineteenth century, but is fraught with twentieth-century politics. When the state of Czechoslovakia

was created in the aftermath of World War I, "Sudeten" was used by ethno-nationalist Germans to distinguish the majority (*c.* 3 million) ethnic Germans from the minority Czechs in those parts of Czechoslovakia they had started calling the "Sudetenland," instead of, as before, "Bohemia." In the 1920s and '30s, "Sudeten" became the rallying cry for an anti-Czech, anti-Semitic politics that ultimately led to the incorporation of the so-called Sudetenland into Nazi Germany, where it became the administrative region Sudetengau.

2   Derived from medieval Germanic law, *Sippenhaft* was invoked as a principle of Nazi law and deployed as a form of state terror.

3   The National Socialist Party adopted the black, white, and red of the imperial German flag to distinguish itself from the black, red, and gold flag of the Weimar Republic. The black, red, and gold color scheme was restored in both postwar German republics, West and East.

4   In the 1930s, the vast majority of Germans identified as Christian: around 54–60 percent as Protestant (officially called the German Evangelical Church) and around 40 percent as Roman Catholic, with most of the rest declaring themselves either deists/creationists or non-religious. Less than 1 percent of the German population in the 1930s identified as Jewish.

5   The persecution of Roma and Sinti during the Nazi years resulted in the death of up to 220,000 people. An estimated 25 percent of all European Roma were killed by Nazi Germany and its allies. Officially considered to represent two distinctive "tribes" or "nations" of a particular ethnic minority in Europe, Roma and Sinti have popularly been referred to as "gypsies." In Germany, "gypsies" are known as *Zigeuner*, a term derived from a Greek root meaning "untouchable."

6   About half the children in Vienna at the time were said to be born to unwed mothers.

7   Croats and Slovenes are considered southern Slavs and Slovaks western Slavs. Despite the fact that it forged a strategic alliance with Croatia and the so-called Slovak State and annexed Slovenia, Nazi Germany argued that Slavs were not only inferior, but subhuman, and should be exterminated, removed from their lands, or enslaved. The equation of Slavs and gypsies was based on the fact that about half the Roma came from a majority Slav part of Eastern Europe.

Part Two

1   "Shemà," translated by Jonathan Galassi. Copyright © 2015 by Jonathan Galassi, from *The Complete Works of Primo Levi*. Used by permission of Liveright Publishing Corporation. Levi dated this poem January 10, 1946 (the outset of the Nuremberg trials) and chose it as the epigraph to his autobiographical novel *If This is a Man* (translated by Stuart Woolf in *The Complete Works of Primo Levi*, vol. I. New York and London: Liveright Publishing, 2015, pp. 1–165, p. 7.)

Into the Past

1 Kluger, *Still Alive*, p. 87.
2 Data compiled by the United States Holocaust Memorial Museum and Yad Vashem estimate that around 90 percent of the total number of Jews sent to Theresienstadt (around 15,000 of them children) perished. Around 90,000 were deported east, where most were killed in other Nazi camps; between 33,000 and 36,000 died in Theresienstadt itself.
3 Kluger, *Still Alive*, p. 70.
4 Today's Krásná Lípa.
5 Heinz Vatter's cousin, Fred Vatter, restarted the family business in the Bavarian town where he resettled after the war. Bellinda, as he named his hosiery factory (a Latin rendering of the Vatter's hometown in Bohemia, Schönlinde), became one of the most successful enterprises in postwar Germany, producing up to 90 million stockings a year and earning Fred Vatter the moniker "Stocking King" (*Strumpfkönig*).
6 Alongside his professional work as a lawyer, Walter's father was actively engaged in the arts as a composer and pianist. Decrees such as the October 1938 decree prohibiting Aryan musicians from teaching Jewish students affected his own work both directly and indirectly. For a biography of Johannes Bammer, see Widmar Hader, *Johannes Bammer*. Geislingen/ Steige: Verlag des Südmährischen Landschaftsrates, 1989.
7 R.M. Douglas, *Orderly and Humane: The Expulsion of Germans After the Second World War*. New Haven and London: Yale University Press, 2012, p. 96.
8 There is no confirmed account of the number killed; estimates range from several hundred to several thousand. Douglas proposes a figure of around 100–150 deaths (Douglas, *Orderly and Humane*, p. 114).
9 Douglas, *Orderly and Humane*, p. 38.
10 See Article XII of the Potsdam Agreement, "Orderly Transfer of German Populations." http://www.nato.int/ebookshop/video/declassified/doc_files/ Potsdam%20Agreement.pdf.
11 Nicholas Stargardt, *The German War: A Nation Under Arms, 1939–1945. Citizens and Soldiers*. New York; Perseus Books, 2015, p. 549.
12 The official designation was *Mischling zweiten Grades* (mixed race, second degree).
13 In 1938, the Reich Citizenship Law was amended to declare that "a business was Jewish if the proprietor was a Jew, if a partner was a Jew, or if, on January 1, 1938, a member of the board of directors was a Jew." Saul Friedlander, *Nazi Germany and the Jews*. Volume I: *The Years of Persecution, 1933–1939*. New York: Harper Perennial, 1998, p. 257.
14 The decree of November 12, 1938 ("Verordnung zur Ausschaltung der Juden aus dem deutschen Wirtschaftsleben") was followed by the decree of December 14, 1938 ("Verordnung zur Durchführung der Verordnung

zur Ausschaltung der Juden aus dem deutschen Wirtschaftsleben").
Joseph Walk, *Das Sonderrecht für die Juden im NS-Staat: Eine Sammlung der gesetzlichen Maßnahmen und Richtlinien – Inhalt und Bedeutung,* 2nd edition. Heidelberg: C.F. Müller Verlag, pp. 254, 267.

15   Manfred and Gerhard Förster died in 1952 and 1966, respectively.

Walking to Buchenwald

1   Goethe played a defining role in the literary and cultural life of Weimar from his early twenties on. Appointed in 1792 as the first director of the newly founded Hoftheater (Court Theater), he envisioned theater as a synthesis between dramatic art and philosophical debate. Sharing a similar vision, Schiller moved to Weimar to begin a collaboration that lasted until his death in 1805. In 1919, the Court Theater officially became the German National Theater in Weimar. During the Third Reich, it was administered by the Nazi Party and provided with lavish resources, including Hitler's personal funds.

2   Franz Ehrlich, the designer and architect of the famous Buchenwald entrance gate with the cynical slogan *Jedem das Seine* (To Each His Own), was sent to Buchenwald in 1937 for his Communist activities. Trained as a machine fitter and architect (Ehrlich had worked with the Dessau Bauhaus Group, along with Lászlo Moholy-Nagy, Paul Klee, Wassily Kandinsky, and the sculptor and typographer Joost Schmidt), he advanced to a paid position in the camp, where he designed numerous facilities, including a small zoo and domestic interiors for resident SS officers.

3   The camp opened in July 1937 and became operational in November 1938.

4   The exact number of people who perished at Buchenwald is unknown.

5   Imre Kertész, *Fateless*, translated by Christopher C. Wilson and Katharina M. Wilson. Evanston, IL: Northwestern University Press, 1992, p. 94.

6   Kertész won the 2002 Nobel Prize in Literature for works like *Fateless* and *Kaddish for an Unborn Child*, translated by Christopher C. Wilson and Katharina M. Wilson. New York: Hydra Books, 1997, based on his experience as a Hungarian Jew during the Nazi years, including imprisonment at Auschwitz and Buchenwald. Wiesel, a Romanian-born Jew, won the Nobel Peace Prize in 1986. His memoir, *Night*, translated by Stella Rodway, New York: Hill & Wang, 1960, is an account of his imprisonment at Auschwitz and Buchenwald as a teenage boy. The Austrian-born Améry (who repudiated his German roots by changing his name, Hanns Mayer, to the French anagram, Jean Améry), wrote about his internment, first at Auschwitz and then at Buchenwald, in *At the Mind's Limits: Contemplations by a Survivor on Auschwitz and Its Realities*, translated by Sidney and Stella P. Rosenfeld. Bloomington, IN: Indiana University Press, 1980. Bettelheim, an Austrian-born Jew, who went on to become a renowned child

psychologist, was interned at Dachau and then at Buchenwald in the early years of the camp. He was released in the wake of an amnesty announced on Hitler's 1939 birthday. Bonhoeffer, a German Protestant theologian and one of the leading figures in the Christian resistance to Nazism, the Confessing Church, was arrested after the failed 1944 plot to assassinate Hitler. He was sent first to Buchenwald before being executed in the Flössenburg camp. Halbwachs, a French sociologist, was arrested when he protested the Gestapo's arrest of his Jewish father-in-law. He died of dysentery at Buchenwald in 1945. Léon Blum, a socialist and a Jew, was imprisoned at Buchenwald in a special section for high-ranking prisoners. He served three times as French Prime Minister (1936–1937, 1938, 1946–1947).

7 Jean Améry, "Die Tortur," my translation. In *Jenseits von Schuld und Sühne: Bewältigungsversuche eines Überwältigten*. Stuttgart: Klett-Cotta, 1977, pp. 62–63, 68.

8 In Auschwitz, "the liberation of the last surviving Jewish inmates of the main camp (Auschwitz I) and the arrival of the first ethnic Germans was separated by less than a fortnight." Douglas, *Orderly and Humane*, p. 134.

9 Purchased by a wealthy patron in 1897, the house was donated as a residence for the ailing Nietzsche and an archive for his work.

10 Friedrich Nietzsche, "First Essay: 'Good' and 'Evil'; 'Good' and 'Bad,'" translated by Carol Diethe. In *On the Genealogy of Morality*. Cambridge, UK: Cambridge University Press, 1994, pp. 25–26. Nietzsche contends that the wild power of the "blond beast" has historically evoked both fear and admiration.

The Quiet Dignity of Being True

1 The school was officially named the Annette School after World War I, when the school's administration devolved to the city.

2 April 25, 1933, "Gesetz gegen die Überfüllung deutscher Schulen und Hochschulen." See Walk, *Das Sonderrecht für die Juden im NS-Staat*, pp. 17–18.

3 "… *kann es keinem deutschen Lehrer … mehr zugemutet werden, an jüdische Schulkinder Unterricht zu erteilen. Auch versteht es sich von selbst, daß es für deutsche Schüler unerträglich ist, mit Juden in einem Klassenraum zu sitzen … Juden ist der Besuch deutscher Schulen nicht gestattet.*" Walk, *Das Sonderrecht für die Juden im NS-Staat*, p. 256.

4 The so-called *Hitlergruss* (the address, "Heil Hitler," with the right arm fully extended upwards) became mandatory for all active civil servants after Hitler's 1933 election as Reich Chancellor. Teachers in Germany, including at private schools, were civil servants, credentialed and regulated by the state.

5 These small commemorative plaques, called *Stolpersteine* (stumbling blocks or stones), are the work of Gunter Demnig, who created the *Stolperstein*

project in the early 1990s to remember the victims of National Socialism. In the spirit of the Talmudic belief that "a person is only forgotten when his or her name is forgotten," each stone remembers a single person by name, date of birth, date of deportation, and place of death. Each stone is a concrete cube, identical in form and size (10 × 10 cm.), that is inserted into the sidewalk in front of the last known residence of the person deported. Brass plaques affixed to the surface of the stone provide the information. Both a public art installation and a decentralized memorial, the *Stolperstein* project extends across Germany and the landscape of former Nazi-occupied Europe. By April 2017, over 61,000 stones had been placed.

6   Ursula Möllenhoff and Rita Schlautmann-Overmeyer, *Jüdische Familien in Münster, 1918–1945.* Münster: Westfälisches Dampfboot, 1995.

7   Ursula Meyer was adopted by an English family in Middlesex. She married their son and they had two daughters.

8   Entry of 8 July 1941. Anneliese Stöbis, *Tagebuch des Grauens, 1940–1944*, edited by Joachim Stöbis, 2006. http://geschichte-reckenfeld.de/kapitel/ entwicklung/00_pdf_dateien/1945_tagebuch_anneliese_stoebis.pdf.

9   In the painting by Gerhard van der Grinten, the male figure, to the right of Edith Stein, is Niels Stensen (1638–1686). A renowned scholar, Stensen was affiliated with the Ludgeri Church between 1680 and 1683, when he was appointed Bishop of Münster. He left Münster after just three years in protest over the venality and greed of the ruling clergy. Eventually, he also left his bishopric to spend the last year of his life as a simple village priest.

10   The decree that all Jews in the German Reich over six years old be identified by the so-called Jewish star affixed to their outer clothing went into effect on September 19, 1941.

11   Edith Stein, *Life in a Jewish Family: Her Unfinished Autobiographical Account*, edited by L. Gelber and Romaeus Leuven and translated by Josephine Koeppel. In *The Collected Works of Edith Stein, Sister Teresa Benedicta of the Cross, Discalced Carmelite*, vol. I. Washington, DC: ICS Publications, 1986, pp. 23–24.

12   Stein, *Life*, pp. 63, 51, 44.

13   Stein, *Life*, p. 269.

14   "*Ich will die Probe machen, ob ich in Philosophie etwas Selbständiges leisten kann.*" Maria Antonia Sondermann, "Einführung." In Edith Stein, *Zum Problem der Einfühlung.* Freiburg: Herder Verlag, 2008, p. xiv.

15   Stein's dissertation on *Das Problem der Einfühlung in seiner geschichtlichen Entwicklung und in phänomenologischer Betrachtung* (The Problem of Empathy in Its Historical Development and From a Phenomenological Perspective) was supervised by Husserl and dedicated to Stein's mother, Auguste Stein.

16   Sondermann, "Einführung," p. xviii, fn. 36.

17   "*es sind uns fremde Subjekte und ihr Erleben gegeben*" ("foreign subjects and their experience are given to us"). Stein, *Zum Problem der Einfühlung*, p. 11.

18 This was Hobsbawm's view of Europe in "[t]he decades from the outbreak of the First World War to the aftermath of the Second." Eric Hobsbawm, *The Age of Extremes: A History of the World, 1914–1991*. New York: Pantheon, p. 7.

19 Just two years older than Stein, Martin Heidegger (1889–1976) was part of Stein's cohort at the University of Freiburg, where he also studied with Edmund Husserl. After Husserl's retirement in 1928, Heidegger was appointed to fill his position as Professor of Philosophy in Freiburg, and between April 1933 and April 1934, he served as Rector of the university. He died in 1976 aged eighty-six.

20 Originally published in 1917, it was reissued on the tenth anniversary of Edith Stein's beatification.

21 Edith Stein, *Endliches und ewiges Sein: Versuch eines Aufstiegs zum Sinn des Seins* (Temporal and Eternal Being: An Attempt to Approach the Meaning of Being-ness). In *Edith Stein: Gesamtausgabe*, vols. 12 & 13. Cologne: Edith Stein-Archiv. http://www.edith-stein-archiv.de/ wp-content/uploads/2014/10/11_12_EdithSteinGesamtausgabe_ EndlichesUndEwigesSein.pdf.

22 Being a Jew was not the only obstacle in Stein's way. Being a woman was another. Husserl's letter of reference for Stein candidly acknowledges this gender barrier. "Should academic careers be opened to ladies," he wrote (the conditional mode highlighting the unlikelihood of such a future anytime soon), "then I can recommend her whole-heartedly and as my first choice for admission to a professorship."

23 April 7, 1933, "Gesetz zur Wiederherstellung des Berufsbeamtentums." Walk, *Das Sonderrecht für die Juden im NS-Staat*, p. 12.

24 Teresa of Avila (1515–1582) was canonized by Pope Gregory XV in 1622.

25 For these and the following details I am indebted to Stein, "Chronology," 430–435.

26 The term "planet Auschwitz" was coined by the Jewish writer and Auschwitz survivor Yehiel De-Nur, when called as a witness in the 1961 Eichmann Trial. De-Nur is known for the lurid and often grotesque fictions that he published after the war under the pen name Ka-Tzetnik 135633, the number assigned to him as a prisoner in Auschwitz.

27 In 1998, Pope John Paul II canonized Edith Stein as Saint Teresa Benedicta of the Cross. Members of the Stein family and the Carmelite community were present, and an official delegation of the West German government included the German Chancellor Helmut Kohl. In his homily, the pope recognized the two faith communities, Jewish and Catholic, that had been formative in Stein's life.

In Love and on Trains

1 In 1911, the Prussian Ministry of Science, Art, and Culture commissioned the graphic artist, Ludwig Sütterlin, to develop a modern script for public

use in Germany. Although Sütterlin's "modern" script was just an updated version of the traditional German script known as *Kurrent*, it became the official German script between 1915 and 1941, when it was discontinued and replaced by Latin script to facilitate communication with other countries during wartime. However, many Germans continued to use Sütterlin well into the postwar period.

2 The War Relief Service (*Kriegshilfsdienst*) was created in July 1941 as a voluntary, half-year extension of the Reich Labor Service (*Reichsarbeitsdienst*). Officially intended to provide social services and clerical help to various government agencies, over half of the approximately 50,000 young woman who enlisted in it were put to work in the arms industry.

3 Jeanette Winterson, *Art Objects: Essays on Ecstasy and Effrontery*. New York: Vintage, 1997, p. 26.

4 Saul Friedlander, *Nazi Germany and the Jews, 1939–1945: The Years of Extermination*. New York: HarperCollins, p. 263.

5 Friedlander, *Extermination*, p. 340.

6 Found in Ian Kershaw, *Hitler, the Germans, and the Final Solution*. New Haven: Yale University Press, 2008, p. 144.

7 Data taken from the *American Jewish Yearbook*'s "Statistics of Jews": http://www.ajcarchives.org/AJC_DATA/Files/1941_1942_9_Statistics. pdf: 663.

8 Until spring 1944, when train tracks were laid through the gate house at Auschwitz to accommodate the mass transport of Hungarian Jews deported directly to the extermination center at Birkenau, the camp entrance was designed for motor vehicle and pedestrian traffic.

9 Designed by the architect team Nicolaus Hirsch, Wolfgang Lorch, and Andrea Wandel, the Track 17 Memorial (*Mahnmal Gleis 17*) was inaugurated on January 27, 1998.

10 Friedlander, *Extermination*, p. 491.

11 A single, two-axle car was designed for 50 and a double, four-axle car for 100 passengers.

12 This and the following quotes are from Levi's *If This is a Man*, p. 11.

13 The so-called Jewish Star that all Jews in the Reich and Reich-annexed territories were required to wear had to include the word "Jew" in the language of the respective country. In German-speaking lands, *Jude* was spelled out in faux-Hebraic letters.

14 Kershaw, *Hitler, the Germans, and the Final Solution*, p. 186.

Once Upon a Wartime

1 Ian Kershaw, *To Hell and Back: Europe 1914–1949*. New York: Penguin, 2015, p. 352.

2 Kershaw, *To Hell and Back*, pp. 350–351.

3 Through the 1941 Russian campaign Wehrmacht officers often still wore the old-style foldable field cap (*Feldmütze*) dubbed a "crusher," instead of the high, stiff peaked cap (*Schirmmütze*) worn for official occasions.

4 Walter Benjamin, "The Storyteller: Observations on the Works of Nikolai Leskov," translated by Harry Zohn. In *Walter Benjamin: Selected Writings*. Vol. 3: *1935–1938*, edited by Howard Eiland and Michael W. Jennings. Cambridge, MA: The Belknap Press, 2002, p. 144.

5 Non-ethnic Germans (which, in the Sudetengau, meant Jews and Czechs) were relegated to the second-class and increasingly rightless status of "citizens of a racially-foreign ethnicity" (*Angehörige rassefremden Volkstums*).

6 In the German military, the *Soldbuch*, commonly translated as "military paybook," doubled as the official identification papers that a soldier was required to carry with him at all times.

7 William B. Hanford, *Dangerous Assignment: An Artillery Forward Observer in WWII*. Mechanicsburg, PA: Stackpole Books, 2008, p. 4.

8 Wound badges were both among the most common and most respected military awards, as they were "paid with blood." They were awarded in three ranked categories: Black (wounded once or twice or frostbitten in action), Silver (wounded three or four times or severely), and Gold (wounded five or more times or with traumatic injuries, such as total blindness, loss of limbs, severe brain damage, or "loss of manhood"). Gold Wound badges were often awarded posthumously.

9 W.G. Sebald, *The Emigrants*, translated by Michael Hulse. New York: New Directions Books, 1997, p. 30.

10 The first cited use of "carpet bombing" is in the *New York Times* on January 26, 1944.

11 Stargardt, *The German War*, pp. 367–368.

12 Kurt Vonnegut, *Slaughterhouse-Five, or The Children's Crusade: A Duty-Dance with Death*. New York: Dell Publishing, 1969, pp. 146, 148.

13 Vonnegut, *Slaughterhouse-Five*, p. 149.

14 Vonnegut, *Slaughterhouse-Five*, p. 179.

15 Ruth Andreas-Friedrich, *Der Schattenmann: Tagebuchaufzeichnungen 1938–1945*. Berlin: Suhrkamp, 1947, p. 202.

16 The number of undocumented refugees that had recently flooded the city and the catastrophic circumstances allowed only a rough estimate of the total casualties.

17 Ian Kershaw, *The End: The Defiance and Destruction of Hitler's Germany, 1944–1945*. New York: Penguin, 2011, p. 237.

18 Desmond Tutu, "Chairperson's Foreword," *Truth and Reconciliation Commission of South Africa Report*, vol. 1 (1998), section 27, p. 7.

19 The exhibition opened in April 1995 and ran until October 1999. In response to charges that critical materials, both photographs and

documents, had been misidentified or incorrectly labeled, the exhibition was suspended and subjected to rigorous scholarly review. It reopened in 2001, in revised form, as "Crimes of the Wehrmacht: Dimensions of the War of Annihilation, 1941–1944" (*Verbrechen der Wehrmacht: Dimensionen des Vernichtungskrieges 1941–1944*). The exhibition traveled across German-speaking countries (Germany, Austria, Luxembourg) until March 2004. It is permanently housed in the German Historical Museum, Berlin. See Wildt et al., *Crimes of the Wehrmacht*.

20 Commonly rendered in English as the Historians' Debate, the German term, *Historikerstreit*, better captures its acrimonious tenor: it was not just a "debate" but an argument (*Streit*).

21 The German premiere of *Schindler's List* was in Frankfurt, which before the Holocaust was second only to Berlin in terms of the size and influence of its Jewish community.

22 Tutu, "Chairperson's Foreword," section 27, p. 7; emphasis added.

23 Goldhagen's book appeared in German translation the same year as the American original. Daniel Goldhagen, *Hitler's Willing Executioners: Ordinary Germans and the Holocaust*. New York: Alfred A. Knopf, 1996. (German translation by Klaus Kochmann, *Hitlers willige Vollstrecker: Ganz gewöhnliche Deutsche und der Holocaust.*)

24 His critics included Christopher Browning, Raul Hilberg, Yehuda Bauer, Omer Bartov, and Ian Kershaw.

25 "Combat report on Unternehmen Dreieck und Viereck from September 17 to October 2, 1942." Bundesarchiv/Militärarchiv, RH 23/ 25, BL. 3.52, Quotation BL. 51f. Excerpted in Wildt et al., *Crimes of the Wehrmacht*, p. 23.

26 Photographs found on Sergeant Fritz Lawen (Regiment 679, 12th Company) when taken into Soviet military custody in 1944. Found in Wildt et al., *Crimes of the Wehrmacht*, pp. 318–319. The German caption reads: "*Sie wollten nicht für Deutschland arbeiten*" (They didn't want to work for Germany").

27 The German Military Law of 1935 required every German male between eighteen and forty-five to do military service. During wartime, this service requirement, modified for gender, also applied to women. Article 26 specifically addressed political engagement: "Soldiers may not be politically active. Membership in the NSDAP [Nazi Party] or any of its affiliated organizations is suspended for the duration of their military service." Even the right to vote was suspended during active military service. http://www.verfassungen.ch/de/de33-45/wehr35.htm.

28 Johannes Rau served as President of the German Federal Republic from 1999 to 2004.

29 The German word, *Schweinereien*, is almost untranslatable in this context. Literally, "the things that pigs (*Schweine*) do," it can mean anything from a physical or moral mess to acts of gross, even obscene, transgression. The word always carries an element of contempt.

A World in Letters

1 Founded in the early 1920s and organized along paramilitary lines, the Hitler Youth was the Nazi Party's official youth organization. In 1926, it was incorporated into the League of German Worker Youth.

2 Founded in 1930 for girls aged between ten and eighteen, the League of German Girls (Bund Deutscher Mädel, BDM) was the female wing of the Nazi Party youth movement.

3 Many members of the Waffen-SS had their blood type tattooed on the underside of their left arm near the armpit. After the war, these tattoos were used as prima facie evidence of SS membership. To evade prosecution, some former SS members tried to surgically remove their tattoo, even resorting to self-inflicted burns or gunshot wounds.

4 Philip Levine, "Innocence." In *News of the World: Poems*. New York: Alfred A. Knopf, 2010, p. 15.

Part Three

1 Walter Benjamin, "The Meaning of Time in the Moral Universe," translated by Rodney Livingstone. In *Walter Benjamin: Selected Writings*. Vol. I: *1913–1926*, edited by Marcus Bullock and Michael W. Jennings. Boston: The Belknap Press, 1996, p. 286.

2 This relief sculpture of a charred female body on a massive bronze plate is featured in the "Hamburg Firestorm" section of Alfred Hrdlicka's "Countermemorial" (*Gegendenkmal*) in Hamburg. While this section of the memorial refers most explicitly to Operation Gomorrah, the 1943 air raid on Hamburg that destroyed the greater part of the city and left some 35,000 people dead, its depiction of burned and tortured bodies also carries an unmistakable Holocaust resonance. Located a stone's throw from the Hamburg Dammtor train station, from which deportation trains departed regularly toward destinations east, its figures evoke the horror of bodies burned in Nazi crematoria. "Hamburg Firestorm" (1985) was the first of four planned sections of the memorial to be completed; a second was completed the following year. The last two parts were never finished. The memorial thus stands as a melancholic work of incomplete remembering and unfinished mourning.

A Longing Called Home

1 Freud died in September 1939, a year after moving to London.

2 A West Germanic language officially known as *Plattdeutsch* (literally Flat or Low German), *Platt*, as native speakers call it, was traditionally spoken throughout most of Westphalia, in parts of northern Germany, and the eastern part of the Netherlands. With only around 2 percent of the younger generation still able to speak it in the early twenty-first century, it is now classified as a "vulnerable language." Standard German, unmarked by any regional affiliation, is called *Hochdeutsch* (High German).

3 In September 1945, 326 people—the first contingent of ethnic German refugees, mostly from Silesia—were repatriated to Velen.

Memories of War

1 *The HarperCollins Study Bible*, New Revised Edition, edited by Wayne A. Meeks, Jouette M. Bassler, Werner E. Lemke. Susan Niditch, Eileen M. Schuller. New York: HarperCollins, 1998, p. 1912.

2 Annette von Droste-Hülshoff, "The Boy on the Moor," translated by David Paley. http://www.poemswithoutfrontiers.com/Der_Knabe_im_Moor.html.

3 What, if anything, these men and boys were actually charged with is unclear. "Complicity" was Anna's term, as she assumed a direct connection between their wartime *Volkssturm* participation and their postwar punishment.

4 This Honor Book (*Ehrenbuch*) was dedicated on November 19, 1961 by the local affiliate of the Association of Returnees (*Verband der Heimkehrer*) "in gratitude for the safe return home from the war of 1939–1945 and in memory of the fallen/missing and civilian dead of both World Wars."

5 The 1939 census count for Velen was 1,294. If roughly half of those were men, of whom roughly a third would have been of military age, we get a sense of the relative numbers.

6 Founded in 1897 in Vilna as the Algemeyner Yidisher Arbeter Bund (Universal Jewish Worker's Association), the Bund was a labor organization for Jews in eastern Europe. In 1917, an independent Polish Bund was formed that in the course of the 1920s eventually became a political party in its own right (the Jewish Socialist Party), simultaneously functioning broadly as a Jewish cultural and social organization, providing schools and medical facilities, and sponsoring sports and cultural activities for Polish Jews. By the mid-1930s, the Bund had become the dominant Jewish organization in Poland.

7 Historians estimate that during the Warsaw Uprising some 200,000 Poles were killed and another 800,000 captured. The city of Warsaw was looted and burned.

8 According to German records some 56,000 Jews were captured. Around 7,000 of them were killed directly and the rest deported to various camps.

9 "it is not possible to remember the future ... memory is of the past" (from *De Memoria et Reminiscentia*). Aristotle, *Aristotle on Memory*, translated

with interpretive summaries by Richard Sorabji. Providence, RI: Brown
University Press, 1972, p. 47. For Aristotle's discussion of the work of the
imagination, see his *De Anima*, particularly II.6 – III.2 and III.3.

10 Davoine and Gaudillière, *History Beyond Trauma*, p. 105.

11 Anna Bancken, née Jägering, died on June 9, 2014, at the age of eighty-two.

Memories of Betrayal

1 In modern German, the word for peace is *Frieden*, from the Germanic root
fried (=peace).

2 This and the following, Klemperer, *The Language of the Third Reich*,
pp. 155, 157.

3 Anna never mentioned it, but I learned later that it was her father who built
the gate for the Frank's back yard fence.

4 Anna got these details wrong. The Laumanns had already come to Velen and
acquired the Franks' butcher shop and house in 1937, several years before
the aerial bombings of German cities. Anna's confusion probably stemmed
from the fact that in the wake of the bombings, families (sometimes just the
children) were evacuated from urban areas to the countryside, including Velen.

5 *Bahnhof Straße* literally means train station (*Bahnhof*) road or street (*Straße*).

6 Amalie Landau was deported on a Monday (July 27, 1942).

7 According to Nazi law, Günther was a "half-Jew" (or *Mischling*, first degree).
However, he was not deported with his Jewish mother, but remained in
Velen with his father.

8 Helene Frank's sister, Frieda, married Adolf Terhoch, a merchant from
Ramsdorf, and had twin sons. They fled first to Holland, then to Canada,
where they settled in Winnipeg.

9 Ida's husband, a cattle trader, died in 1939. Their daughters, young women
in their twenties, escaped to England and found work in domestic service.
Their widowed mother was deported to Riga on the same transport as her
brother, Abraham Frank, and sister-in-law, Helene.

10 Halbwachs, *On Collective Memory*, p. 194.

There Was a Butcher Here, Once

1 A possible factor in their move was the progressive status afforded
Westphalian Jews at the time. At the height of his power, after the 1807
Peace of Tilsit, the French emperor Napoleon Bonaparte founded the
Kingdom of Westphalia, which he envisioned as a model state of the
modern age. Within this framework, under the Napoleonic Code, Jews
were emancipated and granted full citizenship rights.

2   Friederika Frank (née Abraham) had eight children. The six Landau
    children were born to two mothers. Hermann Landau's first wife, Julie (née
    Gumpers), died after the birth of her first child. His second wife, Helena (née
    Levi), had five children. She died after the birth of her last child, perhaps as
    a result of complications following childbirth. Hermann Landau married a
    third time, but there appears to have been no issue from this last marriage.
3   Helena Frank never married and had no children. She died in Velen aged
    fifty-two. The fate of the other four Frank daughters (Antonette, Henriette,
    Elizabeth, and Adelheid) is not known. The second son, Abraham, died
    aged two, and the third son, Moyses (also a butcher by trade), moved to a
    neighboring town, Weseke.
4   The record is unclear whether Meyer Landau and his first wife, Marianne,
    had two or three sons. The first son, Salomon, died at birth or very young.
    In 1864, when Marianne Landau was almost forty, the Landaus either had
    twin sons, Liefmann and Leopold (one of whom, Liefmann, died), or one
    son, whose Jewish name, Liefmann, was later Germanized to Leopold. This
    son, Leopold Landau, died in 1887 aged twenty-three.
5   Amalia's parents, Samuel and Julie Frank, were by then in their seventies and
    sixties, respectively. Amalia's youngest sister, Ida Frank, was still in her teens.
6   Meyer Landau's first wife, Marianne Canters, had also been thirty-five when
    she married him.
7   The eldest son, Louis, had moved away from Velen. The five other
    remaining Frank children were daughters.
8   At the time of Meyer Landau's death, Amalia Landau was fifty; her
    unmarried sisters—Ida, Bertha, and Dora Frank—were forty-nine,
    forty-six, and forty-four respectively. The youngest Frank sister, Ida
    (by then, Ida Cohen), had married and moved away from Velen the
    previous year.
9   Since some critical dates are not available—both birth and death dates of
    Hermann Landau's third wife, Johanna Besack, and the death dates of the
    Landau's first sons, Salomon and Liefmann (assuming that Liefmann was
    the twin of Leopold, not the same person, registered under two names)—it
    is impossible to accurately gauge who would have been living in the Landau
    household at a given time. Seven to nine persons is a realistic estimate.
10 Abraham and Helene Frank and their two children, Siegfried and Edith;
    Abraham's unmarried sisters, the "three old aunts"; Abraham's widowed
    sister, Amalia Landau, and her two daughters, Helene and Ida.
11 In 1928 Helene Landau married a Catholic merchant from Coesfeld,
    Johannes Tiwisina; she was thirty-three and he was twenty-six. Dora Frank
    died the following year aged sixty-two.
12 I am indebted to Norbert Fasse's exhaustive research for many of the
    details in this chapter. Norbert Fasse, *Katholiken und NS-Herrschaft im
    Münsterland: Das Amt Velen-Ramsdorf. 1918–1945*, 2nd edition. Bielefeld:
    Verlag für Regionalgeschichte, 1997.

13 Walk, *Das Sonderrecht für die Juden im NS-Staat*, pp. 15, 88. The Baden "Ordinance for the Restitution of Honesty in the Cattle Trade" was passed on April 19, 1933. The Bavarian "Prohibition of the Hebrew Language on Cattle Markets" was passed on August 2, 1934.

14 Decree issued February 6, 1936 by the Württemberg Rural Political Police. Walk, *Das Sonderrecht für die Juden im NS-Staat*, p. 154.

15 Issued by the mayor of Königsdorf, Bavaria on September 28, 1935, the directive stated that "1) Cows and cattle that have been acquired, directly or indirectly, from Jews, are excluded from servicing by the community bull. 2) Cows and cattle from barns that also house livestock acquired from Jews are subject to observation for the period of one year. During this time, they are excluded from servicing by the community bull." Walk, *Das Sonderrecht für die Juden im NS-Staat*, p. 133.

16 In particular, Abraham Frank had assigned the slaughter of pigs to his apprentice, enabling him to avoid contact with an animal he was forbidden by Jewish law from eating.

17 "Laumann application for permission to assume ownership of a vacant establishment." Velen, March 20, 1937.

18 Helene's brothers, Ernst and Siegmund, as well as her sister, Frieda Cohen, and family emigrated to Canada. Her brother, Willi, and his family fled to the Netherlands.

19 Walk, *Das Sonderrecht für die Juden im NS-Staat*, p. 353. The decree regulating the "Behavior of Persons of German Blood [*Deutschblütige*] Toward Jews" was issued by the Reich Security Main Office on October 24, 1941.

20 Fasse, *Katholiken und NS-Herrschaft im Münsterland*, p. 619. Directive issued and sent to local authorities, November 11, 1941.

21 In the town registry, each person's profession (e.g. "butcher") or, if they have no profession, status (e.g. "wife") is specified. In their final entry, both Abraham and Helene Frank are identified as "o.B" (*ohne Beruf*, without profession), presumably on the grounds that Abraham had been deprived of the right to practice his profession.

22 Winfried Nachtwei, "Nachbarn von nebenan—verschollen in Riga," edited by I. Bardenmeier and A. Schulte-Hemming. In *Mythos Münster: Schwarze Löcher—Weiße Flecken*. Münster: Unrast Press, 1993.

23 Many items that deportees had been told to pack, particularly clothing, bedding, and assorted household goods, were confiscated at the assembly places and given to non-Jewish Germans who had lost their homes and possession during the air raids.

24 Fasse, *Katholiken und NS-Herrschaft im Münsterland*, p. 633.

25 Amalia Landau died March 13, 1944.

26 Fasse, *Katholiken und NS-Herrschaft im Münsterland*, p. 635.

27 The fact that Ida Sandmann's husband, Franz, was a master electrician, with responsibility for Velen's electrical grid, was surely an additional factor extending protection to his family.

28 Kertész, *Fateless*, pp. 180, 186, 188–189.

29 Personal conversation with Johannes and Cäcilia Liesner, Velen, June 2012. Liesel Sandmann died on January 19, 1944.

30 Alfons Wellerman, Personal conversation, Velen, June 2012. The Wellermans lived and worked as tenant farmers on the Wiechert farm, not far from the Sandmanns. In 1945, Franz Sandmann wasn't an "old man" yet (he was in his early forties), but to the young Alfons, he probably appeared old. Moreover, the events he had suffered had likely aged him.

31 Personal conversation, Cäcilia Liesner, Velen, June 2012.

32 When Ida's sister, Lene, returned to Coesfeld after seven months in a Nazi labor camp and found that everything in her home was gone—confiscated, stolen, or plundered—she moved to Velen to live with Ida and her family until her husband, Johannes Tiwisina, returned from the war. Lene Tiwisina died in Velen aged eighty-nine.

33 The request is dated May 29, 1953 and identifies Edith's aunt, Helene Tivisina (*sic*) as witness. Information about the outcome of her request was not available. Edith died in Shaftesbury, England, in the 1980s. Found in Franz Schrief, ed. *Das Schicksal der jüdischen Familien in Velen und Ramsdorf, 1933–1945*, vol. 1. Velen/Ramsdorf: Kleine Edition zum 20-jährigen Schuljubiläum, 2012.

34 "[I]t is to the degree that our individual thought places itself in these frameworks and participates in this memory that it is capable of the act of recollection." Halbwachs, *On Collective Memory*, p. 38.

35 This custom prevailed in Velen until well into the 1950s.

36 The information on the memorial stones for Abraham and Helene Frank is at odds with the information provided in the official Memorial Book (*Gedenkbuch*) compiled by the German federal government and held in the Federal Archive. The *Stolpersteine* give Theresienstadt as the Frank's deportation site, but the Federal Archive confirms their deportation to Riga. There is no official record of where or when they died, but it is most likely that both Franks died in Riga.

37 A commemorative plaque for Amalia Landau was not included with the other *Stolpersteine* memorials in Velen after her grandson, Günther Sandmann, refused permission. He feared drawing renewed anti-Semitic attention to the house he had shared as a child with his parents, sister, and grandmother, Amalia Landau.

My Nazi Family

1 Tony Judt, *The Memory Chalet*. New York: Penguin Books, 2010, p. 149.

2 The photocopier had only recently (1937) been invented and was not put into commercial use until the late 1950s. To keep a record, his only option at the time was a handwritten copy.

3 Heuss was initially appointed by OMGUS to serve as Minister of Education and Cultural Affairs in the state of Württemberg-Baden.

4 *Law for Liberation from National Socialism and Militarism*, Part I, Article 1, sections (1) and (2).

5 Under the command of General Lucius Clay, OMGUS (created January 1, 1946) supervised the transition from a fascist to a democratic Germany and helped the process of reconstruction get underway. OMGUS was disbanded in December 1949.

6 The KPČ was the Czech Communist Party. In April 1946, the Soviet authorities maneuvered a merger between the Communist Party and the Social Democratic Party in the Soviet occupation zone. The result of this merger was a new party, the Socialist Unity Party of Germany (*Sozialistische Einheitspartei Deutschlands*, SED).

7 Velen, where Walter had registered his permanent residence, was under the jurisdiction of the British Military Government. Ordinance No. 79 went into effect in the British Zone on February 24, 1947.

8 Founded in 1931, the NS-Frauenschaft merged a number of different women's organizations under one umbrella. From 1935 on, it was officially integrated into the Nazi party structure. With up to 2.5 million members, its declared mission was "to supply the Führer with ideologically reliable leaders from the world of German women."

9 On the western edge of Westphalia, close to the Dutch border, Kevelaer has been a pilgrimage site for Catholics since the mid-seventeenth century. It is considered the most important Catholic pilgrimage site in northwestern Europe.

10 Fasse, *Katholiken und NS-Herrschaft im Münsterland,* p. 363, figure 159.

11 "P" for *Partei* (Party), "G" for *Genosse* (comrade).

12 His father, Josef Wilhelm August Bushoff, worked as a medical professional for the town of Borken.

13 The Nazi labor camps for political prisoners in Westphalia included the notorious Emsland camps in the border region between the Netherlands and Westphalia. Karl von Ossietzky, who was awarded the Nobel Peace Prize in 1935 for his courageous anti-militarist resistance to Nazi Germany, was a prisoner in one of these camps. Refused release to attend the Nobel ceremony, he died in 1938 from the effects of abusive treatment in the camps.

14 Fasse, *Katholiken und NS-Herrschaft im Münsterland,* p. 681; see also Fasse, *Katholiken und NS-Herrschaft im Münsterland,* p. 857, note 79.

15 Other former Zentrum members made the same argument, claiming that by working not just with, but within, the Nazi party, they were able to wield a moderating influence.

16 By 1938, almost the entire Velen electorate (96.7 percent) voted for the Nazi party, compared with just 10 percent in 1932.

17 Peter Weiss, *The Investigation: Oratorio in 11 Cantos*, translated by Alexander Gross. London: Marion Boyars Publishers, 2010, p. 88.

18 Walter Benjamin locates justice in the realm of historical time and forgiveness in the realm of messianic time. Benjamin, "The Meaning of Time in the Moral Universe," pp. 286–287.

Epilogue
Forgetting Anne Frank

1 Aristotle considers both memory and imagination faculties of the soul. They reside in the same part of the soul (the perceptual—or sensible—part) and cognize things the same way: in terms of time and "by means of images." Where they differ is in relation to time. Imagination can produce images of things that do *not yet exist*, while memory can only produce images of things that *have already happened*. "[M]emory is of the past," Aristotle notes, "a person remembers now what he saw or experienced earlier." "[I]t is not possible to remember the future"; we can only imagine it. Richard Sorabji, *Aristotle on Memory*, Providence, RI: Brown University Press, 1972, pp. 48, 47, 53.

Sources and Acknowledgments

1 Theodor W. Adorno, "Erziehung nach Auschwitz." In *Erziehung zur Mündigkeit. Vorträge und Gespräche mit Hellmut Becker, 1959–1969*. Frankfurt: Suhrkamp Verlag, 1971. Both quotes, p. 90.

2 In this sequence of early essays ("Remembering, Repeating, and Working Through" [1914], "Mourning and Melancholia" [1915], and "The Uncanny" [1919]), all written at a time when Europe was reeling from the catastrophic losses suffered during World War I, Freud explored the psychological costs and consequences of different responses to traumatic pasts. While he proposed that some approaches, notably what he called "memory work" (*Erinnerungsarbeit*) or "mourning work (*Trauerarbeit*), promised to yield significant relief from hitherto unresolved psychic suffering, he also acknowledged that the experience of great loss left lasting traces that might never be completely resolved ("The Uncanny").

3 In addition to his two-volume study of *Nazi Germany and the Jews*, Saul Friedlander's early *Kurt Gerstein; The Ambiguity of Good*. New York: Alfred A. Knopf, 1969, impressed and moved me with its nuanced exploration of the morality of complicity in a criminal regime.

4 Works by Stargardt and Douglas are referenced above. Works by the other authors I drew on include: Marion Kaplan, *Between Dignity and Despair: Jewish Life in Nazi Germany*. New York and Oxford: Oxford University

Press, 1998; Sönke Neitzel and Harald Welzer, *Soldaten: On Fighting, Killing, and Dying: The Secret World War II Transcripts of German POWs.* New York: Vintage, 2013; Ullrich Völklein, *"Mitleid war von niemand zu erwarten": Das Schicksal der deutschen Vertriebenen.* Munich: Droemer Verlag, 2005.

5   Rick Atkinson's *The Guns at Last Light: The War in Western Europe, 1944–1945.* New York: Henry Holt & Company, 2013 and Erik Larson's *Dead Wake: The Last Crossing of the Lusitana.* New York: Crown Publishers, 2015, were of particular relevance for my work in this book. Jonathan Spence's *The Question of Hu.* New York: Alfred D. Knopf, 1988, was a revelation to me and, multiple rereadings later, it still impresses me anew each time. I consider it both a historiographic and literary masterpiece.

6   Tony Judt's *Postwar: A History of Europe Since 1945.* London: Penguin, 2005, sits next to Hobsbawm's *The Age of Extremes* on my bookshelf as an exemplar of history with a capital "H" done brilliantly and compellingly. What makes each work compelling in its own right is the force of the argument underlying it. In Judt's case, the gist of his argument is spelled out in the concluding essay. By the end of the twentieth century and the beginning of the twenty-first, Judt proposes, it is the history and memory of the Holocaust (not just a, but "*the,*" European crime, as he maintains) that defines European identity.

7   The Sütterlinstube-Hamburg, e.V. is a non-profit organization that provides translations of materials written in Sütterlin script into standard Latin script. Their services are free of charge, with voluntary donations used to subsidize a variety of initiatives to aid youth and seniors.

8   Rebecca Solnit, *The Faraway Nearby.* New York: Penguin Books, 2013, p. 3.

9   Particularly useful for my purposes were Daniel Schacter's *Searching for Memory: The Brain, The Mind, and the Past.* New York: Basic Books, 1996 and *The Seven Sins of Memory: How the Mind Forgets and Remembers.* Boston: Houghton Mifflin Harcourt, 2001 and Elizabeth Loftus, "Our Changeable Memories: Legal and Practical Implications," *Neuroscience,* vol. 4, no. 9 (April 2003), pp. 231–234.

10 Ernst Bloch, "Summary Transition: Non-Contemporaneity and Obligation to Its Dialectic," in *Heritage of Our Times,* translated by Neville Plaice and Stephen Plaice. Berkeley, CA: University of California Press, 1991, pp. 97–148.

11 Abraham and Torok, and Fresco are referenced above. Other works of particular use for this book were Marianne Hirsch, *Family Frames: Photography, Narrative and Postmemory.* Cambridge, MA: Harvard University Press, 1997 and *The Generation of Postmemory: Writing and Visual Culture after the Holocaust.* New York: Columbia University Press, 2012; Cathy Caruth, *Unclaimed Experience: Trauma, Narrative, and History.* Baltimore, MD: Johns Hopkins University Press, 1995; Ruth Leys, *Trauma: A Genealogy.* Chicago: University of Chicago Press, 2000; Esther Rashkin, *Family Secrets and the Psychoanalysis*

of Narrative. Princeton, NJ: Princeton University Press, 1992 and *Unspeakable Secrets and the Psychoanalysis of Culture*. Albany, NY: SUNY Press, 2008; Gabriele Schwab, *Haunting Legacies: Violent Histories and Transgenerational Trauma*. New York: Columbia University Press, 2010; and Eva Hoffman, *After Such Knowledge* and *Lost in Translation: A Life in a New Language*. New York: Dutton, 1989.

12   Christa Wolf's 1968 *Nachdenken über Christa T.*, translated as *The Quest for Christa T.* by Christopher Middleton (New York: Farrar, Straus and Giroux, 1970), is one of the earliest and most influential works of German literature attempting to reckon with the experience of Nazi fascism.

13   Uwe Timm's 2003 *Am Beispiel meines Bruders* (My Brother, For Example) was translated by Anthea Bell as *In My Brother's Shadow: A Life and Death in the SS*. New York: Farrar, Straus and Giroux, 2005, unduly sensationalizing the intentionally muted tone of the German original. Roger Frie, see both *Not in My Family: German History and Responsibility After the Holocaust*. Oxford and New York: Oxford University Press, 2017 and *History Flows Through Us: Germany, the Holocaust, and the Importance of Empathy*. New York and London: Routledge, 2017.

14   Sarah Kofman, *Rue Ordener, Rue Labat*, translated by Ann Smock. Lincoln, NE: University of Nebraska Press, 1996. Ruth Kluger's *weiter leben: Eine Jugend*. Göttingen: Wallstein Verlag, 1992 is a variant, not a direct translation, of *Still Alive* (referenced above). Susan Faludi, *In the Darkroom*. New York: Metropolitan Books, 2016.

15   In addition to *The Truce* and *If This Is a Man*, I drew on Primo Levi's essay "The Memory of the Offense." In *The Drowned and the Saved*, translated by Michael F. Moore in *The Complete Works of Primo Levi*, edited by Ann Goldstein, vol. III. New York and London: Liveright Publishing Corporation, 2015, pp. 2405–2567. W.G. Sebald's *Austerlitz*, translated by Anthea Bell. New York: Random House, 2001, has become a classic in the literature of German post-Holocaust memory.

16   See, in particular, Deborah Lipstadt's *Denying the Holocaust: The Growing Assault on Truth and Memory*. New York: Plume, 1994 and *History on Trial: My Day in Court with a Holocaust Denier*. New York: HarperCollins, 2005.

17   See, in particular, Evelyn Torton Beck, *Nice Jewish Girls: A Lesbian Anthology*, revised and updated edition. Boston: Beacon Press, 1989.

Index

Note: Italicized page references indicate illustrations.